Decolonisation, Globalisation

NEW PERSPECTIVES ON LANGUAGE AND EDUCATION
Series Editor: Professor Viv Edwards, *University of Reading, Reading, Great Britain*
Series Advisor: Professor Allan Luke, *Nanyang Technological University, Singapore*

Two decades of research and development in language and literacy education have yielded a broad, multidisciplinary focus. Yet education systems face constant economic and technological change, with attendant issues of identity and power, community and culture. This series will feature critical and interpretive, disciplinary and multidisciplinary perspectives on teaching and learning, language and literacy in new times.

Recent Books in the Series
Distance Education and Languages: Evolution and Change
Börje Holmberg, Monica Shelley and Cynthia White (eds)
Ebonics: The Urban Education Debate (2nd edn)
J.D. Ramirez, T.G .Wiley, G. de Klerk, E. Lee and W.E. Wright (eds)

Other Books of Interest
Beyond the Beginnings: Literacy Interventions for Upper Elementary English Language Learners
Angela Carrasquillo, Stephen B. Kucer and Ruth Abrams
Bilingualism and Language Pedagogy
Janina Brutt-Griffler and Manka Varghese (eds)
Continua of Biliteracy: An Ecological Framework for Educational Policy, Research, and Practice in Multilingual Settings
Nancy H. Hornberger (ed.)
Language and Literacy Teaching for Indigenous Education: A Bilingual Approach
Norbert Francis and Jon Reyhner
Language Learning and Teacher Education: A Sociocultural Approach
Margaret R. Hawkins (ed.)
Language Strategies for Bilingual Families
Suzanne Barron-Hauwaert
Language Minority Students in the Mainstream Classroom (2nd edn)
Angela L. Carrasquillo and Vivian Rodríguez
Making Sense in Sign: A Lifeline for a Deaf Child
Jenny Froude
Multilingual Classroom Ecologies
Angela Creese and Peter Martin (eds)
A Parents' and Teachers' Guide to Bilingualism
Colin Baker
Power, Prestige and Bilingualism: International Perspectives on Elite Bilingual Education
Anne-Marie de Mejía
Understanding Deaf Culture: In Search of Deafhood
Paddy Ladd

For more details of these or any other of our publications, please contact:
Multilingual Matters, Frankfurt Lodge, Clevedon Hall,
Victoria Road, Clevedon, BS21 7HH, England
http://www.multilingual-matters.com

NEW PERSPECTIVES ON LANGUAGE AND EDUCATION
Series Editor: Viv Edwards

Decolonisation, Globalisation
Language-in-Education
Policy and Practice

Edited by
Angel M.Y. Lin and Peter W. Martin

MULTILINGUAL MATTERS LTD
Clevedon • Buffalo • Toronto

Library of Congress Cataloging in Publication Data
Decolonisation, Globalisation: Language-in-Education Policy and Practice
Edited by Angel M.Y. Lin and Peter W. Martin.
New Perspectives on Language and Education
Includes index.
1. Language and education. 2. Language policy. I. Lin, Angel. II. Martin, Peter W.
III. Series.
P40.8.D43 2005
306.44'9–dc22   2004028646

British Library Cataloguing in Publication Data
A catalogue entry for this book is available from the British Library.

ISBN 1-85359-825-9 (hbk)
ISBN 1-85359-824-0 (pbk)
ISBN 1-85359-826-7 (electronic)

Multilingual Matters Ltd
UK: Frankfurt Lodge, Clevedon Hall, Victoria Road, Clevedon BS21 7HH.
USA: UTP, 2250 Military Road, Tonawanda, NY 14150, USA.
Canada: UTP, 5201 Dufferin Street, North York, Ontario M3H 5T8, Canada.

Typeset by Archetype-IT Ltd (http://www.archetype-it.com).
Printed and bound in Great Britain by the Cromwell Press Ltd.

Contents

Author Biodata

Abdolmehdi Riazi holds a PhD in curriculum and second language education from OISE/University of Toronto, Canada. He is currently Associate Professor in the Department of Foreign Languages and Linguistics at Shiraz University, Iran, where he teaches undergraduate and graduate courses in applied linguistics and supervises master's-level theses and doctoral dissertations. His areas of interest include second language curriculum and methodology, academic writing, critical discourse analysis, research paradigms in education, and language assessment. He is the author of three books on research and writing and the translator of two books from English into Persian. He has presented papers in international conferences on different topics related to language teaching and learning.

Contact details
Shiraz University
Shiraz
Iran
Email: ariazi@shirazu.ac.ir

E. Annamalai studied Tamil and Linguistics at Annamalai University and received his PhD from the University of Chicago. He taught in both these places before he joined the Central Institute of Indian Languages, Mysore as Deputy Director. He designed and guided projects to describe, develop and teach the indigenous languages of India. He subsequently became the Director of that Institute and was responsible for developing policy and planning for development of Indian languages, training teachers to teach, and producing materials to learn, Indian languages as a second language in schools. He is a member of the National Council for the Development of Indian Languages, New Dehli. He has been a visiting fellow at Tokyo University of Foreign Studies, Tokyo; International Institute for Asian Studies, Leiden; Max Planck Institute for Psycholinguistics, Nijmegen; Max Planck Institute of Evolutionary Anthropology, Leipzig; The University of

Melbourne, Melbourne. He is a member of the panel of the Endangered Languages Documentation Project, London and UNESCO's World Language Survey, Bilbao, Spain. He is Vice-president of Terralingua, Washington DC. Some of his books are *Language Movements in India, Dynamics of Verbal Extension in Tamil, Adjectival Clauses in Tamil, Lectures on Modern Tamil*, and *Managing Multilingualism in India: Political and Linguistic Manifestations.*

Contact details
4 Canter Court
Nashua
NH 03063
USA
Tel: 1 603 886 3332
Email: annamalai38@yahoo.com

Birgit Brock-Utne is a Professor of Education and Development at the University of Oslo. She is the Norwegian project leader of LOITASA (Language of Instruction in Tanzania and South Africa), of LOISA (Language of Instruction in South Africa), the Norwegian Research Council project *An analysis of policies and practices concerning language in education in primary schools in South Africa and secondary schools in Tanzania* and of NETREED (Network in Research and Evaluation in Education and Development) – a network gathering Norwegian-based researchers and evaluators working with education and development (http://www.netreed.uio.no). She worked as a Professor of Education at the University of Dar es Salaam (1987–1992) and has since written numerous articles on education in Africa. Her latest book is: *Whose Education for All? The Recolonisation of the African Mind*. New York: Falmer Press; 2000. In 2001 she edited a special issue of the *International Review of Education* on Globalisation, Language and Education.

Contact details
Institute for Educational Research
PB 1092 Blindern
0317 Oslo
Norway
Tel: 47 22 85 53 95
Fax: 47 22 85 42 90
Email: birgit.brock-utne@ped.uio.no
birgitbuno@yahoo.no

Grace Bunyi is a curriculum studies Senior Lecturer in Kenyatta University. A PhD graduate of the University of Toronto, her doctoral research was an ethnographic sociolinguistic study of bilingual education and social selection in Kenya. Her general area of interest is multilingualism in education. She has published journal articles and chapters in edited volumes on themes such as language and social inequalities, African indigenous languages in education, the medium of instruction policy and implications for literacy development and language classroom practices. Her other interest is in gender in education and she has published journal articles on gender inequalities in higher education in Kenya and in Africa.

Contact details
Department of Ed. Ad. Plan. & Curr. Development
Kenyatta University
PO Box 43844
Nairobi 00100
Kenya
Tel: + 254 2 810901 ext 496
Fax: + 254 2 2743258
Email: kifaru@kenyaweb.com

Suresh Canagarajah is Professor of English at Baruch College of the City University of New York. His research interests span bilingualism, discourse analysis, academic writing, and critical pedagogy. His research articles have appeared in the professional journals *TESOL Quarterly, College Composition and Communication, Language in Society, Written Communication, World Englishes, Journal of Multilingual and Multicultural Development,* and *Multilingua.* His book *Resisting Linguistic Imperialism in English Teaching* (Oxford University Press; 1999) won the Mina P. Shaughnessy Award (2000) of the Modern Language Association for the best 'research publication in the field of teaching English language, literature, rhetoric, and composition'. His subsequent book *Geopolitics of Academic Literacy and Knowledge Construction* (University of Pittsburgh Press; 2002) won the 2003 Gary Olson Award of the Association of the Teachers of Advanced Composition for the best book in social and rhetorical theory. *Critical Academic Writing and Multilingual Students* (University of Michigan Press; 2002) critiques dominant practices in academic literacy and argues for a place for alternative discourses. He has most recently edited a collection of articles by international scholars on responses to globilisation in *Reclaiming the Local in Language Policy and Practice* (Erlbaum; 2005).

Contact details
Department of English
Box B7-240
Baruch College, CUNY
One Bernard Baruch Way
New York
NY 10010
Tel: 646 312-3991
Fax: 646 312-3911
Email: suresh_canagarajah@baruch.cuny.edu

Angel Lin (http://www.cityu.edu.hk/en/staff/angel/angel.html) is Associate Professor in the Department of English and Communication, City University of Hong Kong. Her research and training have been centred on the connections between local face-to-face interactions and the larger institutional, sociocultural, historical, socio-economic and political contexts in which they are situated. Broadly speaking, she works in the areas of critical discourse analysis, urban and school ethnography, bilingual education policy analysis, feminist cultural studies, and postcolonial studies. With a background in ethnomethodology, conversation analysis and social theory, her theoretical orientations are phenomenological, sociocultural and critical. Her research articles have appeared in *TESOL Quarterly, Linguistics and Education, International Journal of the Sociology of Language, Journal of Pragmatics, Curriculum Inquiry, Language, Culture and Curriculum*, and *Journal of Language, Identity and Education*.

Contact details
Department of English and Communication
City University of Hong Kong
Tat Chee Ave
Kowloon, Hong Kong
Tel: (852) 2788-8122
Fax: (852) 2788-8894
Email: enangel@cityu.edu.hk

Allan Luke is Professor and Dean, Centre for Research in Pedagogy and Practice. National Institute of Education, Singapore. He has worked as a teacher, teacher-educator and researcher in the US, Canada, Australia and Singapore. He was previously Deputy Director General for Queensland state schools and in 2003 he received the Bulletin/IBM Award as Australia's leading educator. He is author and editor of numerous works, including the forthcoming volumes *Struggles over Difference* and *Bourdieu and Literacy Education*.

Contact details
CRPP
National Institute of Education
Nanyang Technological University
Singapore 637616
Tel: 65 6790 3185

Peter Martin is Senior Lecturer and Director of the Centre for English Language Teacher Education and Applied Linguistics in the School of Education at the University of Leicester, where he is involved in the Doctor of Education and Doctor of Philosophy programmes. He has had experience in teaching English at primary, secondary and university level in the UK, and in Malaysia, Brunei, Singapore, Hong Kong and Saudi Arabia. His teaching and research interests include sociolinguistics and discourse analysis. He has been involved in research into language shift and minority and endangered languages, bilingual interaction, multiliteracy, new varieties of English, classroom discourse, complementary schooling, bilingual education and language planning. He has published articles in these areas in *Athropos, International Journal of Sociology of Language, Language and Education, International Journal of Bilingual Education and Bilingualism, Journal of Multilingual and Multicultural Development, International Journal of Educational Development*, and *Oceanic Linguistics*. Recent co-edited volumes include *Language Use and Language Change in Brunei Darussalam* and *Multilingual Classroom Ecologies: Interaction, Ideologies and Interrelationships*.

Contact details
School of Education
University of Leicester
21 University Road
Leicester
LE1 7RF
Tel: 0116 252 3679
Fax: 0116 252 3653
Email: pwm4@le.ac.uk

Margie Probyn has a background in teaching English as an additional language in a township school. She is currently the Alan Macintosh Research Fellow at the Institute for the Study of English in Africa (ISEA), Rhodes

University, South Africa. Her research interests are language in education policy and practice, and the role of English second language as a medium of instruction in learning across the curriculum. She runs in-service teacher-development courses for English second language teachers and for science teachers teaching through the medium of English as a second language.

Contact details
Institute for the Study of English in Africa
Rhodes University
PO Box 94,
Grahamstown 6140
South Africa
Tel: + 27 (0) 46 6226093 / 6038565
Fax: + 27 (0) 46 6038566
Email: M.Probyn@ru.ac.za

Timothy Reagan is currently Dean of the School of Education and Professor of Linguistics and Education at Roger Williams University in Bristol, Rhode Island, USA. His areas of research include foreign language education, TESOL, applied and educational linguistics, and the linguistics of natural sign language. He is the author of _Language, Education and Ideology: Mapping the Linguistic Landscape of US Schools_ (2002), the co-author, with Terry A. Osborn, of _The Foreign Language Educator in Society: Toward a Critical Pedagogy_ (2002), and the co-editor, with Humphrey Tonkin, of _Language in the 21st Century_ (2003).

Contact details
Dean
School of Education
Roger Williams University
One Old Ferry Road
Bristol, RI 02809-2921
USA
Tel: 401 254 3309
Fax: 401 254 3710
Email: treagan@rwu.edu

Rani Rubdy is Senior Fellow in the Department of English Language and Literature at the National Institute of Education, Nanyang Technological University, Singapore. Until recently, she was Director of TESOL at the Institute for English Language Education, Assumption University, Bangkok. She taught for several years as Senior Lecturer at the National

University of Singapore and as Professor in the Department of Extension Services at the Central Institute of English and Foreign Languages, Hyderabad, India. Her research interests include ideological issues in world Englishes, the management of educational change, second language teacher education, process and task-based approaches to language teaching, literacy studies and classroom discourse. Her research articles have appeared in *Applied Linguistics, ELT Journal, ESP Journal, RELC Journal, TESOL Quarterly, SYSTEM* and *World Englishes.* Currently, with Mario Saraceni, she is co-editing '*English in the World: Global Rules, Global Roles*'.

Contact details
Department of English Language and Literature
National Institute of Education
Nanyang Technological University
1 Nanyang Walk
Singapore 637 616
Tel: 65 6790 3437
Fax: 65 6896 9274
Email: rsrubdy@nie. edu.sg

Sandra B. Schreffler is currently Associate Dean and Associate Professor of Foreign Language Education in the School of Education at Roger Williams University. She received her MA from the University of Houston, in Applied Spanish Linguistics/Second Language Pedagogy in 1989 and her Doctorate from the University of Florida, in Theoretical and Hispanic Linguistics in 1995. She spent a year as Academic Head of the College of Foreign Languages at Istanbul Technical University. She previously worked in the Department of Foreign Languages and Literatures at Appalachian State University, where she coordinated a programme in Spanish and French education. Her research interests include a variety of pedagogical issues, languages in contact and discourse analysis related to Romance Languages.

Contact details
School of Education
Roger Williams University
One Old Ferry Road
Bristol, RI 02809-2921
USA
Tel: 401 254 3309
Fax: 401 254 3719
Email: sschreffler@rwu.edu

Foreword: On the Possibilities of a Post-postcolonial Language Education

ALLAN LUKE

What would it mean to speak of a 'post-postcolonial moment' in educational theory and practice? What might be the reconstructive and constitutive focus of language and literacy education, cultural studies and social sciences, educational practice and social policy *after* 'orientalism' and 'postcolonialism'? Where do the systems of Asia, the Americas, and the South Pacific go from here, in the face of rapid forces of cultural and economic globalisation, shifting and recentring of capital, and emergent new blends of language and discourse? What kind of 'eduscapes' can and should be constructed in response to these conditions?

Reading through the essays here, brought together by Angel Lin and Peter Martin, I was both reassured and disturbed by the axiom that all research and scholarship, theory and practice is at once biographical and autobiographical. The choices these authors have made in theory and practice are indeed tied to their historical standpoints as researchers and writers. The decisions we make about how to play the pedagogies of everyday life likewise depend upon our historical positions and dispositions as teachers and learners. But as soon as we venture into the complexities of state, identity, politics and power that are and must be the contexts for discussions of language and education in the Asia Pacific, the Middle East, and Africa, this is a bit trickier than 'finding a voice', supporting retention and opposing loss, or uncovering and serving the needs of 'the community'. Changing the web of everyday practices about us, intervening in applied domains of social science such as language and literacy education requires something more than identity politics, however necessary and powerful a starting point they might be.

Much of the work of scholars from historically marginalised communities or writers from political and cultural diaspora is tied to local and regional struggles to secure and elaborate speaking positions. This is not just an unproblematic matter of 'voice', of speaking from and of a specific historical and cultural location, of the establishing of a psychic and political identity. It is as much a matter of figuring out which theories have explanatory power over local contexts, which theories might matter. At the same time, we struggle over the larger question of whether or if indeed there is *a* theory (however grand or ungrand, North/South, East/West) sufficient for the building of coalitions of action, for the reform and renewal, deconstruction and reconstruction of educational and civic institutions. We see such attempts across this volume 'grab' at the critical application of larger social and cultural theory that either have been ignored or have eluded much of the descriptive work in language planning and education to date.

This will to theory is in part, Bourdieu and colleagues (1994) remind us, required by entry into the academy: our identity papers must be stamped. It shouldn't be surprising, then, that one of the moves since 1968 among scholars of 'difference' working in education, linguistics and literacy studies, language planning, cultural studies and social theory has been a shared effort to bring together our strategies and resources for the enfranchisement and engagement of historically marginalised communities.

In the face of such complexity, it is tempting to in effect 'give up' trying to find larger theoretical constructs that might enable us to work through what in its rawest form is and always has been a matter of cultural and linguistic 'contact' mediated by unequal economic and political force. Indeed, there is much in postmodern scepticism of grand narrative, in a sanctification of the local by opponents of globalisation, and indeed in cultural essentialism of 'voice' that would discourage us from undertaking such a search. With this in mind, let's reconsider the case of postcolonialism. Does it, or its host of affiliated works, have the capacity to 'fuse' our analyses of the Asia Pacific, the Middle East and Africa into common cause, commensurate discourses or complementary strategies?

One of the most robust and suspect theoretical moves of Western philosophy is to assume historical, temporal and spatial synchronicity – that indeed we might live in a 'universal' world where singular theoretical constructs and textual conceits might have generalisable explanatory and practicable power. Yet the answers obviously depend on where, to whom, by whom, when, with which available discourses and in which material conditions. Cameron McCarthy's (1991) seminal discussions of race and curriculum argued that cultural and curriculum histories were 'non-synchronous'. The logic was that particular educational approaches and interventions necessarily played out unevenly and idiosyncratically across very different local educational institutions, discourse sites and political economies. This is equally the case when we attempt to speak of a 'postcolonial' approach to education and it might indeed be the case when we attempt to generalise across language and literacy-in-education planning contexts.

If there is a lesson to be learned from attempts to apply 'postcolonialism' to educational critique and intervention, it would be not only about the difficulties in achieving some kind of consensus about what might count as 'postcolonialism' but also about the slippery, non-synchrony of the places, spaces and times where we might apply such theory.

What this means is that the host of 'postcolonial' theories and models are both historically produced and have particular residual power both to explain educational phenomena and for intervention in particular contexts. Paulo Freire's model of critical pedagogy, for example, stands as a remarkable 'point of decolonisation' theorising (Luke, 2004). As such, its variants are relevant in those educational contexts where systems of domination/oppression still operate in identifiable binary patterns. But, as the feminist critique of radical pedagogy in the 1990s showed, they require significant revision to deal with multiple subjectivities, and complex forms, systems and discourses of domination and subordination that aren't amenable to simple binary analysis.

It is this set of contingencies that the work of Gayatri Spivak and colleagues addressed. A political and theoretical response to the binary simplicity and masculinism of European theory, it is a remarkable bringing together of materialist and poststructuralist, feminist and postcolonial analyses. Yet the subaltern group struggles to offer practicable and normative educational agendas other than the self-production of deconstructive capacity: that is, for educationists, the moment of analytically 'writing back' against master colonialist and masculinist narratives, and of showing their moments of contradiction and unintended consequences as a precursor to a normative educational agenda that involves the respecification and reconstruction of knowledge and power among teachers and students. In the face of new and difficult material conditions, the educational production of critique and deconstruction is necessary but not sufficient for secular education systems faced with the task of opening up new life pathways and social futures. But, at the same time, the risk is that a deconstructive educational agenda can lead very clearly to the self-reproduction of a sophisticated critical intelligentsia but fail to address the need for rudimentary large-scale educational engagement – precisely Freire's emphasis.

This is not to say that what we might argue 'counts' as canonical postcolonial theory does not continue to have salience and power. But its potential educational power depends upon the demands, constraints and revolutionary possibilities of particular local material and cultural conditions. Freirian radical pedagogy might indeed be a strategy of choice in political economies that are characterised by point-of-decolonisation binary political, racial/ethnic, or ideological division. The deconstruction of master narratives and their hybrid theoretical reconstruction might be particularly significant in those national and regional contexts building indigenous intelligentsia and reconnoitring the division and hierarchy of academic, scientific and theoretical knowledge. A focus on identity politics and 'strategic essentialism' could be *the* powerful educational move in a system where the historical silencing and suppression of difference has been enforced. It would be a mistake to write off any of these as productive educational moves.

But it also might mean that there are other educational strategies that need to be considered in the reconstruction of knowledge, cultural capital and subjectivity *after* the ostensive achievement of national, regional or local juridical or cultural autonomy. This depends on the local and situated responses to forces of globalisation, residual and adjacent colonial and neocolonial powers, and the immediate practical demands for reform and revision of systems of governance, basic material infrastructure, viable economies for communities and, indeed, the building of sustainable educational capacity and resources in the broadest senses.

In this way, the normative answers for education systems might indeed be blended, hybrid and laminated – like the languages and discourses that are the objects of study here. But blended not in the now clichéd 'two cultures' sense, but rather in the coming-together of complex and potentially contradictory contingencies of nation-building, educational systems development and, indeed, the forging of new social contracts and cohesions that might make for sustainable and equitable patterns of material distribution. However theoretically impure and politically polemical this might sound, it could mean that the most pragmatic and revolutionary educational strategy is to bring together, for example, identity politics with basic technical/vocational skills training; bilingual education with scientific training for new economies; 'heritage' or 'mother-tongue' programmes with media studies; or training in local school management and leadership with preparation for radical pedagogies. My point is that the complex and contradictory push/pull demands upon governance and education in postcolonial and globalising conditions may require very edgy hybrid blends of policy and practice, curriculum and pedagogy that do not jump out of the pages of canonical postcolonial theory or educational theory and do not sit well on the academic whiteboards of linguists or anthropologists, much less the wish lists of senior systems bureaucrats.

To return to the original question: Where to after 'orientalism' and 'postcolonialism'? This turns out to be a scarier proposition than at first glance. For it is the principal issue facing varied nation-state contexts and their educational systems that are having to cope with unprecedented economic conditions, secular and non-secular volatility, and their own internal heteroglossic dynamics of difference and diversity – from Hong Kong, Malaysia, Singapore, India to parts of the Middle East, from Kenya, Tanzania to South Africa. It is a question not only about the competitive production of human capital – as dominant neoliberal models of education advocated by the West and North, by NGOs and aid agencies suggest – but also about the maintenance and building of intercultural understandings, social cohesions and identities, and new social and linguistic contracts between and within national populations, some of which arguably have cases that they were victimised by intranational colonialism long after the British and Europeans departed.

It asks what kinds of educational and linguistic practice, what kinds of text and discourse, and what kinds of educated subject can and should be constructed to forge new critical and contingent relationships with globalising economies and mass cultures – long after the departure of colonial masters, and well after decades of reconstruction of postcolonial curricula and educational infrastructures. The issues of which languages, whose languages, which texts and discourses cannot be considered in isolation from these other questions about the amelioration and recon- struction of material conditions.

At the same time, we face a moment where such systems must at once deal with the spectre of new forms of empire and with indigenous and fun- damentalist responses, without the rhetorical and political capacity to explain away such struggles by reference to a 'first-wave' colonial master long departed but still holding a significant place in the political and educa- tional imaginary. It is a moment of few excuses and fewer pat answers. But, however theoretically vexing it might appear, it is also a moment where teachers and students, scholars and civil servants working within these educational systems stitch and suture together answers, however provi- sional and local, on a daily basis. It is the interpretive *and* empirical study of *their* work, its consequences and effects that should be the focus of 'post- postcolonial' educational studies.

References

Bourdieu, P., Passeron, J-C., de Saint Martin, M., Baudelot, C. and Vincent, G. (1994) *Academic Discourse: Linguistic Misunderstanding and Professorial Power.* Cambridge: Polity Press.

Luke, A. (2004) Two takes on the critical. In B. Norton and K. Toohey (eds) *Critical Pedagogy and Language Teaching* (pp. 22–30). Cambridge: Cambridge University Press.

McCarthy, C. (1991) *Race and Curriculum*. London: Falmer.

Chapter 1

From a Critical Deconstruction Paradigm to a Critical Construction Paradigm: An Introduction to Decolonisation, Globalisation and Language-in-Education Policy and Practice

ANGEL M.Y. LIN and PETER MARTIN

The turn of this century has witnessed a heightened sense among language educators and researchers of the need for critical analytical approaches to language-in-education (LIE) and language planning and policy (LPP) issues in diverse contexts of the world. There are many recent important and useful anthologies embodying such approaches. The question arises why the present volume is needed, or indeed what new kind of insights or contributions will it make theoretically, politically, educationally and practically? Is it just another addition to the already burgeoning critical academic discourses on LIE and LPP issues?

As all good questions do, they push us to go further than just putting together a collection of regional reports on LIE and LPP issues in a range of postcolonial contexts. We endeavour to do more than that. From the outset, we are committed to both theorising and problematising issues in these contexts, to provide the reader with more than just an encyclopaedic walk through the uneven histories and developments of LIE and LPP in different postcolonial contexts. We do not want to provide the reader with an excursion like that of a cultural tourist (and in this case an 'intellectual tourist') – a neocolonialist textual journey into different 'exotic' temporalities and localities – without also raising thorny, uncomfortable questions about the political and educational dilemmas and the new subtle ways of

1

marginalisation and collusion under new forces of globalisation. Fully aware of such a risk and trap (of providing just another comfortable, exotic cultural and academic tour) in embarking on this textual-political project (as all textual projects are simultaneously implicit political projects), we have contracted critical educators and researchers working in different postcolonial contexts who have a track record of not stopping at a comfortable academic excursion only, and who are committed to asking bold questions about existing social, cultural, economic, political and educational formations which in new complex ways effect new forms of educational, social and material inequalities under new forces of globalisation and global capitalism.

What stands out as a key distinguishing feature of this collection of essays is the attempt by the authors to link old colonisation processes with new globalisation processes, seeing the latter as in many ways a continuation of the former and yet not in a simple binary imperialism-resistance logic, but in new, complex ways that also offer new opportunities of collusion and interpenetration, hybridisation and postcolonial reinvention, ways that go beyond the essentialist, nationalist identity and 'two cultures' politics (see Allan Luke's critique in his Foreword to this book) that defined the earlier phases of decolonisation, nationalism and national culturalism in the process of nation-building in many postcolonial societies.[1] In the following sections, we shall propose a framework to see how the different essays in this volume link together and what kinds of new insights they offer to us in current LIE and LPP studies in postcolonial contexts that will allow us to advance from a critical deconstruction paradigm to a critical construction paradigm which will offer not only policy and practice critiques but also practical policy, pedagogy and curriculum alternatives.

'The Empire Strikes Back'? The Global Spread and Hegemony of English Riding on New Wings of Globalisation

The papers in this volume cover an array of societies which are at different historical and economic conjunctures of their respective developmental trajectories, with both similar and distinct pathways. It is important that they are not seen as merely lying on different points of a singular, linear developmental pathway, as Western modernism might have us believe. Having said that, one has to note that they do, however, seem to share a similar moment in their respective histories: that in all their encounters with the West, now dispersed into the globe in various forms of global capitalism, global mass-media flows and global technological and communications penetration, English has often been perceived as an indispensable resource which many postcolonial peoples and governments seek for themselves and their younger generations in their respective socioeconomic contexts. This is often infused with a strong desire for economic development, technological and material modernisation, and human-resource capital investment for current and future successful participation in the new global economic order (that is, the desire to have one's cake and eat it). Such capital includes English communication skills, information technology, business management and commercial know-how and so on, and very often English comes in a package with all these desirable 'goodies', or it is the indispensable medium for bringing in and acquiring these goodies. How to make English linguistic capital accessible to more of the school population and how to spread English capital more efficiently and evenly across different social sectors in the society become important issues in critical (if not always government) research in policy, curriculum and pedagogy, and very often occupy priority places in national development agendas. The main initiatives (sometimes coming from government, sometimes coming from local communities or both) found in different societies to reform their former largely structure- and drill-based English curricula, to introduce communicative, task- and function-based pedagogies, to develop the kinds of English interactive/productive competencies required of new generations of the workforce in economically modernising contexts are similar in their spirit if different in their particularities of implementation.

Thus, we see in India (see Annamalai's chapter) and Malaysia (see Martin's chapter) that English has returned with renewed force as a strongly desired (by parents) and officially desirable medium of instruction in both higher and basic education (for perceived needs of economic, technological modernisation and globalisation). In Singapore (see Rudby's chapter) and Hong Kong (see Lin's chapter), exonormic English (that is, English varieties oriented to external Anglo norms, not counting Singlish or Hong Kong English) continues to be the single most important language for socioeconomic advancement for accessing higher professional education and the globalised, knowledge-intensive job market, and thus a tool of social stratification. In Turkey (see Reagan and Schreffler's chapter) and Iran (see Riazi's chapter), both local communities and the governments (albeit in different manners) recognise the need for learning English to a greater extent and the prestige and value of mastering English under new forces of globalisation (for example, a major state university in Turkey installing English as a medium of instruction in more courses to compete with private English-medium institutions; middle-class Iranian parents sending children to private English tutorial schools to acquire more globally marketable communicative competences in English which the public schools' old English curricula cannot provide). In South Africa (see

Probyn's chapter and Brock-Utne's chapter), despite the post-apartheid constitutional commitment to linguistic diversity and multilingualism, research evidence indicates that this policy has not been implemented and, where schools' language practices have changed, the shift has been towards an even earlier introduction of English as a medium of instruction. In Tanzania and South Africa (see Brock-Utne's chapter), we see the painful cost paid by schoolchildren sitting year after year in English-medium lessons, often repeating a class, without learning anything. In Kenya (see Bunyi's chapter), we see how the policy of installing English as the medium of instruction from Primary Four onwards presents enormous challenges to the majority of Kenyan children and teachers, particularly those living in rural and poor urban communities, where there is little access to English outside school. The forceful, legitimate (and legitimised) 'return' (if it has ever departed, perhaps only temporarily, as in the history of postcolonial Malaysia) of English as a dominant language and/or medium of instruction in the education system to postcolonial contexts riding on new wings of global capitalism cannot be described simply as 'the Empire strikes back' – for this time the 'Empire' is both invisible and non-monolithic, as it is dissolved into the 'Globe' taking the form of various (sometimes conflictual) forces of globalisation, and is not necessarily one-sidedly against national and local community interests (as seen in the postcolonial governments' and local communities' growing desire for English for both national and personal interest, as described in the chapters of this book).

'The Postcolonial Puzzle'? Renewed Desires for English in Education in Postcolonial Contexts

In the Afterword to this volume, Suresh Canagarajah succinctly and vividly notes how the carpet has been pulled from under the feet of those non-Western countries that were undergoing the 'project' of decolonisation, by another 'project', that of globalisation. Whereas decolonisation entailed resisting English, globalisation 'has made the borders of the nation state porous and reinserted the importance of English language' (Canagarajah, this volume).

To understand the new desires, new phenomena, new interests and new hybrid identities in diverse postcolonial contexts, we can no longer use the old binary logic that characterises the old imperialism-resistance analytical model. Pennycook (2000) captures this point well when, with reference to Michel Foucault (1980) and Judith Butler (1999), he argues for a notion of postcolonial performativity, which means:

> ... first, viewing the global dominance of English not ultimately as an a priori imperialism but rather as a product of the local hegemonies of

English. As Foucault (1980: 94) puts it, in the context of arguing for a notion of power not as something owned by some and not by others but as something that operates on and through all points of society, 'major dominations are the hegemonic effects that are sustained by all these confrontations'. Any concept of the global hegemony of English must therefore be understood in terms of the complex sum of contextualised understandings of social hegemonies. . . . but such hegemonies are also filled with complex local contradictions, with the resistance and appropriations that are a crucial part of the postcolonial context. (Pennycook, 2000: 117)

Under Pennycook's notion of postcolonial performativity, English is neither a Western monolithic entity nor necessarily an imposed reality, and local peoples are capable of penetrating English with their own intentions and social styles. English as appropriated by local agents serves diverse sets of intentions and purposes in their respective local contexts, whether it be the acquiring of a socially-upward identity, or the creation of a bilingual space for critical explorations of self and society (see Lin *et al.*, 2002).

The debates revolving around the apparent puzzle of why postcolonial governments and local communities in many postcolonial contexts today seem to desire English with such renewed and unashamed enthusiasm, the phenomenon that we may describe as 'the postcolonial puzzle', can be tackled by recourse to the postcolonial theorists' discourses on postcolonial hybridity, performative agency, multiple subjectivities and new global identities, upon which Pennycook and Canagarajah's sophisticated analyses have drawn.

In the Foreword to this volume, Allan Luke points out insightfully that all research and scholarship, theory and practice is at once biographical and autobiographical. We cite Luke here as we wish to engage dialogically with him:

Reading through the essays here, brought together by Angel Lin and Peter Martin, I was both reassured and disturbed by the axiom that all research and scholarship, theory and practice is at once biographical and autobiographical. The choices these authors have made in theory and practice are indeed tied to their historical standpoints as researchers and writers. The decisions we make about how to play the pedagogies of everyday life likewise depend upon our historical positions and dispositions as teachers and learners. But as soon as we venture into the complexities of state, identity, politics and power that are and must be the contexts for discussions of language and education in the Asia Pacific, the Middle East, and Africa, this is a bit trickier than 'finding a voice', supporting retention and opposing loss, or uncovering and serving the needs of 'the community'. Changing the web of everyday practices about us, intervening in applied domains of social science such as language and literacy education requires something more than identity politics, however necessary and powerful a starting point they might be. (Luke, this volume)

We would like to add a theoretical twist by responding to Luke's words. We agree with him that it is important to go beyond merely doing identity politics – that enterprise of finding and giving voice to hitherto marginal-ised groups. However, we also appreciate the fact that the writers and researchers in the different postcolonial contexts contributing to this book seem to be echoing similar voices – voices of the subalterns, for example, the marginalised children (and sometimes also teachers) who struggle in the English-medium classrooms in an English-dominant education system, those social actors confronted with the social stratification and selection mechanisms based on a mastery of English, university people faced with the dilemmas created by the perceived need for local cultural and linguis-tic preservation and the parents' overwhelming desire for global English. It would seem to be too much of a theoretical reduction to see the writers and researchers as merely trapped by old nationalistic or culturalistic dis-courses of identity politics or polemics born of personal, biographical histories, as yet uninformed by theories of postcolonial hybridity, peformativity and multisubjectivity.

So here lies both our theoretical and our practical question: Are there any alternative theoretical and political discourses and praxis which will allow us not to fall into the trap of old European, masculine binarism (the 'Empire-Resistance' binary analytical framework, the simplistic theoretical analysis as caricatured by 'the Empire strikes back' or 'renewed imperial-ism' discourses) while at the same time allowing us to analyse the new forms of marginalisation and new productions of subaltern subjectivities amid the new possibilities and opportunities of postcolonial hybridity, performativity and cosmopolitanism under new forces of globalisation?

We see the above question as a driving force for this book and for bringing out the unique contribution of this book to existing discourses on issues in LIE policy and practice in postcolonial contexts. Going beyond the debate between 'imperialism-resistance' discourses and 'postcolonial performativity' discourses, we have to find a way of understanding and exposing new forms of inequalities in education and society and new pro-ductions of subaltern subjectivities under globalisation. While doing critical education analysis we must also be wary of falling into the trap of doing merely essentialist identity politics; rather, we must struggle to study the new material conditions and to explore practical alternatives in LIE policy and practice.

The New Cosmopolitan Multilingual Elites and the Newly Ghetto-ised Locals under Globalisation

As much as we would want to celebrate the new opportunities that globalisation has seemed to offer us in reworking and refashioning our identities as new transnational, global cosmopolitans, unbound by old forms of essentialist nationalism and culturalism and binary frameworks of identity politics, we however also see the anxieties created by globalisation forces. Zygmunt Bauman (1998) points out this economic underside of globalisation in his book, *Globalization – The Human Consequences*:

> The creation of wealth is on the way to finally emancipating itself from its perennial – constraining and vexing – connections with making things, processing materials, creating jobs and managing people. The old rich needed the poor to make and keep them rich. That dependency at all times mitigated the conflict of interest and prompted some effort, however tenuous, to care. The new rich do not need the poor any more. (Bauman, 1998: 72)

Thus, increasingly under the forces of economic globalisation, entire factories and jobs can disappear overnight from one locality as fast, nomadic global capital holds no allegiance to communities in any locality and roams from one locality to another across the globe searching for ever-cheaper land and labour (Bauman, 1998). Also, while the cosmopolitan multilingual elite well-versed in global English and new knowledge technologies (often mediated through global English) can find jobs anywhere across the globe (i.e. gaining transnational mobility), those monolingual locals who never catch on to the new skills and new languages (often due to lack of class-based capital and habitus; see discussion below) are ever more locked up in non-mobility both geographically and socioeconomically.

In his plenary paper given at the Crossroads Conference of the International Association of Cultural Studies on 25 June 2004, Larry Grossberg urged cultural studies scholars and critical theorists to go beyond the mere analysis of expressive culture (e.g. popular culture and media), and also to pay attention to the policies of the state and the global flows of capital. He urged critical theorists, educators and cultural researchers to do what he called 'conjunctual analysis' – to analyse the historical conjunctures formed by both cultural and material, economic and political forces. We also see a parallel in critical education analysis in postcolonial studies of LIE and LPP contexts. While the contributors to this book have largely focused on LIE and LPP issues, they have also attempted to situate them in the larger socio-economic and political contexts. For instance, Rani Rubdy in her chapter on Singapore has given us a sharp analysis of how the state's English-dominant LIE policy has been driven by both agendas of economic globalisation and political management of different ethnic groups. This has resulted in the wiping-out of Chinese dialects (including Hokkien, which used to be the mother tongue of the majority of Chinese in Singapore), creating cross-generational linguistic and cultural discontinuities (e.g. English-speaking grandchildren cannot communicate with Hokkien-speaking grandparents), and indirectly fostering the development of 'Singlish', an officially denigrated but popularly embraced hybridised Hokkien-sounding variety of English (see Rubdy's chapter). Singlish, as a hybridised linguistic variety, is certainly not a language and trademark of the high-flying cosmopolitan Singaporean identity, but instead a marker of local Singaporean identity and a medium for parodying official discourses (Chua, 2003). While the cosmopolitan, global Singaporean can sometimes switch to Singlish for a joke or to show their 'authentic' Singaporeanness, what socially stratifies the cosmopolitan multilingual high-flyer from the monolingual Singlish/Hokkien-speaking ghetto-ised local is their differ-ential access to and differential degrees of mastery of global or 'standard' English. In the words of Singaporean sociologist and cultural theorist Chua Beng-huat:

> The consequence, after 20 years [of the state's language policies], is that Hokkien, along with all other Chinese languages, has become a language spoken by those who have never received a formal education and/or those who did not make the grade in the highly-competitive bilingual education system. It is thus reduced to a language of the lowest-educated section of the working class and the illiterate. The lin-guistic hierarchy, in order of economic and political advantages, is thus English, Mandarin and Hokkien, as depicted in the film, 'Money' (Chua, 2003: 169)
> . . . Ah Beng and his female counterpart, Ah Lian [in a popular TV sitcom] are two caricatures of the Singlish-speaking Singaporeans who are 'adoringly' laughable to the middle-class English-educated writers and audience, for whom switching code from standard English to Singlish is a marker of 'authentic' Singaporean identity. (Chua, 2003: 162)

We must point out that our concern here lies not so much in a nostalgic mourning for the loss of linguistic diversity (though this is a legitimate concern to many) as in the production of socioeconomic disadvantage and new subaltern identities – consequences of Singapore's cosmopolitan-oriented ruling elite's emptying out of the 'local' (e.g. local languages) in their thorough-going pursuit of the 'global' (e.g. standard English, standard Mandarin Chinese) under their linguistic engineering policies driven by globalisation desires. The emergence of Singlish as a surrogate for the 'linguistic local', and in some sense as a reincarnation of Hokkien, is certainly not anticipated by the state's linguistic engineers and might represent the poor's linguistic resistant 'weapon', a local linguistic spectre that lingers on to continue to embarrass and haunt the authorities (see Rubdy, this volume). However, as the acquisition of standard English correlates with family-based capital and 'habitus' (see Lin, 1999 and Lin, this volume), we can expect new forms of socioeconomic stratification along the lines of social class mediated by the (un)availability of family capital predisposing the use and acquisition of global, standard forms of English versus local hybridised forms of English such as Singlish in Singapore or 'mixed codes' in Hong Kong (see Lin, 2000). Here, we find Bourdieu's critical analytic tools very useful, as delineated by British sociologist Nick Crossley:

> Class-based cultural advantages are passed from parents to children through the habitus, but as pre-reflective and habitual acquisitions they are generally misrecognized within the school system as 'natural talents' and are rewarded 'appropriately'. The school thus launders cultural advantages, albeit unwittingly, transforming them into the hard and clean currency of qualifications. (Crossley, 2003: 43)

We see parallel social and linguistic processes taking shape in Iran (see Riazi, this volume) when parents who can afford it send their children to private schools to acquire globally marketable communicative competences in English that the state schools cannot offer, and in Turkey when private institutions that teach in the English medium multiply and compete with state universities which struggle to offer a balance of local languages and English. The economic drive (from both the local communities and the postcolonial governments) towards the emptying-out of the 'linguistic local' and the one-sided pursuit of the 'linguistic global' must be problematised in our study of the consequences of globalisation. While taking care not to embrace linguistic and cultural essentialism as a simple, reductionist reaction to these globalising forces, we have to both critically examine these processes in their consequences (e.g. new forms of social stratification and new productions of subaltern subjectivities; see Lin, this volume), and explore new alternatives in policy, pedagogy and curriculum drawing on theoretical frameworks that go beyond traditional discrete models of languages, cultures and literacies and beyond the traditional top-down models of LIE policy planning.

New Intellectual Breakthroughs and What They Can Offer Us in LIE Policy and Practice in Postcolonial Contexts

Suresh Canagarajah offers us insightful theoretical and practical directions in LIE policy, pedagogy and curriculum in his Afterword to this volume. To engage with his views we cite them below. On language policy and planning (LPP) he states:

> Since community needs and attitudes may be ambivalent, the processes of implementing policy can be multifarious and the outcomes of policy surprising. Therefore, the field of LPP is now moving towards a more localised orientation that takes these tensions, ambiguities, and paradoxes seriously to construct policies from ground-up, along micro social domains (see Cooper, 1989: 182). Hence the growing popularity of ethnographic approaches in LPP (as we see exemplified so well in many chapters in this volume). (Canagarajah, this volume)

As good ethnographers do, many of the contributors to this book show us that the languages in the everyday lives of students and teachers both inside and outside of the classrooms do not exist in neat, discrete categories but in fact are used in fluid, creative, intertwined ways. Pennycook (2004) reminds us that the notion of discrete languages is in fact a product of colonialists' and orientalists' project of oriental knowledge production:

> First that the objects of study of linguistics (languages), like cultures, are not pre-given entities but rather are the products of the mode of study; and second, this process of forming languages is deeply embedded within colonial projects of knowledge formation. . . . The invention of Indian languages has to be seen in the context of this larger colonial archive of knowledge. The British, as Lelyfeld (1993) points out, 'developed from their study of Indian languages not only practical advantage but an ideology of languages as separate, autonomous objects in the world, things that could be classified, arranged, and deployed as media of exchange' (p. 194). Central to this process, then, were a series of assumptions about languages as bounded territorial entities. (Pennycook, 2004: 3–4)

Suresh Canagarajah expresses a similar idea in his critique of traditional LPP models in his Afterword to this book. He refers to how multiple languages 'jostle together in many domains of communication, functioning in a complementary, integrated, and fluid manner' (Canagarajah, this volume). Thus, we see that the postcolonial state's top-down language-planning models have often unwittingly followed in the steps of their colonial masters: treating languages as discrete entities that can be neatly classified and manipulated in their policy models. As an alternative to these traditional, colonialist LPP models, Suresh Canagarajah draws on Nancy Hornberger's (2003) model of *continua of biliteracy* as a useful alternative policy orientation to literacy, which provides an ecological framework for educational policy, research and practice in multilingual settings. In particular, the continua model 'provides a heuristic for addressing the unequal balance of power across language and literacies' (Hornberger, 2003: xvi), and for understanding how communities negotiate the mix of languages, literacies and discourses that best suits their interests (Canagarajah, this volume).

It is important to note, though, that this negotiation process has seldom taken place in entirely democratic, constraint-free ways (as in Habermas's idealised rational speech situation; see Habermas, 1984), but has often been subject to the hegemonic effect of the already-in-place normative valuation mechanisms born of the habitus and subjectivities of the postcolonial state's elite. The liberalist idea that each local community can always be 'free' to negotiate its own language and education needs must be problematised. For instance, in postcolonial Hong Kong, the habitus and subjectivity of the English-educated ruling elite in the post-1997 era are not much different from those in the pre-1997 era. As fluent bilinguals who graduated from former colonial prestigious English-medium schools (many of which are missionary schools with a history dating from the early colonial times of Hong Kong in the 19th century), they embody a special consciousness and habitus born of the colonial times. With all the social selection mechanisms unchanged (across the 1997 boundary) which use a mastery of standard English as a chief screening and gate-keeping measure for access to higher education (see Lin, 1997 and Lin, this volume), the parents', students', teachers' and principals' choices are necessarily constrained under the hegemonic effect of the dominance of English in the society's social mobility mechanisms, which are newly re-legitimised in the postcolonial era by globalisation discourses. Thus we see the local communities in Hong Kong voluntarily choosing English-medium schools for their children despite the fact that many of these children can hardly function in an English medium classroom (see Lin, 1997; Lin, this volume, and Lin & Man, forthcoming). Similar processes are also seen in African postcolonial contexts, as shown in chapters by Probyn, Brock-Utne and Bunyi in this volume. Thus we are in complete agreement with Canagarajah's (this volume) remarks on the need for institutional changes in language status in LIE policies. We would add that our rationale for advocating proactive status planning that is backed up by concrete institutional changes in the state's policy to give a place to all languages (instead of just the globally valued standard languages) is more than that of cultural and linguistic preservation for cultural and linguistic preservation's sake. Pennycook, in his plenary paper given in the *International Conference on Language, Education and Diversity* (at University of Waikato, New Zealand, 26–29 November 2003), problematised the latter position. Without going into the details of the debates at this conference, we would point out that from a critical sociological perspective inspired by Bourdieusian analyses of habitus and capital, it is important to advocate institutional changes that can result in a re-shaping of the social selection mechanisms (or 'fields' in Bourdieu's terms) in a postcolonial society that will allow people who, due to family habitus, excel more in local than global languages to have a chance for socioeconomic mobility.

To illustrate the above point we revisit the Singaporean scene outlined above. The production of new subaltern identities and subjectivities is captured in the popular TV characters of 'Ah Beng' and 'Ah Lian'. These 'Singlish-speaking Singaporeans who are "adoringly" laughable to the middle-class English-educated writers and audience' (Chua, 2003: 162) embody the new subaltern habitus and subjectivities which are a result of Singapore's economic globalisation-driven LIE policies in the past 20 years (see Rubdi, this volume). As mentioned above, we argue that in any postcolonial society the chances are that the English-educated middle classes who have had the closest links with their former colonial masters have the best cultural advantages (in the form of pre-reflective habitus; see Crossley, 2003) that predispose them to excel in an education system that privileges global, standard forms of languages and literacies.

While exposing the possibilities of internal colonialism as analysed above in postcolonial contexts, we must not stop there but must try to construct positive policy, pedagogical and curriculum alternatives that will do more than just argue for essentialist, culturalist identity and linguistic rights. We see this mission as both a theoretical and a pedagogical driving force for this book. As Allan Luke reminds us in the Foreword to this volume:

> My point is that the complex and contradictory push/pull demands upon governance and education in postcolonial and globalising conditions may require very edgy hybrid blends of policy and practice, curriculum and pedagogy that do not jump out of the pages of canonical postcolonial theory or educational theory and do not sit well on the academic whiteboards of linguists or anthropologists, much less the wish lists of senior systems bureaucrats. (Luke, this volume)

We would add that these 'edgy hybrid blends of policy and practice, curriculum and pedagogy' do not automatically jump out of the pages of the critical sociologist's deconstructionist paradigm, either. We have to do more than mere critical deconstruction of existing policies and practices and conduct careful research into the nitty-gritty of the everyday realities of students and teachers to come up with constructive suggestions for policy and practice alternatives. Thus we find the suggestions made by Canagarajah (this volume) regarding the necessity of observing practices in local situations extremely timely.

Exploring the potential of bilingual pedagogical strategies must be seen as a pedagogical breakthrough in the research on how to help rural or poor urban working-class schoolchildren to acquire global, standard languages and literacies for wider communication and socioeconomic mobility. While agreeing with Canagarajah on this pedagogical suggestion, we want to point out that there is a diverse range of bi- and multilingual pedagogical practices in different classroom contexts. While some of these practices are pedagogically effective, some of them might be reproductive of the lack of linguistic capital of both teachers and students (for example, Chick, 1996; for detailed analyses of both the risks and the rich potential of these different classroom practices, see Lin, 1999, 2000; Lin & Luk, 2002, 2004; Martin, 1996, 1999, 2003). Again the positive bi- and multilingual pedagogical and curriculum practices do not simply jump out of the pages of educational theorists or critical deconstructionists, but are the hard-gained results of careful, situated classroom and curriculum studies in different sociocultural and institutional contexts. We thus echo the views of Luke and Canagarajah that much more multilingual pedagogical and curriculum research needs to be conducted in the future as this kind of research tends to be dismissed or marginalised in traditional educational research paradigms. For instance, one useful kind of study would be to look at how hybridised local languages such as Singlish in Singapore or 'mixed codes' in Hong Kong can be capitalised on in teaching school languages and literacies as well as content subjects in bilingual education programmes. As many contributors to this book attempted to uncover the everyday classroom realities in different postcolonial contexts, we must encourage them not to stop there but to continue with their ethnographic projects until their initial largely deconstruction projects (e.g. exposing problems of existing policies and practices), worthwhile as they are, ultimately develop into construction projects (e.g. delineating and uncovering effective policy and practice alternatives).

Finally, on the curriculum front, we echo Luke's assertion that much more new and innovative curriculum thinking and research is needed, and that the 'normative answers for education systems might indeed be blended, hybrid and laminated – like the languages and discourses which are the objects of study here' (Luke, this volume).

In our dialogue with Luke, Canagarajah and the other contributors to this book, we hope that our discussions do not stop here and will stimulate contributors and readers alike to start planning and doing the kinds of 'blended, hybrid and laminated', 'theoretically impure and politically polemical' educational research that is urgently needed to advance our projects from a critical deconstruction paradigm to a critical construction paradigm.

To provide the reader with an overall sense of the contents of the book, chapter summaries are provided below.

The chapter by E. Annamalai provides an historical account of language choice and education in India, focusing on colonial educational policies and how these policies have affected education in postcolonial India, as well as on the whole issue of nation-building in the country. In India, localised educational control and content were centralised by the colonial rulers in order to standardise education throughout the country. This created an indigenous elite who became mediators between the rulers and the masses. In the postcolonial period, the educational aim was to combine imparting the skills and knowledge needed for an industrial economy with inculcating national pride and building national solidarity. This aim, as well as the exponential growth in the scientific knowledge created in English and the growth in its international political and economic power, delayed the replacement of English with Indian languages. The delay was rationalised as helping the global integration of the people. A consequence of this was ambivalence in the policy of medium change in education from English. Annamalai points out that the widespread preference for English-medium education contributes to the acquisition of poor and imitative knowledge. In addition, the policy of every student in school learning three languages, which means the regional language, Hindi and English, does not provide a place for the mother tongue (when it is different from the regional language), or for a classical language like Sanskrit. According to Annamalai, the students, abetted by the states, ignore one or more of the three languages except English. In this way, the dilution of the language-in-education policy in practice defeats both the instrumental and the integrative purposes of the policy and subordinates them to global aspirations.

Angel Lin critically examines several different disciplinary approaches to the analysis of language-in-education policies and practices in Hong Kong. She illustrates how different epistemological perspectives, with their different emphases, privilege the construction of different kinds of understanding and knowledge about language education policies and practices in a former colonial context. In the chapter, she argues for the importance of the need for researchers researching on language-in-education policies and practices in different sociopolitical contexts to constantly recognise the *partial* and *positioned* nature of the knowledge and understandings that they construct as researchers who are always themselves historically and sociopolitically located in a certain *interested* position (Ang, 1996). According to Lin, all these point to the need for researchers to become increasingly more like a postmodernist, reflexive, '*tweener*' (Luke, 2002), readily travelling between different disciplines and different ideological positions, critically self-reflexive on these positions, as well as travelling between the roles of academic knowledge-producers/consumers and political participants in a world still full of both blatant and subtle forms of social injustice and relations of domination and subordination.

The chapter by Rani Rubdy attempts to unravel some of the contradictions and conflicts of interest underlying official ideology in modern-day Singapore when compared with what is found to be the case in the everyday life of Singaporeans. In particular, it focuses on the ideology of pragmatism, of multilingualism and meritocracy – all of which are rife with potentially fractious tendencies. If modern-day Singapore can boast of a highly efficient education system it is mainly owing to its carefully monitored and proactive management of language policies and language planning, which occupy a central place in education, as in all of its nation-building projects. The Singaporean leadership's prime focus in a post-September 11, SARS-spectred world today is how to reinvent itself in order to successfully stay at the forefront of global economic competition. Given the crucial role that language-in-education has to play in achieving this goal, official ideology constructs its own preferred view of reality by prioritising issues of language choice and maintenance in the Singaporean consciousness in particular ways. This is done by manipulating the Singaporean psyche, although in not too subtle yet in powerfully effective ways, through a series of vigorous campaigns, through language debates in political forums and in the media. By playing up Singapore's need to become a viable player on the global stage in the face of stiffening regional competition, and prioritising economic issues over social, cultural and personal concerns, and by bringing language centre stage in all of this, the leadership effectively determines and maintains control over the choice of linguistic resources in Singapore. However, the realities of practice on the ground reveal that none of these policies are entirely unproblematic.

The chapter from Peter Martin provides a micro-ethnographic and discourse-analytic study of two classrooms in rural communities in the East Malaysian state of Sarawak. The study juxtaposes the observed classroom language practices alongside the historical conditions shaped by colonialism, neocolonialism, and the complex processes of globalisation. It examines classroom practices in the light of the current tensions between, on the one hand, local, cultural and nationalist imperatives, and 'global' imperatives on the other. Of particular relevance to the discussion in this chapter is the recent policy decision in Malaysia to change the language of instruction in science and mathematics from Malay to English.

The chapter by Abdolmehdi Riazi discusses the 'four language stages' in the history of Iran. The significance of each of these four stages lies in their treatment of indigenous and other languages in the development of the country. The four stages include the early Persian Empire of the Achaemenian and Sassanid dynasties followed by an Islamic stage when Arabs took over Persia and brought Islam to the country in the 7th century. The third stage was the Pahlavi dynasty (1925–1979) and the fourth started with the Islamic Revolution in 1979 and resulted in the establishment of the Islamic Republic of Iran, which continues to the present time. Language has played an important role in all four of these stages. Moreover, the ruling powers in each of these stages treated language in a way that distinguished them from each other in terms of sociopolitical and educational policies. The chapter ends with a discussion of how the language policies in Iran have responded to the challenges of globalisation.

Reagan and Schreffler, with reference to Turkey, look at the dilemma for many universities in the so-called developing world: whether to utilise English (or some other language of wider communication) as the principal medium of instruction, or to make provision for the use of an indigenous language. In this chapter, a third alternative is explored. It explores the case of a major state university in Turkey with a long, well-established tradition of instruction in the national language which is in the process of a significant status change with respect to language-medium policy. Faced with growing competition from English-medium institutions in the private sector, this university is undertaking what is intended to be a middle path: in order to ensure that students have the necessary language skills to compete both nationally and internationally, all students are now required to complete approximately one-third of their university courses in English. The policy is intended to ensure English-language competence while at the same time maintaining a scholarly and academic context in which Turkish remains a significant and necessary language.

Within the African context, Grace Bunyi focuses on language practices in Kenya. In the current language-in-education policy in Kenya, English is the medium of instruction from Standard Four onwards. Bunyi relates how this policy presents enormous challenges to the majority of Kenyan children and teachers, particularly those who live in rural and poor urban neighbourhoods, where there is little access to English outside the school. Using ethnographic data from Standard One and Standard Four classrooms in a rural school, Bunyi demonstrates that linguistic routines, choral responses, strict Initiation-Response-Feedback episodes and code-switching are the dominant linguistic and interactional practices in these schools. She argues that pupils do not experience meaningful learning in school. One area that needs to be given more emphasis is in-service teacher education, in order that teachers can be better equipped to organise meaningful learning activities for their pupils.

Margie Probyn looks at 'language and the struggle to learn' in her chapter on South Africa. Following the democratic elections in 1994, which brought South Africa into the global mainstream, the new government set about dismantling apartheid institutions, and embarked on an ambitious programme of transforming civil society – to redress the imbalances of the past, and to prepare for active involvement in the global economy. This included the transformation of education with a range of new policies, including a Language-in-Education Policy which reflects the constitutional commitment to linguistic diversity and multilingualism. However, research evidence indicates that the Language-in-Education Policy has not been implemented and, where schools' language practices have changed, the shift has been towards an even earlier introduction of English as a medium of instruction. In this chapter, Probyn seeks to explore how national efforts to promote previously marginalised languages and multilingualism, as a means to reconciliation and nation building, have come up against the realities of globalisation: both in its impact on economic policies and what this means in terms of the allocation of limited resources, and in relation to the need of people to access English as the perceived language of global social, political and economic power.

The chapter by Birgit Brock-Utne reports on a five-year research project (conducted with researchers from the University of Western Cape, South Africa, and the University of Dar es Salaam, Tanzania) focusing on languages-of-instruction issues in Tanzania and South Africa. Using mainly observation, the research reported in this chapter exposes several commonly-held beliefs about languages and education in Africa. For example, the author proposes that economists should try to figure out how much it costs to have African children sit year after year in school, often repeating a class, without learning anything, and she puts this against the cost of producing texts in African languages. She relates how the African continent abounds with examples of the low pass rate and high attrition rate in schools. She refutes the argument that the African languages do not possess a sufficient vocabulary to be used for science and technology. Brock-Utne takes the reader inside the African classroom and shows how pupils and teachers try to cope in a near hopeless situation by using such strategies as code-mixing, code-switching and full translation.

The final part of the volume is an Afterword by Suresh Canagajarah. After reviewing the contributions to the volume, Canagarajah draws together the strands running through them, focusing particularly on the tensions in the language policies and practices in the communities represented in the chapters of the volume. He discusses the different types of tension and points to commonalities and differences within the different contexts.

Note
1. Technically Turkey and Iran cannot be described as postcolonial states as they have not been colonized like the other societies described in this book. However, in their respective histories, Anglo-European influences, especially recent American political and economic hegemony in the Middle East, has cast a colonial shadow over them which they are still struggling to resist with both oppositional and collusion strategies (with Iran more often than Turkey taking up the former stance towards the West).

References

Ang, I. (1996) *Living Room Wars: Rethinking Media Audience for a Postmodern World.* London: Routledge.

Bauman, Z. (1998) *Globalization: The Human Consequences.* New York: Columbia University Press.

Butler, J. (1999) Performativity's social magic. In R. Shusterman (ed.) *Bourdieu: A Critical Reader* (pp. 113–28). Oxford: Blackwell.

Chick, J.K. (1996) Safe talk: Collusion in apartheid education. In H. Coleman (ed.) *Society and the Language Classroom* (pp. 21–39). Cambridge: Cambridge University Press.

Chua, B.H. (2003) *Life is not Complete without Shopping: Consumption Culture in Singapore.* Singapore: Singapore University Press.

Cooper, R.L. (1989) *Language Planning and Social Change.* Cambridge: Cambridge University Press.

Crossley, N. (2003) From reproduction to transformation: Social movement fields and the radical habitus. *Theory, Culture & Society* 20 (6), 1–20.

Foucault, M. (1980) *Power/Knowledge: Selected Interviews and Other Writings, 1972–1977.* New York: Pantheon.

Habermas, J. (1984) *The Theory of Communicative Action.* (T. McCarthy, trans.) Boston: Beacon Press.

Hornberger, N. (2003) Multilingual language policies and the continua of biliteracy: An ecological approach. In N.H. Hornberger (ed.) *Continua of Biliteracy: An Ecological Framework for Educational Policy, Research, and Practice* (pp. 315–39). Clevedon: Multilingual Matters.

Lelyfeld, D. (1993) The fate of Hindustani: Colonial knowledge and the project of a national language. In C.A. Breckenridge and P. van der Veer (eds) *Orientalism and the Postcolonial Predicament: Perspectives on South Asia* (pp. 189–214). Philadelphia, PA: University of Pennsylvania Press.

Lin, A. (1997) Bilingual education in Hong Kong. In J. Cummins and D. Corson (eds) *Encyclopedia of Language and Education, Volume 5: Bilingual Education* (pp. 281–89). Dordrecht, the Netherlands: Kluwer Academic Publishers.

Lin, A. (1999) Doing-English-lessons in the reproduction or transformation of social worlds? *TESOL Quarterly* 33 (3), 393–412.

Lin, A. (2000) Deconstructing 'mixed code'. In D.C.S Li, A.M.Y Lin and W.K. Tsang (eds) *Language and Education in Post-colonial Hong Kong* (pp. 179–94). Hong Kong: Linguistic Society of Hong Kong.

Lin, A., Wang, W., Akamatsu, A. and Riazi, M. (2002) Appropriating English, expanding identities, and revisioning the field: From TESOL to Teaching English for Glocalized Communication (TEGCOM). *Journal of Language, Identity and Education* 1 (4), 295–316.

Lin, A. and Luk, J. (2002) Beyond progressive liberalism and cultural relativism: Towards critical postmodernist and sociohistorically situated perspectives in ethnographic classroom studies. *Canadian Modern Language Review* 59 (1), 97–124.

Lin, A. and Luk, J. (2004) Local creativity in the face of global domination: Insights of Bakhtin for teaching English for dialogic communication. In J.K. Hall, G. Vitanova and L. Marchenkova (eds) *Contributions of Mikhail Bakhtin to Understanding Second and Foreign Language Learning*. Mahwah, New Jersey: Lawrence Erlbaum.

Lin, A. and Man, E. (forthcoming) *Bilingual Education: Southeast Asian Perspectives*. Hong Kong: Hong Kong University Press.

Luke, A. (2002) Educational futures. Plenary speech delivered at the 13th World Congress of Applied Linguistics, 16–21 December 2002, Singapore.

Martin, P.W. (1996) Code-switching in the primary classroom: One response to the planned and unplanned language environment in Brunei. *Journal of Multilingual and Multicultural Development* 17 (2–4), 128–44.

Martin, P.W. (1999) Bilingual unpacking of monolingual texts in two primary classrooms in Brunei Darussalam. *Language and Education* 13 (1), 38–58.

Martin, P.W. (2003) Bilingual encounters in the classroom. In J-M. Dewaele, A. Housen and Li Wei (eds) *Bilingualism: Beyond Basic Principles* (pp. 67–88). Clevedon: Multilingual Matters.

Pennycook, A. (2000) English, politics, ideology: From colonial celebration to postcolonial performativity. In T. Ricento (ed.) *Ideology, Politics and Language Policies: Focus on English* (pp. 107–119). Amsterdam: John Benjamins.

Pennycook, A. (2004) Performativity and language studies. *Critical Inquiry in Language Studies* 1 (1), 1–26.

Chapter 2

Nation-building in a Globalised World: Language Choice and Education in India

E. ANNAMALAI

Education in Ancient India

Education in precolonial India was localized. Although the ruler and other locally powerful and wealthy people influenced education through patronage, they did not control it. There were non-local education centres (for example, Nalanda, from the 5th century to the 12th century) that provided religious education, which included teaching of philosophy, logic and grammar (Gosh, 2001). The medium of education in them was a non-local language like Sanskrit or Pali. Locally, the centre of education was the teacher, who decided the curricular content and the learning outcome, but who did not deviate from the broad desires of the community he served. The educational needs of caste groups differed along the lines of the social roles prescribed for them and so did the curricular content including the language taught. The language taught was also the medium of teaching. It was Sanskrit for the priestly Brahmins, Pali for Buddhist monks, and the local language for others engaged in farming, trade and artisan work. Education served the purpose of preparing the different groups of people to perform their socially ascribed roles, and the choice of language to be taught was the one needed for those roles. The choices whether to have an education and what language in which to have this education in precolonial India were dictated by the hierarchical nature of the society organized on the basis of ascription of sacred and various kinds of secular work to groups of people by their birth.

The Colonial Education Policy

In colonial India, education became centralized in order to standardize the educational outcome across the country and came to be controlled by

20

the state politically and bureaucratically (Shahidullah, 1987). The curricular content and language choice in education were decided on political grounds and were meant to be common to all social groups. The political objectives of education and the choice of language were made in order to improve the colonial subjects in their temporal usefulness and behavioral morals, and to have a cadre of people to assist the colonial government by working in subordinate positions and by being the buffer between the rulers and the masses. To improve their usefulness, the subjects had to acquire the knowledge and skills needed for assisting the colonial government and for providing resources in terms of materials and labour for the industrial economy of the colonizing country. To improve their morals, the subjects had to acquire the values and world-view of the English and, consequently, allegiance to the colonial government. To meet these objectives, it was believed that education should impart to the colonial subjects the European values and knowledge, scientific and social, of that time. The content and goal of education were dictated by the need to produce consenting subjects to serve the interests of the colonial government. They also aimed at moulding their minds by negating their native values and knowledge and substituting them with European values that were accepted as superior.

Given this objective, English, in which the European values and knowledge were available and in which the administrative skills must be developed for governance, was the obvious choice as the language taught and as the medium of teaching. The colonial rulers, however, debated the need for a strategy for the execution of their educational objectives that would have minimal financial cost to the government, and minimal political cost arising out of social tensions from the educational changes. Three strategies were debated about the medium, while English would be taught as a language for developing language skills and cultural attitudes (Annamalai, 2001). The first strategy was to modify the content of the education imparted to the traditional elite through classical languages, primarily Sanskrit and Persian, by adding to it the works that codified European knowledge and values through translation (Sharma, 1986: 183). The educational objective would reach the masses through their own languages, called vernaculars, with the aid of this newly oriented traditional elite. This strategy would co-opt the traditional elite to the colonial project, help them partially retain their control over education and avoid a major social disruption. The ideological position of the educators and administrators who advocated this strategy was known as the Orientalist position.

The second strategy was to give education through the medium of English to a small percentage of the population, who in turn, as teachers and opinion-makers, would help spread European knowledge and values to the rest of the population through their own languages. This strategy would create a new elite, who would be loyal to the colonial government and would be the mediators between it and its subjects. By keeping small the population educated through English, the demand for jobs in the government would be under control and, consequently, social unrest arising out of being unable to get white-collar jobs after English education would be kept in check. This position was known as the Anglicist position and it became the official policy in 1835, when Governor General William Bentinck accepted the recommendation of the Committee on Public Instruction headed by Thomas Macaulay. The recommendation clearly articulated the assimilatory goal of education for the natives to be 'educated in the same way, interested in the same objects, engaged in the same pursuits with ourselves [the English, to] become more English than Hindus' (McCully, 1966: 72).

The third strategy was to impart European knowledge and values directly to most of the population in their native languages through schools funded by the government. There were not many supporters of this position in the government, as it was considered too expensive and impractical. This strategy underlies the policy position adopted by the postcolonial government with the rhetorical change of European to modern with regard to knowledge and values, supplementing with more Indian historical and cultural content. The cost of providing universal education was accepted to be primarily the responsibility of the government of the independent country. The essence, however, of the Anglicist position, that those educated through English would be a small, new elite, would be granted access to power, wealth and status, and would be the agents of change towards a modernized society, continues to be found in the postcolonial educational system (Annamalai, 2001). The private schools, on the other hand, explicitly adopt this position and offer English-medium education, as in the colonial period. The conflict between the goal of mass education through native languages and elitist education through English creates a tension between the policy of the government and the demands of the people, between government schools that implement the policy and the private schools that fulfill popular demands. The tension leads to divergence between policy and practice with regard to the medium of education, as will be discussed later.

The Colonial Construction of Knowledge

The European knowledge imparted in colonial education was not just the knowledge developed out of experience and experiments in Europe from the Renaissance and the Industrial Revolution. It was also the knowledge constructed by Europeans about the Orient from their perspective and for their purpose (Said, 1978). New knowledge was created about Indian history, mythology, religions, society and culture as well as about the physical and natural things of India, which were surveyed and categorized to make sense of the colonized country and to interpret it in European terms. New disciplines were developed moulded in the European intellectual tradition and theoretical framework to understand the unfamiliar colonized people and lands. Native knowledge systems about health care and environment were replaced with European ones (Chatterjee, 1996).

The basic premise of constructing knowledge about the colonized country and its people was the dichotomy of the self and the other. The colonized people were the other and the purpose of the colonial education was to reduce this otherness in the people. This perverted the universal educational goal of the making aware of the self to condemnation of the self. Postcolonial education has the task of reversing this perspective of self and of deconstructing the colonial knowledge of the people now independent and thus decolonizing their mind. This exercise goes beyond replacing, for example, the History or Sociology of Britain with the History or Sociology of India and involves reconstructing Indian History and Sociology. The choice of language in education provides the necessary first step and frame of mind to engage in this process.

Indeterminate Medium Policy in Independent India

Any commission (Bhatt & Aggarwal, 1977) appointed from a decade before Independence until the present to study the prevailing educational system and to make recommendations for a new educational framework has considered change of medium fundamental for building a new nation. This change is the accepted educational policy and it is to be implemented at all levels of education. The major Indian languages were optional media of education from the 1920s when the political power was shared by the colonial government with Indian political parties. The education portfolio was under the charge of an Indian minister and the Indian-language medium reflected a political objective different from that of the colonial government mentioned above. About half of the schools provided an Indian language medium as an alternative by the year 1937 (Nurullah & Naik, 1951: 650), and so it was a question of extending it to all schools ('gradually' [item V: 1], according to the Secondary Education Commission of 1953 [also called Mudaliar Commission by its chair]), after the colonial government ended in 1947. In the case of colleges, it was a new policy to change the medium. The education commissions hedged the policy when it came to the time line for implementing the new policy in higher education with platitudes like 'the medium will be changed as early as practicable' (8: 3) (University Education Commission of 1949 [also called Radhakrishnan Commission by its chair]), 'urgent steps should be taken for the change of medium' (Indian Education Commission of 1968 [also called Kothari Commission by its chair]). It is the same in the current National Policy in Education as reformulated in 1986. The absence of pre-scription of a time line in the policy dilutes the accountability of the government for its implementation.

The ambivalence of the policy at the tertiary level affects the choice of medium at both secondary and primary levels. The students with English medium at the lower level are advantaged at the higher level and this pushes the English medium down to lower classes, even to pre-school, by demand from parents. There are political reasons (such as class interests and regional interests) for promoting English in education and other domains and they have been discussed elsewhere (Annamalai, 2003). The promotion of English in the context of the education policy for nation building alone will be discussed in this chapter.

The recommendations of expert commissions about language policy in education mentioned above stem from a vision of building a nation out of a colony, which is based on a sense of pride in its cultures and languages and on skills and knowledge needed for an industrial economy. It is to be built by repudiating what the colonial rule did with regard to the first policy goal (national pride and solidarity) and by refurbishing with regard to the second (skills and knowledge needed for an industrial economy). The natural language policy for achieving the first was replacement of English and the recommended language policy for achieving the second was retention of English. There is inherent conflict between these two policy propositions and it is pronounced in education, which prepares the citizens of the country for their cultural and their economic lives. The solution to the conflict was to give a statutory recognition and elevation to Indian languages as the medium in the domains of power such as public adminis-tration, law and education, but in practice to delay their actual use until they became ready through internal development to perform the assigned roles. A corollary to this policy of delayed implementation was to calibrate the implementation to come later at college and university levels. This conflict resolution was a recipe for policy failure, as it brought pressure to continue English-medium education at the school level.

Focusing on preparing the Indian languages to take the place of English, the governments at the federal and state levels created through subject spe-cialist committees millions of technical terms in science and other academic subjects, law and administration, and wrote or translated hundreds of textbooks and glossaries in them. This was considered an exercise in language development, but it was a development devoid of use and so was useless. The premise underlying the replacement of English was that the Indian languages must first become like English to play its role, not its converse that the Indian languages must first assume the role of English to become like it in course of practice. It is planning language development that goes against the principle of natural language evolution. With the exponential increase in knowledge created in English and the explosive increase in the power of English globally in the postcolonial world, the goal of catching up with English will be perpetually delayed.

Dissonance between Policy and Practice

Coupled with the globally heightened pull of English, the differential implementation of the replacement of English domestically in India, which put the change on hold at the higher levels of education, brought popular pressure on the policy to have English-medium education at the lower levels, as mentioned above. It also made unattractive the Indian-language medium optionally offered at the tertiary level of education, commonly for subjects in humanities and social sciences. The choice of the Indian-language medium at the college level is made primarily by students who are poor economically and scholastically (Shanmugan & Pandian (n.d.). This stigmatizes this medium in the competitive educational and economic environments, undermines its validity and diminishes its appeal.

The national solidarity dimension of the policy does not allow the pressure, global and local, to discard the policy, but the pressure has brought divergence between policy and practice. The deferred implementation of medium change at the college level built into the policy has become *de facto* non-implementation. At school level, the special situations allowed in the policy for the continued use of the English medium have been extended to include students who are not specially placed. Children of parents, primarily employed in the federal government and in the armed forces, who move on the job from one state to another, which have different media of education, have special schools with English and Hindi media. These schools are administered by the Central Board of School Education (as different from the State Boards of School Education), which has a provision for accrediting private schools. Private schools established to satisfy the demand from the public for English medium (and to make a profit) are accredited to the Central Board and they provide education through English. Though the number of English-medium schools in the country is small (about 10%) (NCERT, 1999: Ch.11) compared to the schools of Indian-language medium, which provide free or highly subsidized education and are mostly run or funded by the state governments, they cater to the needs of the influential urban middle and upper classes, which produce the decision makers and opinion-makers of the country. The demand for English-medium schools, however, is percolating to the urban working class and rural farming class, for whom the middle-class ways are the model for success.

Another factor exploited to establish English-medium schools that results in divergence between policy and practice is the constitutional provision for the minorities to establish and administer educational institutions to further their educational and cultural interests and to maintain the cultural and linguistic diversity of the country. The minorities have the freedom to have a modified curriculum including the languages taught and to choose the medium of instruction, which could be their mother tongue and different from the official language of the state, which is the medium of instruction in government schools. Very many minority communities, however, choose English medium as it is perceived to give an advantage to the minority students over those students whose mother tongue is the state official language, and who have their education in the official language (Annamalai, 1998). The minority schools can admit students from the majority community and the majority community comes to have English-medium education in this way.

The continuance of English medium in education concurrently at school level and near exclusively at college level defeats the policy goal of nation-building with equal educational opportunities for all. The apprehension expressed by educational commissions recommending policy to the government that dual medium will create two nations on the basis of language, one in which life is defined by English and the other where it is defined by the many Indian languages, has become real in spite of the accepted policy for changing the medium from English (Srivastava & Sharma, 1991). The dual medium produces students with different aspirations, world views and personal attitudes about self and society (Krishna Kumar, 1996). This divisiveness in the population is not conducive to building a cohesive nation.

Failure of Policy Goals

Education through the medium of English is detrimental also to the knowledge development necessary to build the nation economically. Learning subjects through a poorly commanded language encourages learning through memorization, which gives knowledge that is not critical, creative and applicable to the problems of real life and the needs of the society. The knowledge is imitative, and not interpretive. Learning English takes precedence over learning the subjects in the subject classes. Any English learnt in the subject classes turns out bookish, with minimal communicative potential. The students who are successful, intellectually and communicatively, in English-medium education are from socioeconomically privileged homes and schools. A universal educational system built on outcomes that are exceptions does not provide the input needed for national development. It contributes to elite formation, as colonial education did, with the difference that the elite are rulers themselves, and not mediators between the rulers and the masses.

The classroom practices in the majority of schools show that instruction through the medium of English is rather symbolic, not substantive. The teachers, who are not very proficient in English, prepare questions and answers in advance and dictate them to the students, who commit them to memory by copying them many times. There is no classroom interaction in which students express themselves and ask questions on the subjects taught because of 'silencing by English', the way the teacher makes use of the students' inability in English in order to keep them quiet in the class, i.e. by not permitting questions in the students' language. The English used by the teacher does not provide an acceptable model to follow for the students. The inadequate proficiency of teachers in English is inevitable, given the number of teachers required. It means that most students come out of English-medium education with poor English skills, which does not help them or the country. The situation will be far worse if English medium becomes universal by changing the policy. All teachers at all levels (classes one to 12) in schools, numbering 4.5 million (93% of whom work in rural schools), must then be proficient in English to use it as the medium of instruction in the school (NCERT, 1999: Ch.11).

Languages in the School

There is no widespread disagreement in India about the need for learning English for the advancement of individuals and the nation. The primary reason for the public demand for English medium in education is the belief that it will give proficiency in English, which matters most in education even in the postcolonial period. It is a total immersion program in popular perception. Learning English in this way is high in social and intellectual cost, as mentioned above. It is counter-productive not even achieving the narrow goal of proficiency in English for the majority of students. Hence the policy is to teach English as a subject and it is included as one of the languages taught in schools.

Historically, the choice of languages in education was dictated by educational objectives, which were locally defined. For religious or spiritual education, the choice of Sanskrit or Arabic was common. There could be other languages for the needs of the temporal life, which varied in different regions. English was the temporal language *par excellence* during the colonial period in the British-administered provinces as well as in the princely states under the tutelage of the British. Though the colonial policy was to limit the choice of English, as mentioned earlier, it was increasingly available in a wide spectrum of schools, including the missionary schools.

At the time of independence, the administrative units of the Indian Union were historical formations of the colonial rule. They reflected the history of the annexation of territories by the British, and not any natural basis. Each unit had speakers of many languages with no one with a superior status; the educational system offered a list of languages for the students to choose from. When the administrative units were reorganized into linguistic states in the 1950s with one majority language in each state, other languages in that state became minority languages. The majority language generally became the official language of the state and also the official medium of education. A policy of language choice known as 'Three-Language Formula' was evolved as a political consensus arrived at by the chief ministers to be implemented in the states (Aggarwal, 1991). The three languages are the regional language, which is generally the majority language of the state, English and Hindi or another Indian language. It is Hindi in the states where it is not the regional language. It is another Indian language in the states where Hindi is the regional language. The policy pre-scribes that it must be one of the modern languages, not a classical language of India and prefers it to be a language from the southern region of the country. Though this is the formula enunciated in the policy, there is variation and flexibility in the languages actually chosen by the students because of historical and political reasons.

The three languages are called first, second and third language in a cur-ricular sense. Their teaching starts at different classes or grades; they have different quantum of instructional hours and different weights in grade points or credits. The regional language is the first language; it is taught from class one and is generally the medium of instruction. The first language is English in English-medium schools. English is the second language all over the country, but its teaching begins in different classes in different states. It is taught from a primary-level class (classes one to four or five) in many states, and in some from class one. The third language is taught from the post-primary level. All three languages are taught up to the end of the secondary level (class ten). In the higher secondary level (classes 11 and 12), there is no third language. It is the language taught for the least number of years.

Political Versus Cultural Factors in Language Choice

The three languages prescribed in the policy are the official languages of the state (the regional language) and of the Union (Hindi and English). It is clear that the policy is motivated by the instrumental objective in the choice of languages. The mother tongue of the linguistic minorities in the states does not find a place in the formula, though the Constitution enjoins the states to endeavour to use it as the medium of instruction at the primary level under certain conditions of numerical strength in the class of students speaking the minority language. The classical language symbolizing cultural and religious heritage (Sanskrit for Hindus, primarily of upper castes and Arabic for Muslims), which had pride of place in traditional education, is not included in the formula either. Exclusion of these two categories of language from the formula is one of the factors causing deviation in practice from the policy.

The linguistic minorities that have political strength in the state call for the inclusion of their language in the formula as the first language at the primary level, and beyond if their strength is considerable. Since learning four languages is argued to be an unequal educational burden for the minorities, the inclusion of the minority language tends to exclude the regional language from the formula. The call for the inclusion of a classical language, commonly Sanskrit, as the third language in Hindi states excludes non-Hindi regional languages. The exclusion of regional languages from the formula in practice, which are not the mother tongues of the students, whether they are minorities in the states and the majority in the country (the latter are Hindi speakers, who are actually the largest minority in the strict numerical sense), raises questions about the national integration aimed at in the policy as regards the nature of integration. The integration envisaged in nation-building is multidirectional and multi-layered, with reciprocal integration between linguistic communities at the state level and between states at the national level. The integration is to evolve not by losing language diversity, but by strengthening it through learning others' languages. When geographic contiguity or social proximity is not there for learning through interaction, education provides the opportunity to learn. The minorities in the states have economic motivation to learn the regional language of the state they live in and they are willing to learn it when there is no cost to their cultural and political interests. But the Three-Language Formula does not provide for the minorities to learn both their language and the official language of the state. The formula is not flexible. Its rigidity, built on its premise of unidirectional vertical integration, leads to its non-adherence in practice by the minorities in the states.

The students in Hindi states do not have the economic motivation to learn another Indian language. Any economic opportunity in other states for them is likely to be available because of their knowledge of English rather than their knowledge of regional languages. This is owing to the nature of the job market and the place of English in it. The policy is formulated with the aim of national integration resulting from the knowledge of the language of another culture. It also has a defensive side to it as an answer to the political charge that the language load is less for the students speaking Hindi, which doubles as the regional language and as an official language of the Union. The students and their parents would be expected to have less of a problem in travelling the same distance as the rest of the students in the county. They prefer to choose Sanskrit, as mentioned above, for its heritage value and for its 'score value', which is that it is easier to score high marks in the Sanskrit examination, which tests mechanical skills (such as declension and conjugation) and receptive skills (like translation) in the teaching of this text-based language, and not productive skills, as in the teaching of a living language. The minority of Hindi-speaking students who choose a regional language of other states, particularly of southern states, as intended by the policy, end up with a sketchy grasp of it. They do not go beyond acquiring rudimentary skills in the language, which are lost after school. The formula with regard to the third language is not even symbolic of its purpose in the Hindi states. It is just an examination ritual, which is also dispensed with in some states by declaring the third language as a non-examination subject.

Hindi in the formula is not to equip the people to be ready for the nation-building tasks when it replaces English in the process of decolonization, as originally envisaged at the time of Independence. English was not replaced by Hindi in 1965 when the time line given for it in the Constitution ended, and it will continue to be the additional official language of the Union along with Hindi until non-Hindi speakers agree to its complete replacement. This means that students will have to have both languages and this is reflected in having both in the formula. But English is given more weight as a second language than Hindi, which is a third language. The purpose of learning Hindi is not cultural integration, nor even political integration, as much as it is administrative consolidation. Indian cultural integration has been, historically and contemporarily, not through one language but through multiple languages. There is no one language designated as the national language in the Constitution and so allegiance to one language (Hindi) is not expected for integrating the country politically. There is therefore no reason connected with political integration for learning Hindi, though many educated people may feel that knowing Hindi is part of Indian identity and nationalistic spirit. Hindi is learned in schools through the formula (and outside schools) to increase economic opportunities, particularly for employment in and transactions with the central government, and educational institutions and commercial establishments under it. It is also learned, though not its formal variety, for communicating with speakers of another Indian language, who do not know English.

The Soft Power of English

The purpose of learning English is clearly not the cultural integration of the nation. The attitudinal integration with English culture through English language in education during the colonial period is politically irrelevant (and incorrect) in postcolonial India. It is for the economic progress of the individual from the point of view of the learner and also of the country from the point of view of the policy. English finds a place in the language policy for that part of it that aims at developing the skills and knowledge needed for nation-building. The overall policy of national development is to supplement the skills and knowledge at the advanced level with English, which would be basically developed with Indian languages. Because of the retention of English as the medium at the tertiary level of education, as mentioned above, English has assumed a primary role in the minds of the people to achieve this policy goal.

There is, however, a new kind of cultural integration in which English plays a pivotal role. It is class culture, with its distinctive group behavior, ideas about life and view of the world of others, and it is disseminated to the members of the class by English. English is the cross-linguistic symbol of the identity and solidarity of this class, which is economically the middle and upper class of the country. The national integration intended in the policy, though, is of integrating primordial differences between communities into an Indian community at an abstract level. English has also assumed a role in another kind of cultural integration in the globalized world, which puts a premium on what is called a global culture but which is heavily drawn from Western cultural values. The global culture supersedes the national and ethnic cultures; it does not add to them. English is the key to this overpowering culture that offers material rewards to its adherents. This cultural role of English marks down the value of nation-building in the cultural sphere through identification with Indian languages. The ideological and behavioral integration with Europe planned though the language policy in education in the colonial period re-enters in the disguise of global integration, with English playing the same instrumental role.

The primary role of English in the economic dimension of nation-building has been strengthened in recent times by the forces of a global economy with a common market, where the supply and demand of goods and services go over national boundaries with minimal checks. English is the language of the global market, and its attendant job market. The new global economic order has similarities to the colonial order of the past. The developed countries, led by USA, most of which are former colonists, exercise control over the developing countries, most of which are former colonies. The control is not physical and political but structural and economic, the method used is not physical force, but the offer of surplus money and the superior technology available with it to further interests. As the army of a country made its language dominant in the past, so the financial and technological muscle of a country makes its language dominant in the present. English has gained global dominance by both, which is not a historical coincidence. A vital instrument of the soft power (Nye, 2002) of neocolonialism exercised by remote control is English, which controls not by coercion but by seduction. The image of English as the language of oppression in the colonial era has come to be projected as the language for freedom from poverty in the postcolonial world.

The Impact of the Power of English on Policy

The soft power and economic ideology of English have improved its political desirability in postcolonial countries. The twin goals of language policy, to promote self-pride and self-progress of the individual and the nation, were planned to be achieved in postcolonial countries by denying English, instantly or gradually, the dominant role it played in the domains of power. The postcolonial change in the perception of English has made it possible to bifurcate the goal and keep English for progress indefinitely. This reinforced the place of English in education, undermining the strategy to redefine its place in this sphere. This fundamental change in perception has contributed to instability and ambivalence in policy, and dissonance between policy and practice in the acts of policy-makers as well as people. An example of instability is frequent changes in the policy. Given the aim of the ultimate replacement of English by Hindi and the resentment of Hindi speakers towards English (with which the speakers of other languages hold power because of their early supremacy over it) as an obstacle to their power, a Hindi state, Bihar, found it politically prudent to remove English from the formula. (By similar political prudence, a non-Hindi state, Tamilnadu, did the converse of removing Hindi from the formula.) Bihar reinstated English in education after a few years when the power of English in its new incarnation could not be rejected. The state of West Bengal, ruled by the Communist Party (which, under a policy of primacy for the language of the proletariat, had postponed the teaching of English to the post-primary level, has recently reversed the policy to teach it from class one.

The case of ambivalence in policy was pointed out earlier in not fixing a definite time line for changing the medium of higher education from English. With regard to language choice, the ambivalence of the policy is revealed when English is the only language made available for study in professional courses and when Indian languages as subjects are progressively removed from courses in science and commerce. It is a reflection of ambivalence when English is allowed to be the first language in school education on the grounds that the first language is the mother tongue of the students, and the parents (not only descendants of mixed marriage with Europeans in the colonial period, but also educated people of interlingual marriage and people who claim to have shifted their primary language at home to English) have the right to declare it as their mother tongue.

The dissonance between policy specification and people's preference was mentioned in the context of the growing number of English-medium schools. The above instances of asking for English as first language, second language and third language indicate dissonance with regard to language choice. The dissonance at the policy level arises by leaving unresolved some contradictions between curricular objectives and pedagogical methods of language teaching. The Indian Education Commission recommended in 1968 that English should be the library language, meaning that it would be the language for knowledge acquisition (Tickoo, 1996), more so for knowledge not available in Indian languages. It also meant that the knowledge available in English would be transferred to Indian languages through translation and other means. The pedagogical method of teaching English with such a curricular objective should concentrate on receptive skills, decoding texts, technical registers, translation, simplifying language, etc. But the actual method of teaching English in the classroom is structural and communicative, which aims at developing productive skills. This stems from the *de facto* use of English in India for communication with other Indians among the middle and upper class and the increasing use of English in business communication. Such a use of English in life does not find due recognition in the policy, which expects Hindi to become the language of wider communication for all classes.

Mismatch between Policy and Pedagogy

Given the *de facto* use of English in the country, the pedagogy of English has adopted the principles of second language teaching (ESL). Second language teaching methods will be used in countries where English has institutionalized status and functions and where one is exposed to English passively, if not actively, outside the classroom at home, in the market place and from the media. This is true of English in India (Kachru, 1983), but India is heterogeneous with regard to exposure to English. The first-generation learners from rural areas, who form a large percentage of students in government schools, have nil or severely limited exposure to English before and after school. The ESL method is not best suited for teaching English to them; it must be combined with the principles of teaching English as a foreign language (EFL). The language policy does not a make a pedagogical distinction of social conditions when English will be taught as a second language and as a foreign language in India.

While the place of English in education is becoming strengthened, the content of the English taught is changed to reflect the Indian ethos and milieu and it incorporates Indian themes including the mythological and situations including the traditional in the lessons. The pragmatics of the use of English in India is accepted in the lessons. The writings by Indian authors form part of the English textbooks. The English language used in them admits some collocations, vocabulary and grammatical constructions that are not found in 'native' English. It is one aspect of decolonizing the English language by nativizing it in the normative teaching context to some degree and in some respects. Nativization gives a sense of ownership of English to Indians and voids any nationalistic antipathy to it. But it disjoins the teaching of English in the classroom from the policy of using it, during and after education, as a language for accessing the knowledge codified in its international standard form.

Nativized English in India naturally has a range of variation from the standard native variety of newspapers to the pidgin of the tourist guide. The English of students from socially disadvantaged castes (the first-generation students mentioned earlier predominantly come from these social groups) has diverged from the Indian standard by the end of their schooling. This variety of English prevents them from acquiring the social status and economic benefits English offers to others, thereby leading to social and political tension. This is a somewhat different manifestation of the social unrest feared by the colonial rulers about the use of English in universal education that was mentioned earlier. It is a matter of political ideology whether such 'deficient' English is interpreted as a subversive act by the low-caste students to unsettle the purity and hegemony of English monopolized by the upper castes (Dasgupta, 1993, 2000), or a conspiratorial act of the upper-caste teachers to keep the lower-caste students from entering into the sanctum of English and thus from the status and other rewards the entry bestows (Anand, 1999). It could be simply a matter of pedagogical failure caused by the universal method of teaching of English that fails to take cognizance of its alien nature in their socialization process and class moorings for the students socially marginalized for generations and lacking the lineage of colonial English education. The net result is that English does not equalize opportunities as projected, but it actually reproduces inequality, not only by that language *per se* but also by its varieties.

If nativization of English formally and functionally is decolonizing it by using it natively, decolonizing it in teaching takes place by nativizing the content of the English course, as mentioned above. This process is Janus-faced, looking East and West, in the English courses meant for those specializing in English language and literature at the college and university level to become teachers of English among other things. These courses teach the canons of English literature as developed during the colonial period (after experimentation first in the colony (Viswanathan, 1989)) and as modified periodically in the home country of English. The curricular objective of such a course in English does not reflect the needs and aspirations of the free, sovereign country. The curricular content of specialist courses in English has been gradually changing, in the midst of some resistance, to include the study of literature in English written by non-native speakers, comparative study of English literature with literature in Indian languages, application of Western literary theories to the literature in Indian languages and of classical Indian literary theories to English literature, and the social and political dimensions of teaching the English language to non-natives. After training, the students are encouraged to contribute to their native language's literary development. The courses for specializing in English are trying to be relevant to the postcolonial society while maintaining the link with the colonial past.

Deconstruction of Language Pedagogy

Deconstruction of the colonial bodies of knowledge created from the colonial perspective and for colonial interests, which continue to be transmitted through education irrespective of medium change, is a challenging task. The challenge is to keep the postcolonial reconstruction of bodies of knowledge objective and free of nationalistic ideology. Some efforts in this direction include reworking the focus of the discipline, highlighting the sidelined facts and finding a place for the traditional knowledge; they are tangible in humanities and social science disciplines compared to physical and natural sciences. They are in general more like repairing and renovating with additions and substitutions than redesigning the basic architecture. The content of the Indian-language curriculum is geared towards linguistic, literary and cultural glorification with the reconstruction of a proud past. The risk in the postcolonial reconstruction of knowledge for the purpose of building national pride as part of nation-building has become evident presently when in the name of cultural nationalism knowledge is fabricated and misrepresented to suit the political agenda of the ruling party. Decolonizing the minds of the politically freed people cannot be done by filling them with cultural fundamentalism. Creation of knowledge fueled by the notion of native (religious) cultural supremacy will be no different in subjugating the minds from the knowledge created by the colonialists with the notion of their (racial) cultural supremacy.

The greatest challenge for education in postcolonial India and the choice of language for delivering new education is in combining inculcation of self-pride with self-criticism, of cultural rootedness with cosmopolitanism, and of modernization with tradition. Tradition is an epistemological construct of the colonialists to put in opposition to modernity, which rationalized their construct of the exotic other. It was constructed to be destroyed by their rule in the self-conceived fulfilment of civilizing duty burdened on them by the destiny. Decolonizing education is to question this dichotomy and to use the dynamics of the 'tradition' to adapt to the modern world, and to use the 'tradition' not to get a sense of superiority or security, but to be the site of confidence to change. To do this, education must undermine the linguistic dichotomy reflected ambivalently in policy and assertively in practice that Indian languages are for keeping the tradition and cultural moorings and English is for embracing modernity and material progress; in other words, the former to keep the people local while the latter makes them global. As long as education perpetuates this dichotomy, nation-building will remain notional.

References

Aggarwal, S. (1991) *Three Language Formula: An Educational Problem*. New Delhi: Gian Publishing House.

Anand, S. (1999) Sanskrit, English and dalits. *Economic and Political Weekly* 34 (30), 2053–56.

Annamalai, E. (1998) Language choice in education: Conflict resolution in Indian courts. *Language Science* 20 (1), 29–43.

Annamalai, E. (2001) The colonial language in multilingualism and the process of modernization. In E. Annamalai (ed.) *Managing Multilingualism in India: Political and Linguistic Manifestations*. New Delhi: Sage.

Annamalai, E. (2003) Medium of power: The question of English in education in India. In J.W. Tollefson and A.B.M. Tsui (eds) *Medium of Instruction Policies: Whose Agenda? Which Agenda?* Mahwah, NJ: Lawrence Erlbaum.

Bhatt, B.T. and Aggarwal, J.C. (1977) *Educational Documents in India (1813–1977)*. New Delhi: Arya Book Depot.

Chatterjee, P. (1996) The disciplines of colonial Bengal. In P. Chatterjee (ed.) *Texts of Power: Emerging Disciplines in Colonial Bengal*. Minneapolis: University of Minnesota Press.

Dasgupta, P. (1993) *The Otherness of English: India's Auntie Tongue Syndrome*. New Delhi: Sage.

Dasgupta, P. (2000) Sanskrit, English and dalits. *Economic and Political Weekly* 35 (16), 1407–11.

Gosh, S.C. (2001) *The History of Education in Ancient India*. New Delhi: Munshiram Manoharlal.

Kachru, B. (ed.) (1983) *The Indianization of English: The English Language in India*. New Delhi: Oxford University Press.

Krishna Kumar (ed.) (1996) Two worlds. In Krishna Kumar *Learning from Conflict*. Hyderabad: Orient Longman.

McCully, B.T. (1966) *English Education and the Origins of Indian Nationalism*. New York: Columbia University Press (reprint by Peter Smith, Gloucester, MA).

NCERT (1999) *Sixth All India Educational Survey: Main Report*. New Delhi: National Council for Educational Training and Research.

Nurullah, S. and Naik, J.P. (1951) *A History of Education in India (during the British Period)*(2nd edn). Bombay: Macmillan.

Nye, J.S., Jr (2002) *The Paradox of American Power: Why the World's Only Superpower Can't Go It Alone*. New York: Oxford University Press.

Said, E. (1978) *Orientalism*. New York: Pantheon Books.

Shahidullah, Kazi (1987) Patshalas into Schools: *The Development of Indigenous Elementary Education in Bengal 1854–1905*. Calcutta: Firma KLM Pvt. Ltd.

Shanmugan, M. and Pandian, S.V. (n.d.) *College Education through Tamil*. Madurai: Muthu Padippagam (in Tamil).

Sharma, N.K. (1976) *Linguistic and Educational Aspirations Under a Colonial System*. Delhi: Concept Publishing House.

Srivastava, R.N. and Sharma, V.P. (1991) Indian English today. In R.S. Gupta and Kapil Kapoor (eds) *English in India: Issues and Problems*. New Delhi: Academic Foundation.

Tickoo, M.L. (1996) English in Asian bilingual education: From hatred to harmony. *Journal of Multilingual and Multicultural Development* 17 (2–4), 225–40.

Viswanathan, Gowri (1989) *Masks of Conquest: Literary Study and British Rule in India*. New York: Columbia University Press.

Chapter 3

Critical, Transdisciplinary Perspectives on Language-in-Education Policy and Practice in Postcolonial Contexts: The Case of Hong Kong

ANGEL M.Y. LIN

A Critical Preamble

I set out to attempt two critical projects in this chapter: first, that of destabilizing the centre-periphery dichotomy in the process of academic knowledge production; and second, that of reflexively problematizing and revisioning the role of the academic researcher researching on language-in-education policies and practices in former/post/neocolonial contexts.

Researchers located in the so-called 'peripheries' of the Anglo-European academic 'centres' are taken seriously mainly (albeit with some significant exceptions, as in this volume) as contributors to the so-called 'area studies'. For instance, in a typical anthology on critical issues in TESOL or language education policies, periphery researchers (i.e. those working in non-Anglo-European contexts) are usually invited to contribute a piece on the language education issues in their own geographical areas. Usually they draw on theoretical and methodological perspectives provided in the core theories of the discipline delineated mostly by theorists and researchers in the Anglo-European centres (e.g. US, UK) and apply these general theories to analyse the particular issues in their respective areas. In such a way, our understanding of the 'regional' issues is already framed by the perspectives of the Anglo-European 'centre' theorists. This 'general-particular', 'centre-periphery' dichotic, hierarchical epistemological relationship in the discipline is produced and reproduced through the conventional ways in which we participate in this knowledge production process. In this chapter, I attempt to temporarily destabilize such a relationship by seeking to illustrate the potential productiveness of inverting such a relationship: i.e. contributing to the development of critical, transdisciplinary theoretical and methodological perspectives on language-in-education policies and practices through the critical examination of particular studies conducted at the 'periphery' – Hong Kong. To do away with the dichotomy of centre-periphery in academic disciplines, I would like to propose in a postmodernist sense the concept of 'multiplying the centres' (cultural studies theorist Kuang-hsing Chen, July 2002, personal communication) and to argue for the multidirectional and multifarious ways in which theories, applications and knowledge are generated, appropriated, reappropriated, circulated and recirculated so that the 'centre-theory-periphery-application' dichotomy in the academic disciplines can be reworked into more fruitful networks of hybrid types of studies which interpenetrate and interilluminate one another (Morris, 1994).

In the next section, I shall first outline the background of Hong Kong for the unfamiliar reader. Following that, I shall illustrate how different (albeit interconnected and interilluminating) approaches to the studies of language-in-education issues in Hong Kong reflect the different epistemological emphases and sociohistorical positions of the researchers. In the concluding section, I shall discuss the importance of developing self-reflexive, transdisciplinary epistemological and political perspectives in a critical project of language-in-education policy and practice research that aims at going beyond mere academic knowledge production and consumption.

Hong Kong: From Colony to Special Administrative Region

Hong Kong defies any attempt at a neat classification of its political status. From 1842 to 1997, under the Western political/juridical system, it was seen and run as a British colony by the British Hong Kong colonial government. However, the People's Republic of China (China for short below) has never officially or formally rectified the unequal treaties signed in the 19th century by the Ching Dynasty. China had only tolerated its existence as 'a problem left by history'. These treaties were signed under British imperialistic military coercion. By these unequal treaties, Hong Kong Island and the Kowloon Peninsula were ceded, and the New Territories were 'loaned', to Britain for 99 years, giving rise to the '1997 problem'.

Since the early colonial days, vernacular or Chinese-medium education (usually practised as Cantonese in speaking and Modern Standard Chinese in writing) has received little government support. By 1911, the government was providing an English-medium education up to university level for children largely from well-to-do families, and a vernacular primary education for children from less well-to-do families (Irving, 1914). In 1935, a British education inspector, Burney, visited Hong Kong and completed the famous Burney Report (1935), in which he criticized the Hong Kong government for neglecting vernacular education. However, government resources continued to be channelled mainly to English-medium schools, cultivating a Westernized, English-conversant elite among the local Chinese population (see historical documentation by Fu, 1975). Despite the lack of government support, in the period between the consolidation of the Chinese Nationalist Government in China in 1928 and its retreat to Taiwan in 1949, private Chinese-medium schools rapidly outnumbered English-medium schools in Hong Kong owing to the influence and support of institutions in China (see historical documentations by Cheng, 1949; Wong, 1982). However, after 1949, with the People's Republic of China adopting a largely self-isolationist stance towards Hong Kong and the rest of the world, Chinese-medium schools declined in popularity in Hong Kong because there no longer existed an alternative, attractive symbolic market offering higher studies and job opportunities for Hong Kong Chinese-medium school graduates. By the 1980s, 90% of secondary-school students in Hong Kong studied in English-medium schools (see historical documentation by Lin, 1997a; So, 1992).

In the early 1980s, Britain tried but failed to negotiate a renewal of the 'lease' with China. Britain then started its preparation for the decolonization of the colony, mainly in the processes of localizing the civil service (with more and more English-educated Hong Kong Chinese taking up high colonial offices; see Hung, 1994), gradually introducing some democratizing elements into its political system (e.g. introducing district-board elections and popularly elected seats in the legislative council; see Ho, 1995), and expanding a largely English-medium higher education – from a formerly elitist two-university system (admitting about 2% of age-appropriate students) to eight publicly funded universities, most of which maintained English as the teaching medium (admitting about 18% of age-appropriate students). All these processes had the effect of expanding and strengthening a local English-educated Hong Kong Chinese bilingual middle class who have benefited from and will continue to have strong investments in English and British-related institutions, whether political, linguistic or educational. These forces have significantly shaped the sociopolitical and socioeconomic contexts of language-in-education policies and practices in Hong Kong.

On 1 July 1997, the sovereignty of Hong Kong was formally handed over by Britain to China as a Special Administrative Region (SAR). China's policies of One-Country-Two-Systems and Hong-Kong-people-ruling-

Hong-Kong were installed by the selection of a local Chinese patriotic business entrepreneur, Tung Chee-hwa, as the Chief Executive. Mrs Anson Chan, a former British Hong Kong colonial high official (and an English major who graduated from the prestigious, English-medium, University of Hong Kong in 1962), became the Chief Secretary under Tung, leading the former colonial civil force in service of the new Hong Kong SAR government. The status of the English language in Hong Kong has remained as important, if not more so, as in the pre-1997 years. This is consistently reflected in the policy speeches of Tung Chee-hwa, who constantly stresses the importance of the schooling system to produce a workforce which is highly proficient in English to maintain Hong Kong's status as an international financial and business centre, and as bridge between China and the world. A 1998 survey (*Sing Tao Jih Pao*, 1998) found that the majority of business corporations in Hong Kong preferred employees with a good command of English to employees with a good command of Chinese. The ruling elite is the English-educated Hong Kong Chinese elite, in both the business and the political arenas. While one might characterize the situation as 'the show may be different, the performers are more or less the same', one also needs to reflexively analyse one's own speaking position and ideological stance as they do shape one's epistemological perspectives.

Different Perspectives on Language-in-Education Policies and Practices

In this section, I shall describe and critically discuss the different (albeit interconnected and interilluminating) perspectives salient in the range of studies on language-in-education issues in Hong Kong with reference to the epistemological and sociohistorical positions of the researchers. These studies include analyses of colonial and public discourses (Lin, 1997b; Pennycook, 1998, 2002), analyses of mechanisms of social stratification (Lin, 1996) and critical ethnographies (Lin, 1996; Poon, 2000a, 2000b). I shall conclude this section with the perspectives of critical cultural studies (Chan, 2002) and discuss what potentially different kinds of understandings it can fruitfully yield.

Critical analysis of colonial and capitalist discourses

Edward Said in his classic study, *Orientalism* (1978), started the postcolonial analytic project of using critical discourse analysis (drawing on Foucault's notions of knowledge, discourse and power) to deconstruct the colonial discursive construction of Self (the colonizer) and Other (the colonized). Located in this theoretical and analytic tradition, Pennycook's (1998, 2002) critical analysis of colonial discourses on language education policies in Hong Kong in the 19th and early 20th centuries has provided us with a rich source of insights into how *both* mother-tongue/vernacular and English-language education policies could be implicit in the discursive construction of Hong Kong Chinese as docile political and cultural bodies:

> Looking principally at colonial language policy in Hong Kong, I shall show how language policy is a crucial cornerstone of cultural governance that both reflects and produces constructions of the Other. *This understanding of language policy has significant implications not just for Hong Kong in the present but for all contexts of language policy.* (Pennycook, 2002: 91; emphasis added)

Pennycook set out to contribute to the production of knowledge and understanding about language policy not just in Hong Kong but also in general (for all contexts) through analysing the British colonial discourses on language policy in a specific historical context: Hong Kong in the 19th and early 20th centuries. His interest appears to be largely critical-scholarly and his analytical tools come from the tradition of critical discourse analysis and Foucault's (1980) critical exegesis of the interrelationships among power, knowledge and discourse.

Pennycook showed that, while the Anglicist colonial discourses stressing the civilizing mission of the British colonizers (e.g. via English-language teaching and English-medium education) produced a grand rhetoric of empire that still has echoes in some current images of English and international relations, it was the Orientalist colonial discourses that had actually shaped language education policies towards vernacular education in Hong Kong. Pennycook pointed out that the colonial government was promoting vernacular education for its conservative ideals (e.g. Confucian ethics of filial piety, respect for the aged and for authority, and emphasis on social hierarchy) to enhance its political and cultural governance of the colonial subjects:

> ... Often far more important, therefore, than the civilizing zeal of English teaching was the conservative use of vernacular education, developed and implemented by colonial administrators and Orientalist scholars. These were the crucial tools of governmentality through language-in-education policies. Conservative Chinese education was the colonial route to the making of docile bodies. (Pennycook, 2002: 108)

Through analysing the colonial language-in-education policies in a particular historical context of Hong Kong, Pennycook contributed to the larger critical scholarly project of enhancing our knowledge and understanding of subtle forms of surveillance and governance as well as the potential pitfalls of indiscriminately subscribing to liberal and pluralistic approaches to language policy in general:

> This understanding of increased modes of surveillance brings into question two widely held views of language policy: That more liberal and pluralistic approaches to language policy necessarily have less governmental implications; and that mother tongue or vernacular education is necessarily preferable to education in other languages.... I am arguing that the model for understanding the relationship between language policy and broader political concerns needs to move away from an understanding of language policy as the imposition or denial of particular languages. A more fruitful perspective may be to view language policy in terms of governmentality, by highlighting the complex relationships among language policies, cultural politics, curriculum, educational practice, and the modes of surveillance of the liberal state. (Pennycook, 2002: 108)

It is apparent from the above account that Pennycook's critical analysis, written mainly for the scholarly readership in the field of language policy studies, has as its chief aim the production and enhancement of the discipline's knowledge about the nature of the pitfalls of indiscriminate subscription to liberalist and pluralist approaches to language policy in general. Has his study also enhanced our understanding of vernacular and English-language education in Hong Kong? The reader might finish reading his study having a sense of a partial picture of the situation in Hong Kong. However, Pennycook is not to blame, for it is not the chief intention of his study to provide an in-depth historical and contemporary analysis of language-in-education policies in Hong Kong. His position in that paper as a critical scholar committed to the production and enhancement of general knowledge in the field of language policy studies has enabled him to provide us with a brilliant analysis of the pitfalls of certain approaches to language policy in general. This *positioned* and *partial* nature of knowledge produced by researchers (Ang, 1996) is necessarily true of any researcher, and thus must not be seen as a pitfall in itself. What is a pitfall is the failure to recognize the inherent partial and positioned nature of every research study inevitably located in a certain sociohistorical and epistemological position. Rather than negatively critiquing individual studies and their positions, then, we should more productively argue for the need to become a 'tweener' (Luke, 2002), readily travelling between different epistemological positions and explicitly acknowledging the necessary partialness of any single position/study. If this is not always possible in our actual research endeavours, perhaps it is possible (at least vicariously) through explicating and reading between a range of differently positioned studies. This brings us to the critical discourse study of Lin (1997b), which is located in a somewhat different sociohistorical position from that of Pennycook (2002).

Lin's (1997b) critical analysis of the public (official, academic and media) discourses on the 'language problem' in Hong Kong in the early to mid-1990s attempted to problematize the public discursive construction and propagation of (1) a politically and economically defined linguistic hierarchy with English at the top, (2) a capitalistic labour production model of education, and (3) a cognitive computer model of the language learner. Lin analysed how the government and capitalist discourses construct and legitimize English as the most important language for Hong Kong students to master, and tried to show:

> ... how these influential discourses impose a labour-production model of education, denigrate the value of the child's mother-tongue, impose a . . . cognitive model of language and language learning, assume an ahistorical, . . . computer-model of the social actor . . . What are left untalked of are the needs of the school, the teacher, and the child. Very often they are on the receiving end of much of the blame for the lamented shortage of English-proficient labour for the labour market. However, what kinds of constraints are they under (e.g. large class size, heavy workload, and lack of staff development opportunities for teachers; a hierarchical school culture . . . ; a top-down approach to the implementation of government education policies)? . . . the labour-market-driven and cognitive models assumed in the public discourses cannot explain why many Hong Kong students are not motivated to learn and use English and Mandarin Chinese. . . . these models also conceal the differential access that students from different socioeconomic and sociocultural backgrounds have to Mandarin Chinese / English linguistic and cultural resources. These models ascribe students' and teachers' lack of English / Mandarin Chinese resources to individual attributes (e.g., lack of competence, industry, initiative). . . . We need to put the child back into the centre of our discussion to see what children need (and not merely what the labour market needs) and what kind of language education curriculum can be developed both to meet their intrinsic needs [for affirmation of their indigenous languages and identities] and to equip them with the necessary resources to survive and succeed in, as well as to contribute to, our society. (Lin, 1997b: 438–39; words in square brackets added for clarity)

Deeply concerned with the difficult situation of Cantonese-dominant students and teachers located in working-class schools in Hong Kong (e.g. lack of English capital in the family and the school; negative attitudes of students towards the learning of standard languages, including both English and Standard Chinese, lack of resources for teachers working with large, limited-English-speaking classes), and increasingly troubled by the ongoing discourses bashing teachers and students in the public and official media for the alleged declining English standards in Hong Kong, Lin's analysis (1997b) was located in a critical pedagogical epistemological position, seeking to generate a counter-discourse that would affirm the indigenous languages and identities of the students, while at the same time acknowledging societal inequalities in the distribution of linguistic resources (capital) across different social groups. Her project was one of advocating more access to the socioeconomic dominant resource of English for the disadvantaged social groups while at the same time seeking to value their L1 (Cantonese) identities and contest the hegemony of English set up by the linguistic hierarchy constructed and propagated in the official and public discourses. Lin's study (1997b) drew on the notion of linguistic, cultural capital of Bourdieu (1991), and the analytical frameworks of critical pedagogy and cultural identity politics as espoused by ethnic-minority educators in North America such as Delpit (1988).

Lin's (1997b) study is necessarily positioned and partial as, like other critical discourse analytic studies, it has a tendency to focus more on what the powerful parties (e.g. the government, the media) in a society say about subordinate groups (e.g. their discursive construction of teachers and students as incompetent and indolent) without also at the same time showing the agency of members of those groups in their local everyday practices. It is at this point that we should turn to a different (but related) type of approach which seeks to show more of the local social actors' agency and tactics.

Analysis of social stratification mechanisms and critical ethnography

Lin's (1996) study is an example of the use of both macro sociological structural analysis and micro critical ethnographic analysis to explicate the role played by English and language-in-education policies in social stratification as well as the local tactics of school participants to enhance their chances of social mobility despite their current unfavourable socioeconomic position. To understand the background of the study I shall first describe the Hong Kong government's implementation of a dual-stream, pure-medium policy in September 1994 – the Medium of Instruction Grouping Assessment (MIGA) policy (Education Department, 1994). The MIGA policy is a precursor of the later linguistic streaming policy enforced in all public-funded secondary schools starting from September 1998. Under MIGA policy, Secondary 1 entrants (aged around 12) are classified into three groups according to their test scores in English and Chinese. Those within the top 40% in both languages are classified as Group I students and labelled as able to learn effectively in either English or Chinese (approximately 33% of all Secondary 1 entrants). Those who are either not within the top 40% in both languages, or are within the top 40% in one language but not within the top 50% in the other language, are classified as Group II students and labelled as able to learn more effectively in Chinese (approximately 60%). The borderline approximately 7% of all Secondary 1 entrants are classified as Group III students and labelled as able to learn better in Chinese but probably also able to learn effectively in English. Secondary schools are advised to adopt one clear medium of instruction based on the MIGA status of their student intakes.

In practice, schools with Group I students mostly chose English as the medium of instruction. The majority of schools that had been advised to switch to Chinese owing to the low grouping of their student intakes also still continued to call themselves 'English-medium schools', while in reality continuing to operate in a Cantonese-English bilingual oral mode and an English written mode.

Lin (1996) analysed the historical, socioeconomic and political forces leading to the institutionalization of specific social selection mechanisms in Hong Kong and the role played by language-in-education policies (chiefly in the institutionalization of a largely English-medium higher and professional education) in socially stratifying different social groups of children, with those without English capital being stratified early on as second-class in the schooling system and the society. In the critical ethnographic tradition of Canagarajah (1993), Lin (1996) also closely analysed the classroom participants' Cantonese-English code-switching practices and delineated various bilingual discourse formats that seemed to serve a variety of sociocultural, educational and linguistic brokering functions. Situating those linguistic brokering classroom practices in their larger embedding historical and socioeconomic context, Lin argued that these practices were the teachers' and students' local, pragmatic, coping tactics and responses to the socioeconomic dominance of English in Hong Kong, where many students from socioeconomically disadvantaged backgrounds with limited access to English resources struggled to acquire an English-medium education for its socioeconomic value. This analysis builds on perspectives expressed in So (1984, 1992) and Yau (1988).

Poon (2000a, 2000b) conducted ethnographic case studies in four secondary schools from different academic backgrounds in the period between September 1994 and November 1995. Through class observations and interviews with school principals, teachers, students and Education

Department officials, Poon addressed the research question of whether and how the MIGA streaming policy of 1994 was actually implemented in the schools. She found that most of the school participants shared the common social values found among the public in Hong Kong: i.e. (a) seeing English-medium (EMI) schools and students as superior to their Chinese-medium (CMI) counterparts, and (b) wanting to have access eventually to some form of English-medium (EMI) education (e.g. the students would like to have the option of a gradual shift from Chinese medium to English medium while the school personnel favoured the option of streaming by subjects). Her respondents also expressed the common view that the inadequate English proficiency of many teachers and students in Hong Kong is a barrier to implementing EMI education in Hong Kong schools. However, for fear of getting poor student intakes if they adopted CMI as a clear medium of instruction, most of the school participants did not want to switch totally to CMI. Many favoured the option of having some subjects taught in English and some subjects taught in Chinese (i.e. partial immersion) in view of the prevalent social prestige assigned to EMI schools. Poon thus recommended the streaming by subject option as better than the streaming by school option.

Both Lin (1996) and Poon (2000a, 2000b) positioned themselves as sympathizers of the local participants (students, teachers and parents) as opposed to the government's socially stratifying language-in-education policy. By choosing to take up the perspectives of the local participants, their ethnographies sought to explicate both the predicaments that the government policy has placed the local school participants into and their agency as expressed in their local tactical strategies and coping practices despite their unfavourable position (e.g. lack of English resources/capital on the part of teachers and students).

While the sociological and critical ethnographic approaches conducted in the tradition of the above-mentioned studies enable the researchers to critically analyse the social selection and social stratification mechanisms of a society as well as the local agency and coping tactics of social actors in the face of socially divisive and gatekeeping policies, these approaches also tend to epistemologically position the researcher in a way that privileges an analytical lens of social class divisions and an explanatory framework in terms of the production and reproduction of 'capitals' (or lack of them) among different social groups. The findings yielded by these approaches are important but also necessarily partial as their social-class analytic lens tends to filter out other important cultural processes. It is helpful at this juncture to turn to a discussion of the critical cultural studies perspectives.

Production of subjectivities through language-in-education policies and practices: Critical cultural studies perspectives
The critical analysis of contemporary, naturalizing and technicalizing, capitalist discourses (see Lin, 1997b) shows us how English has been discursively constructed as the indispensable, natural, neutral and technical vehicle and medium mainly, if not merely, for accessing advanced science and technology, world civilization and both personal and global socioeconomic success. The sociological and critical ethnographic analysis (also discussed above) further shows us how English as a socially unequally distributed linguistic capital plays an important role in the gatekeeping social selection and social stratification mechanisms of a society, as well as how local social actors have themselves recognized (or 'misrecongized' in a situation of 'symbolic violence'; see Bourdieu, 1991; Lin, 1999) the supreme value of English and strive to use local tactics (e.g. classroom linguistic brokering, code-switching practices) to acquire English capital (i.e. 'English-medium education' in name if not in reality) despite their actual lack of English capital (e.g. many teachers and students are not proficient enough to teach and learn entirely in English; see findings by Lin, 1996 and Poon, 2002a, 2002b, summarized above). While these critical discourse analytic and sociological perspectives have enabled us to ask and seek to answer some important questions regarding the naturalization, legitimization and masking of social privilege, inequality and social stratification mechanisms, some other important cultural questions remain unasked and unexplored. For instance, what are the kinds of identities and subjectivities being produced (as well as negotiated and contested) in a schooling system which constructs the possession of an English-medium education and mastery of the English language as the supreme symbol of and key to a person's educational and socioeconomic success in the modern world? What kinds of cultural identities are being included and/or excluded? What kinds of subjectivities are being produced and contested? To address these questions, I am turning to the analytical lens of critical cultural studies researchers in Hong Kong. Cultural studies researcher Stephen Chan, for instance, presented in a recent seminar the following perspectives:

Critical stance on the question of Hong Kong subjectivity:

Hong Kong as a community of needs, aspirations and solidarity could not have taken the form of the dominant culture of modernity we see today without the substantive rule by the British colonizers, especially during the post-War period. In conclusion, colonial rule was not simply about political domination but a persistent rhetoric of colonial dominance that has grown with capitalist modernity itself. This is a situation we may investigate via the case of the global popular in Hong Kong, asking whether colonialism is in effect a complex modern regime of culture, a dynamic mechanism of control in which *power is meant not to prohibit but to produce subjectivity*. (Chan, 2002; italics added)

If 'colonialism is in effect a complex modern regime of culture, a dynamic mechanism of control in which power is meant not to prohibit but to produce subjectivity' (Chan, 2002), then one should also ask the questions of whether and how language-in-education policies and schooling practices are part of that dynamic mechanism of neocolonial control and what kinds of subjectivities are being produced under that mechanism. Work done from this perspective has been little so far and below is a preliminary exploration of the issues from this perspective. First, from the available data, it seems that it is a deep sense of a 'subaltern subjectivity' being felt by working-class schoolchildren located in socioeconomic positions that are not provided with family and community capital for the acquisition of English:

> *'You want to know why I don't pay attention in English lessons? You really want to know? Okay, here's the reason: NO INTEREST!! It's so boring and difficult and I can never master it. But the society wants you to learn English! If you're no good in English, you're no good at finding a job!'* (Original in Cantonese; said by a 14-year-old schoolboy in an informal interview; from Lin, 1999: 407)

What is expressed by the schoolboy seems to be a deep sense of anger, frustration and yet almost helpless resignation to the recognition that he is condemned both to a current identity of school failure and a future identity of social failure. The power of the dominance of English in the education system and the society and his own painful vision of himself never being able to master English illustrate well the role played by English in a neocolonial, complex modern capitalist regime of culture that is 'meant not to prohibit but to produce subjectivity', and in this case, a subaltern subjectivity (Ashcroft *et al.*, 1998) that perceives her/himself as through and through without any hope for social mobility. Students' creative, subversive practices in the classrooms (e.g. see analysis in Lin, 2000) show us how local classroom participants sometimes resist and contest the production of such subaltern identities by engaging in practices that contribute to the building of alternative, counter-identities, perhaps similar to those found in McLaren's analysis of students' counter-cultural practices in the inner city schools of North America:

> . . . the major drama of resistance in schools is an effort on the part of students to bring their street-corner culture into the classroom. . . . it is a

fight against the erasure of their street-corner identities. . . . students resist turning themselves into worker commodities in which their potential is evaluated only as future members of the labor force. *At the same time, however, the images of success manufactured by the dominant culture seem out of reach for most of them.* (McLaren, 1998: 191; italics added)

For the majority of working-class Cantonese-speaking children in Hong Kong, English remains something beyond their reach. Unlike their middle-class counterparts, they typically live in a lifeworld where few will (and can) speak or use English for any authentic communicative or sociocultural purposes. To most of them, English is little more than a difficult and boring school subject which, nonetheless, will have important consequences for their life chances. Many of them have an ambivalent, want-hate relationship with English. While they accept the dominance of English and recognize that English is very important for their future prospects, they also readily believe that they are no good in English; for instance, in the words of a working-class adolescent girl (G) to the ethnographic fieldworker (F) in the study of Candlin *et al.* (2000: 33, original utterances in Cantonese):

F: Yes, yes, and you, do you have any aspiration, what do you want to do?
G: I want to be a teacher.
F: Teacher {chuckling}, Miss Chan {playfully addressing the girl as a teacher}, it's good to be a teacher, it suits you well. At this moment it seems to suit you.
G.   Don't know if it will change in the future.
F.   You have to be patient, you have to proceed gradually.
G: I have to meet the requirement, my English is poor.

The above exchange shows the working-class adolescent girl's lack of confidence in fulfilling her dream of becoming a teacher in the future because of her own self-image as someone with 'poor English'. Her resigned acceptance of both the importance of English for her future and her poor status in terms of her English ability led to her indication of a lack of confidence in fulfilling her aspiration despite the fieldworker's encouraging remarks. Such low self-esteem as a result of their sense of failure in mastering English makes English a subject highly imbued with working-class students' want-hate desires. English plays a chief role in constructing these students' subaltern identities and their own (self-limiting) understanding/ perception of themselves in relation to others and their subaltern position in the society.

The English-dominant education system seems to have produced an elite bilingual social group whose cultural identities are constructed through their successful investments in an English-medium education, a mastery of the English language and their familiarity with and membership in English-based modern professional institutions (e.g. the various English-based professional associations of accountants, lawyers, doctors and engineers, and English-mediated professional accreditation mechanisms). At the same time, alongside the production of these English-oriented successful modern professional, cosmopolitan subjectivities, the English-dominant education system also seems to be producing another much larger group of subalterns, whose own understanding of themselves and their future life trajectories are greatly delimited by a neocolonial, complex capitalist modern regime of culture that seems to have almost stripped them of any possibility of constructing a valuable, legitimate, successful self with other non-English-based cultural resources (such as mastery of the Chinese language and membership of Chinese cultural institutions, or mastery of Cantonese streetwise tactics and Cantonese popular cultural identities, e.g. through participating in underground Canton-pop bands). The post-1997 years have so far not seen any significant changes in the English-dominant education system and society (see the discussion above), and the dominance of English in post-1997 Hong Kong seems to be even more steadfastly maintained by a neocolonial, complex modern capitalist regime of culture, now that any public criticism of English linguistic dominance can be powerfully neutralized by the neocolonial globalizing capitalist economic and technological discourses. In Hong Kong, we seem to inhabit a world where, increasingly, if one does not find oneself an English-conversant, upwardly mobile cosmopolitan, one is very likely to find oneself a limited- or non-English-speaking parochial subaltern located in the lower-end strata of the society.

Beyond Critique: Travelling Between Disciplines and Positions

The preceding sections illustrate how, by travelling between different disciplinary perspectives, we can develop interilluminating, transdisciplinary, critical theoretical and analytic lenses for researching language-in-education policies and practices in (post-/neo) colonial contexts. Located in the position of a university teacher and researcher, my major semiotic work has been that of the production of knowledge for consumption by other similarly located academics in the community. However, while travelling between disciplines can enable us to develop better public critiques of the English-language education polices and practices in different societal contexts, it is increasingly clear that we also need to travel more often between the roles of academic knowledge producers / consumers and political participants in a world still full of both blatant and subtle forms of social injustice and relations of domination and subordination. As Luke points out:

> To what extent does ideology critique stay, indeed, just that – an intellectual exercise lacking a translation into embodied action that might disrupt, interrupt or transform the fields in question. . . . This remains the basis for a very different sense of the critical – not one of abstraction, of distance, of doubling in a logico-analytic sense, of stepping back via a complex linguistic metalanguage, but the 'out-of-body' watching oneself watch oneself as an object of power and naming oneself as such. . . .
> . . . TESOL must do something other than what it currently does. Otherwise, it will remain a technology for domesticating the 'other' . . . , whatever its scientific and humanist pretences. (Luke, 2003: 13–14)

While what to do and how to do TESOL differently will constitute the subject of another series of projects, both textual and political (e.g. see Chui, 2003; Chiu, 2003; Lin, 2003; Lin _et al._, 2003), I hope that in constituting this chapter as a metacritical and political project (see discussion in the first section), I might have accomplished more that just another intellectual exercise of the discipline.

References

Ang, I. (1996) _Living Room Wars: Rethinking Media Audience for a Postmodern World._ London: Routledge.

Ashcroft, B., Griffiths, G. and Tiffin, H. (1998) _Key Concepts in Post-colonial Studies._ London: Routledge.

Bourdieu, P. (1991) _Language and Symbolic Power_ (G. Raymond and M. Adamson, trans.). Cambridge, MA: Cambridge University Press. (Original work published 1982).

Burney, E. (1935) _Report on Education in Hong Kong._ Hong Kong: Government Printer.

Canagarajah, A.S. (1993) Critical ethnography of a Sri Lankan classroom: Ambiguities in student opposition to reproduction through ESOL. _TESOL Quarterly_ 27 (4), 601–26.

Candlin, C.N., Lin, A.M.Y. and Lo, T-W. (2000) The discourse of adolescents in Hong Kong. Final project report (City University of Hong Kong Strategic Research Grant: #7000707). Department of English and Communication, City University of Hong Kong, Hong Kong.

Chan, S.C.K. (2002) Mapping the global popular: An analytical framework for Hong Kong culture. Paper presented at the Cultural Studies Seminars, 13 December 2002, Lingnan University, Hong Kong.

Cheng, T.C. (1949) The education of overseas Chinese: A comparative study of Hong Kong, Singapore and the East Indies. Unpublished MA thesis, London University.

Chiu, J. (2003) Tailor-making an appropriate English curriculum for limited-English-proficiency learners in a prevocational secondary school. TESL-HK Newsletter, 7, p. 6. On WWW at http://www.tesl-hk.org.

Chui, R. (2003) How to capitalize on your students' L1 in English lessons. TESL-HK Newsletter, 7, pp. 4–5. On WWW at http://www.tesl-hk.org.

Delpit, L.D. (1988) The silenced dialogue: Power and pedagogy in educating other people's children. *Harvard Educational Review* 58 (3), 280–98.

Sing Tao Jih Pao (1998) English important for job promotion: Blow to mother-tongue education [in Chinese]. *Sing Tao Jih Pao*, 1998, May 21.

Education Department (1994) An outline of the medium of instruction grouping assessment. Hong Kong: Government Printer.

Foucault, M. (1980) *Power/Knowledge: Selected Interviews and Other Writings, 1972–1977*. New York: Pantheon.

Fu, G.S. (1975) A Hong Kong perspective: English language learning and the Chinese student. Unpublished doctoral dissertation, University of Michigan.

Ho, E. (1995) Decolonization without democratization: A case study of Hong Kong. Research report. Department of Public and Social Administration, City University of Hong Kong.

Hung, W-F.L. (1984) Decolonization and localization of the civil service in Hong Kong. Research report. Department of Public and Social Administration, City University of Hong Kong.

Irving, E.A. (1914) *The Educational System of Hong Kong*. Hong Kong: Government Printer.

Lin, A.M.Y. (1996) Bilingualism or linguistic segregation? Symbolic domination, resistance, and code-switching in Hong Kong schools. *Linguistics and Education* 8 (1), 49–84.

Lin, A.M.Y. (1997a) Bilingual education in Hong Kong. In J. Cummins and D. Corson (eds) *Encyclopedia of Language and Education* (Vol. 5, pp. 281–89). The Netherlands: Kluwer Academic Publishers.

Lin, A.M.Y. (1997b) Analyzing the 'language problem' discourses in Hong Kong: How official, academic, and media discourses construct and perpetuate dominant models of language, learning, and education. *Journal of Pragmatics* 28, 427–40.

Lin, A.M.Y. (1999) Doing-English-lessons in the reproduction or transformation of social worlds? *TESOL Quarterly* 33 (3), 393–412.

Lin, A.M.Y. (2000) Lively children trapped in an island of disadvantage: Verbal play of Cantonese working-class schoolboys in Hong Kong. *International Journal of the Sociology of Language* 143, 63–83.

Lin, A.M.Y. (2004) Introducing a critical pedagogical curriculum in an MATESL programme: A feminist, reflexive account. In B. Norton and K. Toohey (eds) *Critical Pedagogies and Language Learning* (pp. 271–90). Cambridge: Cambridge University Press.

Lin, A.M.Y., Wang, W., Akamatsu, A. and Riazi, M. (2002) Appropriating English, expanding identities, and revisioning the field: From TESOL to teaching English for glocalized communication (TEGCOM). *Journal of Language, Identity and Education* 1 (4), 295–316.

Luke, A. (2002) Educational futures. Plenary speech delivered at the 13th World Congress of Applied Linguistics, 16–21 December 2002, Singapore.

Luke, A. (2003) Two takes on the critical: A foreword. In B. Norton and K. Toohey (eds) *Critical Pedagogies and Language Learning*. Cambridge: Cambridge University Press.

McLaren, P. (1998) *Life in Schools: An Introduction to Critical Pedagogy in the Foundations of Education*. New York: Longman.

Morris, P. (1994) (ed.) *The Bakhtin Reader*. London: Edward Arnold.

Pennycook, A. (1998) *English and the Discourses of Colonialism*. London: Routledge.

Pennycook, A. (2002) Language policy and docile bodies: Hong Kong and governmentality. In J.W. Tollefson (ed.) *Language Policies in Education: Critical Issues* (pp. 91–110). Mahwah, NJ: Lawrence Erlbaum.

Poon, A.Y.K. (2000a) *Medium of Instruction in Hong Kong: Polices and Practices*. Lanham: University Press of America.

Poon, A.Y.K. (2000b) Implementing the medium of instruction policy in Hong Kong schools. In D.C.S. Li, A.M.Y. Lin, and W.K. Tsang (eds) *Language and Education in Postcolonial Hong Kong* (pp. 148–78). Hong Kong: Linguistic Society of Hong Kong.

Said, E.W. (1978) *Orientalism*. London: Routledge and Kegan Paul.

So, D.W.C. (1984) The social selection of an English-dominant bilingual education system in Hong Kong: An ecolinguistic analysis. Unpublished doctoral dissertation, University of Hawaii.

So, D.W.C. (1992) Language-based bifurcation of secondary education in Hong Kong. In K.K. Luke (ed.) *Issues of Language in Education in Hong Kong* (pp. 69–96). Hong Kong: Linguistic Society of Hong Kong.

Wong, C.L. (1982) *A History of the Development of Chinese Education in Hong Kong*. [In Chinese]. Hong Kong: Po Wen Book Co.

Yau, M.S. (1988) Bilingual education and social class: Some speculative observations in the Hong Kong context. *Comparative Education* 24 (2), 217–28.

Chapter 4

Remaking Singapore for the New Age: Official Ideology and the Realities of Practice in Language-in-Education

RANI RUBDY

Forward-looking, decisive and intensely proactive, Singapore is a city-state that is continually engaged in reinventing itself – spurred on by the wheels of globalization to consolidate its successful development as a thriving, cosmopolitan nation in the New World Order. In its current bid to become the knowledge hub par excellence and gain a competitive edge over its neighbours in the region, Singapore seeks to build a highly skilled service sector and a sophisticated technological infrastructure that will help attract and sustain transnational investment and new entrepreneurial initiatives.

The choice of language(s) of education is a central issue – perhaps *the* central issue – in Singapore's education system, unabashedly harnessed in the service of such capitalist interests. The management of Singapore's dramatic success is largely attributed, for instance, to its choice of English as the dominant working language to help Singapore directly 'plug into the global economy' and to its English-knowing bilinguals. Not surprisingly, then, it is in the education system that the government's role in language planning is most clearly manifested. For this reason, language-related issues continue to be a perennial subject of scrutiny and comment by the leading politicians in the country.

Acutely conscious of its economic vulnerability, highlighted recently by the Asian financial crisis and the September 11 incident, and its dependence on outside for its resources, the Singapore leadership recognizes that complacency has no place and that change is the very essence of Singapore's survival as a viable economy on the world stage. Another pressing

55

question is the desire to forge, among a people who speak different mother tongues and come from divergent traditions, a supraethnic national identity, one which serves the government's vision of economic, social and cultural development. Thus in accomplishing these twin goals of economic progress and social cohesion, the management of language planning in education has undergone a series of directional changes ever since Singapore's independence in 1965. Educational policies and practices are constantly reviewed and refined in a process of continuous fine-tuning, as represented by its innumerable campaigns and educational reforms.

However, I wish to argue that none of these policies, or the powerful ideological discourses that are interwoven with them to regulate and reproduce Singaporean life, are entirely unproblematic. Underneath the success story of Singapore's languages-in-education policies there exist in fact a number of potentially fractious tensions and conflicting interests. Three among them will be focused upon in this chapter: those associated with the powerful ideologies of pragmatism, of multilingualism and of meritocracy.

Singapore's Ideology of Pragmatism and its Notion of the 'Practical'

The language policy that has evolved in Singapore is one of 'pragmatic multilingualism'. Based on the guiding principles of multiracialism (covering multilingualism and multiculturalism), which means equal status and treatment for all races, their languages and cultures, Singapore's multilingual model neatly fits the nation's population into four major ethnic blocs, comprising the Chinese, Malays, Indians and 'Others', with Mandarin, Malay, Tamil and English as the respective official languages representing them. However, in effect, English has clearly been the dominant language ever since Singapore's independence in 1965, followed closely by Mandarin among the Chinese community, as a consequence of the success of the pro-Mandarin campaigns launched annually. Increasingly, the sentimental appeal of Mandarin as a language associated with Chinese culture is being overshadowed by its growing economic currency with the opening of China's markets. Although Malay has been designated as the national language for reasons reflecting Singapore's political history and geographical location, its formal role is mainly ceremonial, while the role of Bazaar Malay as a lingua franca for interethnic communication has declined. Hokkien, a southern Chinese dialect which earlier served as a language of local (and regional) commerce and trade, is very likely to meet the same fate.

This present-day scenario has emerged out of a situation previously characterized by a rich linguistic diversity: At the time of the 1957 constitutional conference, 33 mother-tongue groups were reported present, of which 20 were spoken by more than a thousand speakers (Bokhorst-Heng, 1998: 288, citing Chua, 1962). The Chinese community, comprising 75.5% of the population, was the most heterogeneous group and spoke one or more of the following dialects: Hokkien, Teochew, Cantonese, Hainanese, Foochow, Mandarin and other less-known Chinese dialects. The Malay community, representing 13.6% of the population, was quite homogeneous with 85% speaking Malay as their mother tongue. Of the Indian community, comprising 8.8% of the population, 59% spoke Tamil as their mother tongue, while the rest spoke one of seven other dialects. 'Others' included Europeans, Eurasians, Arabs and other expatriates, most of whom listed English as their mother tongue (71.6%). It has been observed that, curiously, the four languages selected to be official languages of the nation were, in total, mother tongue for only 18.6% of the population: Mandarin 0.1%, Malay 11.5%, Tamil 5.2% and English 1.8% (Bokhorst-Heng, 1998: 288). Clearly, the main reason underlying their choice was the government's perception of how these languages could contribute to the social and political progress of the nation, even though this entailed 'reconceptualizing the internally heterogeneous communities as each definable in terms of one single language, paired with one associated culture' (Ho & Alsagoff, 1998: 210), thereby already sowing the seeds of language shift.

A pragmatic philosophy was espoused very early in Singapore's history by the PAP (People's Action Party) leadership, who in embracing English, the language of colonial oppression, clearly saw its supreme value as 'linguistic capital' (Bourdieu & Passeron, 1977), convertible into other forms of capital. Thus while a number of countries from the outer and expanding circles were ambivalent about the continued use of English in the postcolonial era, Singapore, never squeamish about this issue, embraced the language, promoting it to its current dominant position by attempting to make its entire population bilingual and biliterate with English as the cornerstone of its bilingual policy.

The decision to make English, the language of the former colonial rulers, the working language in Singapore, has been defended as a necessity from the early years of Singapore's independence. The key position given to English in Singapore was explained by Professor Jayakumar, then Minister of State (Law and Home Affairs) in this way:

> First, English is the major international language for trade, science and technology and proficiency in the language is essential as Singapore becomes a leading financial and banking centre. Second, education in English is the key to the productivity concept. With increasing mod-

ernization, skilled workers who know English will be in great demand. And third, when it is the common language here, it will enable all Singaporeans – regardless of race – to communicate with one another ... . English is thus the key for both the individual and the nation. For the individual, it is the key to acquisition of skills and training and career advancement; for the nation, it is the key to a better educated and skilled workforce thereby ensuring higher productivity and economic growth. (*The Straits Times*, 19 August 1982)

Bokhorst-Heng (1998: 288) observes how economic growth has always been perceived by the government as tantamount to the viability of nationhood and that virtually all policy action is considered in economic terms, including language. 'Just as the forces of the marketplace dictate economic issues and choices, so do they determine the worth and fate of languages as economic instruments. English, the language of the global marketplace, is crucial to Singapore's survival and success in the global economy – hence its dominance as a working language vis-à-vis the other languages used on the island' (Ho & Alsagoff, 1998: 202).

This perspective informs the ideological rationalizations consistently evoked by the Singapore leadership in justifying the choices and decisions made in the interest of national objectives. As Pennycook (1994, citing Chua, 1983: 33) remarks, the government's success in actively propagating a very particular notion of the 'practical' and in 'convincing even academics and intellectuals to accept this conception of "practical" is indicative of its ideological success'.

Chew (1999), for instance, argues that the early spread of English in Singapore, even though it threatened the loss of ethnic identity, came about as a conscious choice, motivated by the pragmatic realization among parents that the lack of a good command of English would mean the continued marginalization of their children in a world that would continue to use the language to a great degree and denial of access to the extensive resources available in English. 'When it came to the crunch, they valued a situation that left traditional cultures open to risk but with increasing material returns as preferable to the full retention of ethnic pride and culture but with diminishing material returns' (Chew, 1999: 41).

This is reminiscent of the readiness with which parents in Singapore switched to Mandarin when the continued use of the home dialects was identified by the Goh Committee in 1978 as being the key obstacle to the success of the bilingual policy. When it was found that the language of the home did not reinforce the learning of Mandarin in school, to reduce the learning burden, parents were encouraged to sacrifice their dialect for the sake of their children's education.

Interestingly, Singaporeans did not in the least bemoan the inevitable language shift (and the potential language loss) that was to ensue, as long as there were clear economic advantages. Once again, in Chew's view,

> . . . sometimes sacrifices are necessary for future gain. In Singapore many grandparents are unable to communicate with their grandchildren owing to the loss of the mother tongue. However, there has been no strong protest despite swift changes because there has been a shrewd willingness on the part of the older generation to sacrifice – accepting a personal inconvenience for the material well-being of the younger generation in a fast-changing world. (Chew, 1999: 42)

Commenting on this trend, Gupta notes that 'to persuade the population of Singapore to see education in the mother tongue as important would require a radical shift both in educational philosophy and in Singapore's social structure, such that people with skill in English would not be rewarded over people with skill in other languages.' (Gupta, 1994: 182). Indeed, in the Singaporean context an increase in education in the actual mother tongue would be seen as disempowering the lower social classes and as threatening to the minorities. Besides, any objection parents may have had to English education would have been actually pre-empted by the government with the implementation of the bilingual policy (Bokhorst-Heng, 1998: 295), making available as media of instruction a 'choice' of mother-tongue languages, besides English. This is a good example of how language policies in Singapore 'seek to define, consolidate, reproduce and legitimate the status quo in the management of societal consensus', a process made implicit by projecting signs of power asymmetry as 'natural' occurrences in the multiethnic society (Tan, 1998).

Another reason offered in justifying the dominance of English as a lingua franca in Singapore is its so-called 'neutrality'. 'Ethnically neutral', because it does not favour any major community in Singapore, the language ideally serves two main purposes: At the community level, English is seen to be the obvious choice for interethnic communication. In this role, it is crucial in promoting racial harmony and national unity by fostering a shared national (Singaporean) identity. At the individual level, since all members of society have access to English, it is seen as providing equal opportunities for everyone regardless of their ethnic background. As the gap between the English- and Asian-language educated narrows, 'all individuals would have equal access to the benefits that a knowledge of English offered' (Bokhorst Heng, 1998: 290).

The choice of English, rather than any of the vernaculars, as the language accepted for the construction and expression of the Singaporean (i.e. national) identity stems from the consensus that the evolving national culture should be a Singaporean, rather than a Malay, Indian or Chinese, culture. English, perceived as the one common language 'to bring citizens of diverse ethnic origins together and to provide them with opportunities for interaction and mutual understanding, is therefore the ideal language to unify the nation in the building of a common Singaporean-ness. In this regard, the unrivalled role of English in Singapore's nation-building, vis-à-vis all the vernaculars, seems uncontroversial' (Ho & Alsagoff, 1998: 207).

While the dominance of English is thus rationalized in terms of the role it is expected to play in nation-building, its function as a social equalizer, however, is questionable. In the words of Prime Minister Goh, English provides 'an open level playing field' for all Singaporeans to compete equally (Goh Chock Tong, _The Straits Times_, January 1997). However, both historically and within the present-day set-up of Singapore's socioeco-nomic structures there has always been an asymmetry in power between the English-speaking and the non-English-speaking in Singapore. English education was favoured by colonial policies and restricted to an elite minority. Then as now, it opened doors to political and economic opportunities as well as to social prestige. Besides, given that the language is embedded in a system of meritocracy in Singapore, and given the view of education as human capital development, English has not only unifying but also divisive possibilities. Hence, while English is ethnically neutral, ability in it is a class marker, as evidenced by the difficulty experienced by the _silent majority_, a term which refers to the estimated 770,000 low-income 'uncomplaining Chinese-speaking Singaporeans' who have suffered for years a combination of 'economic disadvantage, sociopolitical alienation and cultural dislocation, in communicating with the ruling English-speaking elite because of their language handicap' (Ho & Alsagoff, 1998: 206). The 1990 census showed that English is directly associated with social mobility and socioeconomic status. Furthermore, recent trends are showing that this language-based social hierarchy is beginning to reproduce itself. Therefore, to describe English as a merely neutral, utilitarian language of wider communication (LWC) by depoliticizing its role, is to assume an uncritical understanding of the interconnection between modernisation, globalisation and language policy issues.

Since 1979, when English became the main medium of instruction, Singapore has been undergoing massive language shifts away from a multiplicity of languages and affecting all ethnic groups. English in Singapore has penetrated beyond the formal domains of work into societal spheres, leading inevitably to complex issues of cultural hegemony (Pennycook, 1994; Phillipson, 1992; Tollefson, 1991), to the extent that some scholars believe that 'future generations of English-educated Singaporeans who are less proficient in their ethnic language may only retain surface manifestations of the non-English culture, in the form of token characteristics like foods, dances and folklore elements' (Baetens Beardsmore, 1994: 51). Pennycook's comment, that it is tempting to agree with Catherine Lim that the new generation of Singaporeans is 'more at home with McDonalds and Madonna and Michael Jackson than with the customs of their ancestors' (Lim, 1991: 5) is thus justly warranted.

Nevertheless, the retention of English as the administrative language and the additional role designated for it as the de facto working language in Singapore's formal-public, industrial and modern business sectors have combined to strengthen its purported image as a 'neutral' (non-ethnic) lingua franca in multilingual Singapore. Moreover, the road to techno-economic and educational advancement that Singapore has chosen seems to ensure that useful and important knowledge and the power and status that this knowledge confers will continue to be associated with the English language (Tan, 1998: 46).

The Ideology of Multilingualism and Language Planning in the Schools

One of the first policies to be instituted by the independent government was that of bilingualism, based on the recommendations of the All-Party Committee that the four languages designated as official languages – English, Chinese, Malay and Tamil – be available as media of instruction (Gopinathan, 1980: 181, cited in Pakir, 1994). Bilingual education in Singapore schools has undergone several modifications since then, with English increasingly gaining ascendancy. Today there is no longer the choice of a main medium of education – English is the language of instruction in all schools, and is referred to as the 'first language' (L1), with Chinese, Malay or Tamil ('the mother tongues') designated as the 'second language' or L2. Thus bilingualism in Singapore has uniquely come to be defined as 'proficiency in English and one other official language' (Pakir, 1994: 159). In effect, this policy made English the lingua franca of Singapore, giving the policy the name 'English-knowing bilingualism' (Kachru, 1983: 42).

The bilingual policy has been based essentially on a functional 'division of labour' between languages (Kuo & Jernudd, 1994: 30; Pendley, 1983). In Singapore's official terminology, English is a 'working language', while the other official languages have been assigned 'mother tongue' second-language status, mainly catering to the ethnocultural needs of the three respective ethnic communities.

Thus, on the one hand, English needs to be used for instrumental and pragmatic reasons – for employment and the transfer of technology and exchange of information with the broader global community. In this view, the English language is seen as neutral and cultureless. On the other hand, mother tongues are a demarcation and embodiment of culture, each serving to re-ethnicise and consolidate separate ethnic communities and acting as a cultural bulwark against 'undesirable Western influences'. English is for new knowledge, to keep the nation abreast with its economic and development objectives; mother tongue is for old knowledge, to keep the people anchored and focused amidst the changes around them (Lee Kuan Yew, *The Straits Times*, 24 November 1979).

Official ideology not only clearly demarcates the division of labour between languages but it has, over the years, developed systematic rationales for language roles in the domain of the home, school, social occasions and the economy. In most cases, the reductionist four-race configuration that underpins this multilingual model precludes personal language choices contrary to those laid down by the official policy. As Tan maintains, 'language choice comes to be evaluated as normative typical behaviour oriented around the straightforward "natural" official ethnocultural guidelines . . . Attention is drawn away from the fact that these languages correlate with socioideological dimensions in the larger society and they are really not equal' (Tan, 1999: 50). In addition, the stress on the racial make-up of Singapore has led to a discourse of multiracialism, which stresses an equation between race, language and culture and suggests that conflict between the races is inevitable unless firm control is maintained (Pennycook, 1994).

The Speak Mandarin Campaign

Although English is seen as pivotal for Singapore's survival, it is also seen as potentially harmful to the nation. Since the 1970s, serious concerns have been raised about Singapore's vulnerability to 'undesirable Western influences' because of its heavy dependence on English and the West. Realization that while openness to external influences has made Singaporeans cosmopolitan in outlook, it has also exposed Singaporeans, especially younger Singaporeans, to alien lifestyles and values has made its leaders wary of the effects of such influences.

Ho and Alsagoff (1998) contend that 'Westernization' and, in particular, the shift in 'society's dominant values from communitarianism to individualism has been assiduously thematized by the country's leadership as being a serious threat to national survival'. They suggest that

> [p]olitically, the undesirable Western influences are seen as encouraging disrespect for the government, and fanning public desire for Western-type liberal, pluralist politics. Excessive individualism is perceived as detrimental to the country's economic performance and

competitiveness. Culturally, Westernization is thought to undermine the country's Asian heritage, rendering its people morally weak and directionless. (Ho & Alsagoff, 1998: 203)

One way of countering the negative effects of 'Western decadent values' was to strengthen the policy of bilingualism by promoting, alongside English, the ethnic mother tongues as the agents of the transmission of Asian moral values and cultural traditions.

An obvious example of such deliberate intervention on the part of the leadership is the Speak Mandarin Campaign, which was launched in 1979 by the then Prime Minister Lee Kuan Yew, and continues 'with unabated force to promote the use of Mandarin in place of dialects among all Singaporean Chinese' (Kuo & Jernudd, 1994: 28). Mandarin Chinese, while not the mother tongue of the majority of the Chinese in Singapore, was chosen to represent the largest ethnic community owing to historical, political and economic considerations. The campaign has become so forceful over the years that not knowing Mandarin is seen as being disloyal to one's Chinese ancestry. Commenting on its success, Gupta observes, 'Mandarin is heard from the Chinese in Singapore in volumes unimaginable in the 1970s. Families where parents knew Mandarin but who had chosen to speak their own 'dialects' have switched to a domestic use of Mandarin on a massive scale' (Gupta, 1994: 151). Consequently, the successful implementation of the Speak Mandarin Campaign has improved the extent of use and the standard of Mandarin among the Chinese, making Mandarin the major native language in Singapore; but it has also reduced diversity, and reduced multilingualism.

Indeed, Gupta predicts that in future generations there are likely to be fewer people with knowledge of more than the two school languages. She points out how, ironically, 'this reduction of repertoire is often misleadingly described (by politicians, educationists and sociolinguists) as an *increase* in bilingualism in Singapore', because of the limitation of the term bilingual to 'skill in the official languages, and an equation of bilingualism with biliteracy' – whereas, in fact, multilingualism has decreased (Gupta, 1994: 151).

The interplay between the two dominant official languages becomes even more interesting when we examine the complex array of meanings accorded to these languages in balancing the existing power structure and reproducing the status quo. During the post-independence period, within the conditions of a then underdeveloped internal economy beset with widespread unemployment, illiteracy and suspicion from the non-English-educated majority, it was expedient for the English-educated political elite to ideologize English as a neutral utilitarian language (Tan,

1999: 54). The exalting of English as a practical 'necessity' also helped wean away Chinese youth from Chinese-medium schools, which in the eyes of the government had become hotbeds of Chinese nationalism and revolutionary fervour, especially since the 1949 communist revolution in China (Bokhorst-Heng, 1998: 289). In the campaigning for Mandarin, however, English was no longer presented as neutral, but rather as a carrier of undesirable Western values and habits of thinking, as a threat to the identity and Asian-ness of Singapore. The universalization of English and its increasing encroachment into the more intimate domains and levels of Singaporean social life served to further reiterate its role as the harbinger of certain Western values and habits of thinking. The Speak Mandarin Campaign and the discourse on 'Asian core values', supported by the discourse of Confucianism, can then be seen as a strategy used by the leadership to deculturise a new generation of Singaporeans, dangerously vulnerable to Westernization and the negative effects of English dominance.

However, while the expected outcome of the pro-Mandarin campaign was successfully achieved in terms of wiping out the different Chinese dialects by Mandarin to make it the intraethnic tongue, a totally unplanned effect has been the way English has begun to supplant Hokkien, the dialect of the numerically dominant Chinese group in Singapore, in its intraethnic lingua franca role. It has been hinted that the promotion of Mandarin may have represented an added linguistic burden to dialect speakers, hastening language shift in younger members towards English (T'sou, 1988).

The Speak Good English Movement

Paradoxically, though, it is neither Mandarin Chinese nor Standard English that provides the cultural anchor that holds together the multiethnic, multicultural and multilingual populace of Singapore. Instead, Singlish, Singapore's local brand of colloquial English, has emerged as the symbol of intraethnic identity and cultural integration in Singapore, in total contravention with the ideologies of the language planners. Importantly, Singlish has come to be regarded as the quintessential mark of 'Singaporeanness' by a large majority of young Singaporeans, who now use it freely in informal domains of talk.

It has thus come about that over the last four years a new language debate is being played out in various forums in Singapore – that between Singlish and Standard English. First introduced as an issue worthy of national attention by local politicians in official speeches, the debate was subsequently picked up by the media and further discussed in editorials and letters in the main English daily newspaper, *The Straits Times*. Singlish was defined, especially in official circles, as English 'corrupted by

Singaporeans' that 'will put the less-educated half of the population at a disadvantage'. Lee Kuan Yew called it 'a handicap we must not wish on Singaporeans'. Prime Minister, Goh Chok Tong in his National Day Rally speech (*The Straits Times*, 22 August 1999) echoed a similar sentiment when he said 'We cannot be a first-world economy or go global with Singlish.'

In other words, using Singlish hampers international communication, and, since Singapore's survival as a viable economy on the world stage is a top priority, it has been argued that Singapore cannot afford to maintain Singlish as a dominant linguistic resource (Chng, 2003: 46). In 2000 a campaign known as the Speak Good English Movement (2000) was therefore launched to counter the ill effects of Singlish and re-emphasize the importance of using Standard English.

Used primarily as a spoken form, Singaporeans are generally favourably disposed towards Singlish, with as many as 70% Singaporeans accepting Singlish as a marker of rapport and solidarity (Kang, 1993). Singlish has become so popular and trendy that it has also been exploited in written genres such as local plays and poems, leading to an even greater increase in its popularity. The impact of the use of Singlish became an overt concern for local politicians with the widespread success of 'Phua Chu Kang', one of the most watched Singaporean sitcoms in recent television history, when the younger section of the population began widely to imitate the manner in which the lead character of this sitcom speaks English each week on local TV (Chng, 2003; Rubdy, 2001).

The intention of the policy-makers to manipulate and shape a specific linguistic reality in Singapore is clearly evident in the official rationalizations proffered by key politicians in their attempt to weed out Singlish. In April 2001, Singapore's Deputy Prime Minister, Lee Hsien Loong, urged Singaporeans to 'speak English everyone understands' stating that 'Standard English is a rational trade-off' for Singaporeans who want 'to plug into the global economy' and emphasizing that Singlish is not the (only) way to strengthen Singaporean identity (*The Straits Times Interactive*, 2001). Earlier, Colonel David Wong, who heads the Speak Good English Movement, the machinery set up for a national effort at steering Singaporeans away from Singlish, expressed a similar sentiment in a published interview: 'We are trying to build a sense of pride, that as Singaporeans, we can speak good English as opposed to pride that we can speak Singlish. We are trying to check a trend in which younger Singaporeans are beginning to feel that it is perhaps a way of identifying themselves as Singaporeans if they speak Singlish' (*The Straits Times*, 31 March 2000). As Chng notes, '[i]n short, the encouragement given to Singaporeans to learn "proper" English is a visibly public affair and though the abandonment of Singlish is not spoken of in so many words, in much of the effort to overtly promote Standard English usage, Singlish is understood as the sacrificial lamb' (Chng, 2003: 50). The Singapore leadership's overt attempt to remake Singaporeans and Singaporean identity, linguistically, by rooting out Singlish and aggressively promoting 'proper' English is to be understood in terms of how this is systematically undertaken through the formation of public consensus in ways that equate the use of Standard English with global economic rewards in the Singaporean psyche (see also Rubdy, 2001). 'Happily, Singaporeans buy into a rational economic argument readily. The political leadership has equated correct spoken English with the country's continued economic viability. This alone can boost the campaign' (*The Straits Times, 2000*, cited in Chng, 2003: 52).

As Chng rightly notes, the gap between the official agenda to have every Singaporean speak internationally intelligible English and the opposing desires of the average Singaporean to maintain Singlish as a discourse option represents an ideological conflict. Supporters of Singlish are of the view that Singlish is a crucial part of the Singaporean identity – a concern related to the private domain of individuals. But this issue has now been cast as a national concern that is translated into a rationale for weeding out Singlish, the language of the marginalized community or what has been called 'linguistic working class' – thus blurring the boundaries between the community and the nation, the private and the public (Chng, 2003: 52–53). The considerable disparity between the official concern over international intelligibility and the reality of life on the ground represents clear evidence of the struggle over the determination of choice and control over linguistic resources in Singapore.

The Ideology of Meritocracy and the Reproduction of Inequality

The PAP ideology is unabashedly elitist. The rhetoric of its rationale is primarily 'meritocratic'. The pronounced ideology of meritocracy dictates that the individual's rewards after school are closely linked to success in school (Kuo & Jernudd, 1994: 31). In recent years an element of social elitism has been introduced, connected with the belief that intellectual ability is largely genetic.

The Special Assistance Programme (SAP) for schools, for instance, put in place under the New Education System in 1979 to provide 'effectively bilingual institutions' responsible for protecting the Chinese heritage and producing the next generation of social brokers, became a key marker of an elite leadership, for only the brightest students were offered full opportunities to be effective bilinguals 'key to an internal stabilizer in the form of cultural heritage' (*The Straits Times*, 31 August 1989). The Gifted Education Programme, which caters for the top 3–5% of each cohort, currently run in

16 premier schools, was introduced in 1984 with a similar intent of developing future leaders who possess the drive and commitment to channel some of their energies back into society. Yet another form of elitism is to be found in the University Scholars Programme, an initiative introduced at the National University of Singapore since 2000, for a handpicked, top-5% pool of brilliant, exceptionally talented students zealously being groomed for the leadership of tomorrow's Singapore.

Political rhetoric often articulates that in resource-scarce and land-scarce Singapore, its people are its only resource if Singapore is to survive; hence the need to educate its population and cultivate talent in the country. 'Consequently, education as an issue takes a high priority in the government's domestic policy concerns and is subject to its direct scrutiny. The result generated over the years is an education system that is planned to the last detail with nothing left to chance' (Sankaran & Chng, 2003: 220). Nothing exemplifies this better than the highly complex practice of streaming – an efficient means in actuality of weeding out the less intelligent, who, unable to successfully go through the many educational hoops built within the rigorously competitive education system that exists in Singapore, are automatically eliminated at the examinations placed at every successive stage of the school system. I quote here liberally from Sankaran and Chng, who vividly detail the manner in which this rigidly meritocratic education system translates into practice:

> A Singaporean child entering the school system is subject from Day 1 to a carefully planned curriculum that exacts close to 100% of the child's energy. A seasoned Singaporean student knows about every hurdle she/he has to overcome and the route that is mapped out in front of her/him. Hurdles indeed begin as early as in lower primary in Singapore (US equivalent Grades 1–3). In Primary Three, all schoolchildren need to sit for a special test that enables the government to identify the high-performance children for the gifted education stream. In Primary Four students take a streaming exam that divides then into the average, above average and excellent performers bound for different educational tracks. At the end of their Primary Six they have to take a public exam – The Primary School Leaving Examination (PSLE) – that more or less determines which secondary school (Grades 7–10) they go to. Since secondary schools are ranked according to their performance and have a PSLE grade entry requirement, and also because it is very rarely that a child from a low-ranking secondary school gets into the three (very prestigious) local universities, it is imperative that a Singaporean child gets into the best secondary schools to get a head start. In lower secondary (Grades 7–8) students

once again take a qualifying exam that determines who gets the coveted triple science stream (i.e. pre-med), who gets the double science or the arts stream. After four or five years (depending on whether they are placed in the express or normal tracks respectively) at a secondary school, the students take their Cambridge 'O' level examination, a national exam that has its origin in the UK education system. Their performance determines whether they qualify to go to Junior Colleges (equivalent to Grades 11–12, again ranked) that prepare students to enter university or make it to a local technical college. (Sankaran & Chng, 2003: 220–21)

The phenomenal levels of anxiety and stress generated by this system for students and parents alike, claim some representatives of the foreign press, is equaled only by the growing weariness with Singapore's culture of social 'nannying' felt by 21% of Singaporeans, some of whom in a recent survey expressed the wish to leave the lion city permanently, sufficiently provoking Prime Minister Goh to denounce them as 'quitters' and 'fair-weather Singaporeans', and to blame this development entirely on the sluggish economy.

Recently, the Singapore economy has been less buoyant, forcing it into a reassessment after a long ride on the back of the information technology boom that abruptly ended in 2001. Faced with economic uncertainty and pressed by the swift rise of China, Singapore is asking a hard question: How should it reinvent itself once again?

A government-led national debate is under way, with special panels, including one called the 'Remaking Singapore Committee', expressly created to come up with solutions. Cabinet ministers and business leaders ponder on how they can keep Singapore, with no natural resources and a small population, in a premium global position.

Solutions to the gloom and doom are being sought in several directions, political, economic and educational. The educational system is being over-hauled and the curriculum and methods of teaching restructured to produce Singaporeans who can think creatively and non-conventionally. In the years following independence in 1965, the need for national survival and nation-building had led to the implementation of 'survival-driven' education. This in turn evolved into an 'efficiency-driven' paradigm in the 1980s and 1990s, to meet the growing manpower needs of an expanding economy. Today this thrust has moved to an 'ability-driven' workforce which possesses the creativity and ingenuity to create knowledge that is relevant to the new age. In addition to greater emphasis on the Chinese language, which would facilitate business with China, there is to be less emphasis on rote-learning and more emphasis on critical and creative thinking skills.

Singapore is probably one of the very few nations to have an official Thinking Programme implemented in schools at all levels since 1998, with the aim of equipping its young citizens with the skills and knowledge required to meet the challenges of the new millennium. Secure in the knowledge that education will be the single most important determinant of its future success (or failure) in becoming a first-world economy, slogan-happy Singapore has set at the heart of its current 'ability-driven' educational reforms its vision of 'Thinking Schools and Learning Nation'. These initiatives, intended to create a total learning environment so as to endow the future generation of Singaporeans with the intellectual skills to meet the needs of lifelong learning in a rapidly changing and uncertain world, present yet another paradox, since the larger polity, within which the school curriculum promoting critical thinking is embedded, tends to be largely inimical to the idea of its citizenry adopting a critical or questioning stance, particularly in issues of a sociopolitical nature that really matter.

A telling example of the way in which the sociopolitical context can work to shape the educational ethos of the classroom, and operate at cross-purposes with the aims of Singapore's critical thinking programme, is found in Sankaran and Chng (2003). Frustrated with their students' reluctance to participate in class tutorials while teaching a course on 'Feminist Theory and Feminist Discourse' to graduating majors at the National University of Singapore, they found, on closer examination, that their students, highly intelligent as they were, 'had reasoned themselves into locations of least resistance, with the least need for expending energy' (Sankaran & Chng, 2003: 221), exerting themselves to respond adequately only when they knew the quality of their responses would be assessed and graded. 'To them, engaging in a heated debate about the possible transformations that a feminist consciousness could effect would appear, in the final analysis, wasteful!' Sankaran and Chng conclude that '[t]his entirely utilitarian attitude is the only one that seems to make sense to them' (Sankaran & Chng, 2003: 224). The need to develop critical consciousness that is inherently valued rather than an attitude that is developed for purely pragmatic reasons might go beyond the agenda of a leadership seeking purely utilitarian measures for utilitarian goals.

Perhaps it is recognition of this need that prompted Prime Minister Goh Chock Tong, in his 2002 National Day Rally speech, to urge Singaporeans to change their attitudes and mindsets 'which are holding back progress'. Whereas employers of yore were happy enough to employ diligent and disciplined graduates, unused to being challenged by sudden and unexpected crises, growing capitalist competition from neighbouring countries in the region and the increasing difficulties faced by the business community in Singapore clearly show it can no longer rely merely on the traditional ways of doing business for sustainable growth and survival. Yet, proactive as ever, Singapore is pushing ahead in a mammoth effort of national economic restructuring to build a better future for Singaporeans.

Chief among the new strategies created to meet the growing economic competition is the plan to gain a new technological edge by putting in place a national information infrastructure linking people, business and government through a framework involving telecommunication networks. By the year 2005, the aim is that virtually every home, office, school and factory in Singapore will link their computers. One of the world's most advanced national information infrastructures will be finalized, and Singapore, 'the intelligent island', will realise a vision. Birch (1999) states that this is not an idle vision. Telecoms, for example, has set aside a S$3-billion budget in order to enhance networks and develop new services. Much of the infrastructure is already in place.

Another strategy is to correlate entrepreneurship with a level of cultural vibrancy to make Singapore a cosmopolitan city-state. The Singapore Tourism Board (STB) is now committing $500,000 a year to promote the city's arts events and ventures abroad. The aim is to establish Singapore as the region's unchallenged arts capital – an ambition which it seems nothing can impede, with the opening of the new Esplanade Theatre complex in October 2002. Further, to cushion itself from the economic growth of China, Singapore is cementing its ties with the United States by working to complete a free-trade agreement.

Assuring Singaporeans of the drive undertaken to ensure that the country moves easily in the global economy, Prime Minister Goh asserted in his National Day motivational speech: 'Singaporeans can also take heart from our track record. At every critical point in our history, we have risen to the challenge. *We have been nimble and bold enough to make tough adjustments. We have moved swiftly to seize the opportunities.*' (National Day Rally Speech 2002, Singapore Government Press Release. Emphasis added.)

Singapore, in the new age, is no longer to be judged 'by what it produces, but how it manages and uses information' (The Information Technology Institute of Singapore). As Birch warns, '[w]hat this means is that increasingly politicians, business people and bureaucrats become the cultural managers of a society' (Birch, 1999: 31).

Conclusion

Clearly, the Speak Mandarin Campaign and the Speak Good English Movement privilege the two official languages. And as long as a critical mass of both English and Mandarin speakers is maintained, the power and status of these two languages will continue to grow at the expense of the other minority languages, including Singlish. Issues of social identity and cohesion are thus put at stake here.

Two other social consequences of the adoption of English and Mandarin as dominant languages have been (1) social stratification and divisiveness and (2) language shift, as a consequence of people responding to the demands made on them by a highly successful process of societal diglossia. A totally unplanned effect of the Speak Mandarin Campaign has been the way English has begun to supplant Hokkien in its intraethnic lingua franca role, inadvertently accelerating the development of Singlish. However, the renewed emphasis on Standard Singapore English could well marginalize speakers whose only resource is Singlish. At the same time, although the Singapore leadership would have every Singaporean speak Standard English, the meritocratic system it has spawned, a euphemism for elitism or what Pennycook (1994: 226) has termed 'the planned reproduction of socioeconomic inequality', effectively forecloses such a possibility by legitimizing social and educational exclusion.

Like the Speak Mandarin Campaign before it, which resulted in the exclusion of the minority races by creating linguistic unity among the hitherto linguistically diverse Chinese groups, the Speak Good English Movement holds disturbing separatist implications in its potential to create social division between the English-educated 'cosmopolitans' and the non-English-educated 'heartlanders'. While the intention of policy-makers to manipulate and shape a specific linguistic reality in Singapore is clearly evident from such campaigns, paradoxically launched in the name of 'pragmatic multilingualism', they have invariably resulted in language shift and language loss, leading to the reduction of linguistic diversity, to unequal access to discourse resources and to differential access to power networks.

Thus the rational, rationalized and ideological bases of centralized, top-down official planning in Singapore reveal several discrepancies with the realities on the ground. What is instructive, however, is not just the problematics of these issues in language in education but the way in which, when it comes to the crunch, policy-makers in Singapore tend to privilege the global at the expense of the local, the cultural and nationalist concerns. Invariably, the interests of the citizenry are pitted against relentless market forces in managing such language issues, signifying in the end the triumphal victory of the hegemonic pressures of globalization.

References

Baetens Beardsmore, H. (1994) Language shift and cultural implications in Singapore. In S. Gopinathan *et al.* (ed.) *Language, Society and Education in Singapore* (1st edn) (pp. 47–64). Singapore: Times Academic Press.

Birch, D. (1999) Reading state communication as public culture. In P.G.L. Chew and A. Kramer-Dahl (eds) *Reading Culture* (pp. 19–36). Singapore: Times Academic Press.

Bokhorst-Heng, W. (1998) Language planning and management in Singapore. In J.A. Foley *et al.* (eds) *English in New Cultural Contexts: Reflections from Singapore* (pp. 287–309). Singapore: Oxford University Press.

Bourdieu, P. and Passeron, J.C. (1977) *Reproduction in Education, Society and Culture.* (trans. by R. Nice). California: Sage Publications.

Chew, P.G.L. (1999) Linguistic imperialism, globalism and the English language. In D. Graddol and U.M. Meinhof (eds) *English in a Changing World.* AILA Review 13, 37–47.

Chng H.H. (2003) 'You see me no up': Is Singlish a problem? *Language Problems and Language Planning* 27 (1), 47–62.

Chua Beng-Huat (1983) Reopening ideological discussion in Singapore: A new theoretical direction. *Southeast Asian Journal of Social Science* 11 (2), 31–45.

Chua, S.C. (1962) State of Singapore: Report on the census of population, 1957. Singapore, Department of Statistics: Government Printing Office.

Gopinathan, S. (1980) Language policy in education: A Singapore perspective. In E.A. Affrendas and E.C.Y. Kuo (eds) *Language and Society in Singapore* (pp. 175–202). Singapore: Singapore University Press.

Goh Chock Tong (1997) *The Straits Times*, 5 January.

Gupta, A.F. (1994) *The Step-Tongue: Children's English in Singapore.* Clevedon: Multilingual Matters.

Ho, C.L. and Alsagoff, L. (1998) English as the common language in multicultural Singapore. In J.A. Foley *et al.* (eds) *English in New Cultural Contexts* (pp. 201–17). Singapore: Oxford University Press.

Kachru, B.B. (1983) Models for non-native Englishes. In B.B. Kachru (ed.) *The Other Tongue: English Across Cultures* (pp. 31–57). Oxford: Pergamon Press.

Kang, M.K. (1993) Definitions of attitudes towards Singlish in Singapore. Academic exercise, Department of English Language and Literature, National University of Singapore.

Kuo, E.C.Y. and Jernudd, B.H. (1994) Balancing macro- and micro-sociolintuistic perspectives in language management: The case of Singapore. In S. Gopinathan *et al.* (eds) *Language, Society and Education in Singapore* (1st edn) (pp. 25–46). Singapore: Times Academic Press.

Lim, C. (1991) English for technology – Yes! English for culture – No! A writer's views on a continuing South East Asian dilemma. Paper presented at the International Conference on Language Educational Development and Interaction, Ho Chi Minh City.

Pakir, A. (1994) Education and invisible language planning: The case of English in Singapore. In T. Kandiah and J. Kwan-Terry (eds) *English and Language Planning: A South-East Asian Contribution* (pp. 158–181). Singapore: Times Academic Press.

Pendley, C. (1983) Language policy and social transformation in contemporary Singapore. *South Asian Journal of Social Science* 11 (2), 46–58.

Pennycook, A. (1994) *The Cultural Politics of English as an International Language.* Harlow: Longman.

Phillipson, R. (1992) *Linguistic Imperialism.* Oxford: Oxford University Press.

Rubdy, R. (2001) Creative destruction: Singapore's Speak Good English Movement. *World Englishes* 20 (3), 341–55.

Sankaran, C. and Chng, H.H. (2003) Looking to East and West: Feminist practice in an Asian classroom. In L. Gray-Rosendale and G. Harootunian (eds) *Fractured Feminisms* (pp. 215–29). New York: Suny Press.

Tan S.H. (1998) Theoretical ideals and ideologized reality in language planning. In S. Gopinathan *et al.* (eds) *Language, Society and Education in Singapore* (2nd edn) (pp. 45–64). Singapore: Times Academic Press.

Tollefson, J.W. (1991) *Planning Language, Planning Inequality. Language Policy in the Community.* London: Longman.

T'sou, B.K. (1988) Comparative triglossia in four Chinese speech communities. Paper presented at the International Conference on Language Policy and National Development, Hyderabad, India.

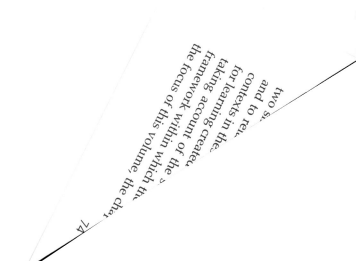

Chapter 5

'Safe' Language Practices in Two Rural Schools in Malaysia: Tensions between Policy and Practice[1]

PETER MARTIN

Introduction

There is a plethora of literature on language planning and policy in a range of contexts, including postcolonial contexts (for example, Ricento, 2000; Tollefson, 2002; Vavrus, 2002; Watson, 1982). More recently, in the last two decades, studies of classroom language practices in many different postcolonial contexts have appeared. While some of these studies (for example, Cleghorn, 1992; Eisemon *et al.*, 1989) provide stand-alone accounts of classroom language practices, with little reference to policy, several recent studies attempt to locate the observed language practices within their wider sociohistorical, sociopolitical and educational contexts (for example, Arthur, 1996; Chick, 1996; Lin, 1996). 'Top-down' approaches, focusing on policy and planning decisions, have been brought together with 'bottom-up' accounts of what is actually happening at the classroom level. This allows an exploration of how practice engages or disengages with policy and the tensions that may pertain. These tensions are not just between local, cultural and nationalist needs, but between what Heller and Martin-Jones (2001: 1) have referred to as the 'new global forms of cultural, economic and social domination' which are increasingly shaping contemporary societies.

The focus of this chapter is to look at the classroom language practices in ⁓mall rural communities in Malaysia away from the 'Malay centre', ¹⁓te these practices to the wider sociopolitical and educational ⁓e communities. The chapter investigates the opportunities ¹ b⁓ the patterns of language use in the two classrooms, ⁓iolinguistic contexts, and the language policy ⁓lassroom participants operate. In line with ⁓ter critically explores the discrepancies between what is officially planned by the ruling elite, and, through an examination of the discourse of two rural classrooms, the voices of the local classroom participants. The tensions and discrepancies are critically discussed within a framework of the historical conditions shaped by the local and global contexts.

In contrast to many studies which juxtapose language policy statements with ethnographic or discourse-analytic studies of classroom practices, the present study gives pre-eminence to the latter. The aim, then, is not to start with an historical account of language policy and planning in Malaysia, but to provide the reader with glimpses of the discourse of two classrooms, allowing the voices of the classroom participants to come through. Subsequently, the chapter shows how the language practices in these classrooms articulate or disarticulate with the language policy. In so doing, the tensions and cleavages of such (dis-)articulation are critically examined.

It is not, then, the intention to provide a full account of language policy in Malaysia in the early part of this chapter. Considerable space has been given to language policy and planning in the literature (Asiah, 1994; Asmah, 1994; Gaudart, 1992; Ożóg, 1990, 1993; Watson, 1983; Wong & James, 2000), and reference will be made to policy issues, in view of the practices described in the two classrooms, in the discussion in the second part of the chapter. Suffice to say here that since independence from Britain in 1957, like several other postcolonial countries, Malaysia has juggled its language education policy, trying to support Malay nationalism and Islamisation on the one hand but at the same time recognising the pragmatic, academic and global importance of English. This is reflected in the twists and turns in policy decisions in the last half century.

This study of the language practices in two rural Malaysian classrooms is written against the backdrop of a recent decision in Malaysia to implement a policy to switch the medium of instruction in mathematics and science from Malay to English, beginning in the year 2003. Although the two lessons that are the focus of this chapter are English lessons, the recent change to the use of English for the teaching (and learning) of science and mathematics has fundamental significance for the discussion in this study. As will be shown later, the discourse surrounding the debate about and implementation of this policy is imbued with issues such as globalisation, economic necessity and communications technologies.

The tension between the new language policy and actual classroom practices comes through forcefully in a recent editorial from *The New Straits Times* (24 April 2003), the major, government-controlled English-medium newspaper in Malaysia, titled 'Tongue-tied teachers'.

The editorial is imbued with critical and political rhetoric. It positions the use of Malay as 'a potential source of trouble' rather than as a natural, pragmatic and spontaneous action by teachers to ensure that some learning is taking place. Statements such as 'a conscious resistance to change', 'teachers who . . . are guilty of sabotaging the policy . . . and short-changing their students', and 'intractable, [teachers who will] have to bear the brunt of disciplinary action' show how deeply classroom practices and language policies are intertwined. Lurking in this text is a viewpoint that language and disciplinary knowledge are best taught and learned monolingually, and the fact that the classroom can necessarily be disassociated from the sociopolitical context in which it exists.

Further discussion of Malaysian language-in-education policy is deferred until after the following section, which looks at how classroom participants do actually use language to teach and learn. This section starts with a brief account of the context of the two communities that are the focus of this study.

Classroom Language Practices in Two Rural Malaysian Schools

The two schools in this study are located in two separate areas in the interior of Sarawak, one of the two states of Malaysia in northern Borneo (East Malaysia). It is important to stress that the communities in both areas are minority groups in the Malaysian context. School A is a primary school in a mixed Sa'ben and Leppo' Ke' Kenyah community, and the main language of communication in the community is Sa'ben. The school also serves a small community of Kelabit speakers. School B is a lower secondary school located in a largely Kelabit speaking area, although ethnic Sa'ben and Penan children come to board in the school. Through their contacts with the Kelabit, both here and in their own communities, these children can speak some Kelabit, the language used in the area. Neither school is accessible by road, though there is a logging track which passes close by School A.

In this chapter, I focus on one lesson in each school. In School A, the focus is on a primary two English class. The teacher was an ethnic Sa'ben. He also spoke Kelabit, Malay and English. In School B, the lesson was an English class at secondary-two level. The teacher was an ethnic Chinese convert to Islam. As well as Malay, Chinese and English, she was also learning Kelabit. This gives some idea of the linguistic complexity of the community and the linguistic resources the participants brought into the classroom.[2]

Although the whole transcripts of the two lessons are available, it is not feasible in a short chapter such as this to discuss lesson transcripts in their entirety. Inevitably, as soon as a lesson is broken up into pieces, the wider picture of the lesson becomes somewhat blurred. However, the aim here is to provide an indication of the linguistic strategies employed by the participants in the classrooms, and to discuss these in the light of the wider educational policies. Transcription conventions are provided at the end of the chapter.

Lesson A: (primary two, English)

This lesson was built around 'Unit 4: I'm Hungry' in the textbook *English 2* (Mutiara & Azly, 1996: 35), particularly the 'Listen and Say' activity, reproduced below:

> *Greg eats a green apple.*
> *Brian eats brown bread.*
> *The cook looks at the cook book.*
> *Glen holds a glass.*
> *There is salt and sugar on Tini's thumbs.*

The text is superimposed over a colour sketch of four children sitting at a table covered in a floral cloth. One boy is eating an apple, another boy is eating a piece of brown bread, and a third is holding a glass. A girl appears to be sifting salt and sugar through her hands and into two containers marked 'salt' and 'sugar'. Behind the table, a woman is stirring the contents of a pan on a raised stove. She is consulting a 'cook book'. The woman is wearing an apron and a chef's hat. Behind the woman is a shelf displaying dinner plates.

After settling the class of 15 pupils, the teacher introduced the text on page 35 of the textbook. Most of the students had copies of the book on their desks. Those that did not shared. The lesson started with the teacher reading the text section by section and the pupils repeating after him (Extract 1, lines 1–14).

Extract 1 (lines 1–14)

1	T:	'Greg eats a green apple'
	Ps:	'Greg eats a green apple'
	T:	'Brian eats brown bread'
	Ps:	'Brian eats brown bread'
5	T:	'The cook looks at the cook book'
	Ps:	'The cook looks at the cook book'
	T:	'Glen holds a glass'

	Ps:	'Glen holds a glass'
	T:	'There is salt'
10	Ps:	'There is salt'
	T:	'and sugar'
	Ps:	'and sugar'
	T:	'on Tini's thumbs'
	Ps:	'on Tini's thumbs'

In the next section of the lesson (Extract 2), the classroom participants negotiate the meaning of the word 'green', which appears in the first part of the text, using both English and Malay. There is some considerable discussion, though it is noticeable that the Malay equivalent for 'green' is not given.

Extract 2 (lines 15–31)

15	T:	**minggu lepas . ah kelmarin . kita baca ini kan . yang pertama tengok** <*last week . ah yesterday . we read this . look at the first one*> 'Greg eats a green apple'. **yang mana** green? <*what is* green?> . **dalam gambar itu . lihat gambar itu . siapa makan** apple **itu?** <*in the picture . look at the picture .*
20		*who is eating the apple?*>
	P:	Greg
	T:	aah . 'Greg eats a green apple' . what is the colour of the apple . what is the colour of apple?
	P:	{green
25	P:	{green
	T:	green . green
	Ps:	green
	T:	**dalam kelas ini ada yang** green <*in this class is there any thing that is* green?
30	Ps:	**ada** <*yes*> .. [inaudible]
	T:	aah . green . [. . .]

These first two extracts demonstrate the pattern of discourse in this classroom. This pattern includes reading through the text, jointly accomplished by teacher and pupils, and bilingual annotation of key words and concepts in the text. The teacher is able to establish, through the interaction that takes place, that the pupils understand the term 'green'.

The interactional strategies seen in these first two extracts continue throughout the lesson. The reading performance is jointly shared by the teacher and the students. The teacher then orchestrates the annotation of particular sections of text, using a range of pedagogical resources, and making use of both English and Malay. Noticeably, Sa'ben (a language common to all in the classroom) is not used as part of the lesson.

It is useful to look more closely at some of the linguistic resources used by the teacher. Extract 3 provides the next section of the lesson.

Extract 3 (lines 31–65)

	T:	aah . green . second one . 'Brian'
	Ps:	'Brian'
	T:	'eats'
	Ps:	'eats'
35	T:	'brown bread'
	Ps:	'brown bread'
	T:	where's Brian . **yang mana** Brian? *<which one is* Brian> . where's Brian? **yang mana** Brian? *(which one is* Brian> **dalam gambar** *<in the picture>* . look **dalam gambar** *<in the*
40		picture> . **apa yang dia makan itu?** *<what is he eating?>*
	P:	bread
	T:	bread . **apa itu?** *<what's that?>*
	P:	**roti** *<bread>*
	T:	**itu yang kita panggil** bread *<that's what's called* bread> .
45		**Bahasa Inggeris** *<English>* bread . **apa warna** bread **yang dia makan?** *<what's the colour of the* bread *he is eating?>* . what is the colour of the bread? . . . what is the colour of the bread?what is the colour of the bread? . **apa warnanya?** *<what's the colour?>*
50	P:	brown
	T:	ah?
	P:	brown
	T:	brown
	Ps:	brown
55	T:	brown bread
	Ps:	brown bread
	T:	**dalam kelas ini apa yang** brown? *<in this class is there anything that's brown?>*
	Ps:	[inaudible]
60	P:	**roti** *<bread>*
	T:	**apa yang** brown? *<what's* brown?>
	P:	**muka** *<face>*
	T:	**ah muka kamu** brown **lah** *<ah your face is* brown>
	P:	**meja** *<table>*

65   T: **itu warna yang dipanggil** brown <*that's the colour called*
                brown>
        P: brown
        T: **roti pun namanya** bread <*the name for roti is* bread>. 'the
                cook'

Focusing specifically on lines 37–46, it is clear that there are different ways
in which the classroom participants organise the exchanges that form the
building blocks of the lesson. The two IRF (Initiation-Response-Feedback)
exchanges below, for example, show that the initiations (by the teacher) in
both exchanges are made in Malay. The pupils' responses, though, are
different, the first one being in English 'bread' and the second one in Malay
'**roti**'.

Exchange 1:   I   T: **apa yang dia makan itu?** <*what is he eating?*>
                  R   P: bread
                  F   T: bread

Exchange 2:   I   T: **apa itu?** <*what's that?*>
                  R   P: **roti** <*bread*>
                  F   T: **itu yang kita panggil** bread <*that's what's called*
                               bread>

The discourse in this classroom, then, allows for either English or Malay in
the response slot, and I would argue that this is an important and pragmatic
discourse strategy in this context. It is also 'safe' in that, potentially, it facilitates comprehension.

In Extract 4, where the particular section of text being discussed is 'the
cook looks at the cook book', the teacher uses a different technique.

Extract 4 (lines 79–97)

        T: **tengok buku kamu** <*look at your books*> .. OK **yang mana**
80   **yang** cook? <*which one is the* cook?>. **apa** cook **itu?** <*what is*
                a cook>.**tukang masak** <*cook*>. **di sekolah sini ada tukang**
                masak? <*in this school is there a cook?*>
        Ps: **ada** <*yes*>
        T: **apa nama dia?** <*what's her name?*>
85   P: Rodiah
        T: Rodiah . **siapa lagi?** <*who else?*>
        Ps: Sepai
        T: Sepai . **jadi . tukang masak itu kami panggil** the cook <*so .*
                we call the tukang masak the cook>. **apa yang dia tengok**

90		**sana**?<*what is she looking at there?*>
	P:	**buku** <*book*>
	P:	**buku** <*book*>
	T:	**buku . apa warna buku itu?** <*what colour is the book?*>
	P:	**coklat** <*brown*>
95	**P:**	pink
	P:	brown
	T:	brown . ah . brown . [inaudible] .. OK the next one . 'Glen'

In this sequence, the teacher is not able to elicit the meaning of 'cook' from the pupils. The picture in the textbook shows a woman, wearing an odd-looking hat (in actual fact, a chef's hat), stirring a pan, and reading a book. It is rather a confusing image for the pupils in this particular context, as cooking and reading at the same time (indeed, the whole cultural concept of 'cook book' and 'recipe') would not be part of their cultural knowledge.

The pupils are not able to provide a response to the teacher's initiation '**apa** cook **itu?**' ('what is a cook?') in line 80. This is clearly an attempt from the teacher to get the pupils to provide the Malay equivalent, as he himself then provides the Malay gloss, **tukang masak** (line 81) in his next statement. That the pupils understand the concept of **tukang masak** ('cook') becomes clear as they provide the names of the two school cooks. As for any discussion about the 'cook book', the teacher focuses simply on the colour of the book. It is highly unlikely that the concept of 'cook book' (i.e. a book containing recipes) will be understood.

Extract 5 shows that, by this stage of the lesson, the interaction between teacher and pupils is mainly in Malay. The sort of pedagogic and linguistic strategies referred to above are demonstrated in this extract, which revolves around the key words 'salt' and 'sugar'.

Extract 5: (lines 133–160)

	T:	**apa yang** salt **itu?** <*what is* salt?>
	P:	salt
135	**T:**	**apa dia** salt? <*what is* salt?>
	P:	**garam** <*salt*>
	T:	**apa?** <*what?*>
	P:	**garam** <*salt*>
	T:	**ga** . {**ram** <*salt*>
140	**Ps:**	{**ram**
	T:	**garam . garam . semua tahu apa garam?** . <*salt . salt . do you all know what is 'garam'?*>
	Ps:	yeh

	T:	**apa** salt **itu?** . **apa guna** salt **itu?** <*what is salt? . what use is salt?*>
145	P:	**buat di sayur** <*to put on vegetables*>
	T:	aah . **buat di sayur** . **buat di sayur** <*to put on vegetables . to put on vegetables*>. **boleh buat di air** . **campur untuk minum?** <*can you put it in water . mix to make a drink?*>
	P:	**tidak** <*no*>
150	P:	**boleh** <*can*>
	T:	**boleh?** <*can you?*>. [laughter] **apa yang buat dalam air minum?** <*what do you put in drinks?*>
	Ps:	**ais** <*ice*>
	T:	**yeh lah** . **buat kopi** . <*yes . to make coffee*>
155	Ps:	**gula** <*sugar*>
	T:	**gula** . **gula** . **apa satu bekas sana?** [pointing to the picture in the book] <*sugar . sugar . what's that container there*> salt . **apa dalam satu bekas lagi?** <*what's in the other container?*>
	P:	**gula** <*sugar*>

Firstly, the key lexical items from the text are embedded in Malay discourse. The teacher's first two initiations in this extract:

line 133   **apa yang** salt **itu?** (*'what is salt?'*)
line 135   **apa dia** salt (*'what is salt?'*)

manage to elicit the desired word **garam** ('salt') from the pupils in lines 136 and 138. The teacher then follows this up using a very common interactional strategy, shown in lines 139–140 below:

line 139 **T:**   **ga** . {**ram** <*salt*>
line 140 **Ps:** {**ram**
line 141 **T:**   **garam** . **garam** . **semua tahu apa garam** . <*salt . salt*
line 142   *do you all know what is 'garam'?*>
line 143 **Ps:** yeh

By elongating the vowel in the first syllable of **garam** and by inflecting his voice, the teacher provides the cue for the pupils to respond in chorus with the second syllable of the word. This is followed up with a check that the pupils understand.

The final extract from this lesson shows how the teacher elicits the term 'yellow' from the pupils.

Extract 6 (lines 175–192)

175	T:	jadi . yang mana yang Tini sini? mana orang yang nama Tini? <*so. which one is Tini here . where's the person called Tini?*>
	P:	sini <*here*> [pointing to the picture of Tini in the book]
	T:	[inaudible] ada garam dengan apa . gula dekat dia punya
180		thumbs .. <*there's salt and . what else . sugar on her* thumbs> bajunya apa warna bajunya? <*what colour is her dress?*>
	Ps:	kuning <*yellow*>
	T:	kuning . apa kuning itu Bahasa Inggeris? <*what's* 'kuning' *in English?*>
185	P:	yellow
	T:	{yellow
	Ps:	{yellow
	T:	yellow
	Ps:	yellow
190	T:	yellow
	Ps:	yellow

What we can see in this lesson is a mixture of two languages: the language of the text, English, and the language of mediation, Malay. No use of Sa'ben was noted, not even in the introduction to the lesson. The pupils' responses were largely limited to single word labels, in either English or Malay. The language practices here, then, are 'safe' in that they allow the classroom participants to accomplish the lesson, albeit by using one school language, Malay, to teach the other school language, English. The juxtaposition of these two languages in the classroom, neither of which has any currency in the communities served by the school, shows the participants' pragmatic response to the policies imposed from above. One other striking feature of this lesson is the text and the accompanying sketch, both of which are culturally loaded.

I now turn to a brief discussion of another English lesson, this time in a secondary-two classroom.

Lesson B: (secondary two, English)

This lesson was built around a unit on 'parts of the body' in the textbook *KBSM English Form 2* (Gaudart, 1989). In the early part of the lesson, the teacher is calling out names of parts of the body and the students are repeating after her, as in Extract 7 below.

Extract 7 (lines 25–40)

25	T:	head
	Ps:	head

	T:	again
	Ps:	head
	T:	again
30	Ps:	head
	T:	forehead
	Ps:	forehead
	T:	again
	Ps:	forehead
35	T:	again
	Ps:	forehead
	T:	hair
	Ps:	hair
	T:	again
40	Ps:	hair

Extract 7 above demonstrates a common feature of this lesson, the repetition of key lexical items. As the teacher calls out names of parts of the body, the pupils repeat after her, in chorus, often three or four times per lexical item. Later in the lesson, as shown in Extract 8 below, the teacher introduces another activity.

Extract 8 (lines 45–64)

45	T:	OK . you two stand up . show me your head
	T:	oh very good .. give them a clap
	T:	show me your tongue .. point to your tongue … touch your tongue
	P:	[aside] **lidah** <*tongue*>
50	T:	tongue . all right . good . thank you very much . OK . Jemi .. touch your nose Jemi
	P:	nose . nose ..
	T:	very good . give him a clap .. Bili . touch your eyebrow
	Ps:	eyebrow
55	T:	OK good [pupils clap] . OK Juel .. touch your cheeks .. Very good [clapping]
	T:	Noni touch your jaw .. [laughter as P touches forehead] .. is that right
	Ps:	no
60	T:	[Writes on b/b 'I touch my … '] Today we want to do some more . some more parts of the body
	T:	shoulder
	Ps:	shoulder

In this part of the lesson, the teacher asks the students to close their eyes and touch various parts of their bodies, such as 'touch your wrist', 'touch your elbow'. I note that several students in the class open their eyes to look at what others are doing. There are also several pupil asides, not all of which I was able to record, where pupils provide translations in Malay or Kelabit for particular parts of the body. One such aside is shown in line 49 in Extract 8. Pupils seem to enjoy the activity, and there is laughter as one pupil mistakenly touches her forehead instead of her jaw (lines 57–58).

The next part of the lesson returns to repetitive naming of parts of the body. Following this, the teacher instructs the students to sit down and write the numbers one to ten in their books. She is planning to give them a spelling test of the words they have used during the lesson. The first part of this 'test' is shown in Extract 9 below.

Extract 9 (lines 175–213)

175	T:	OK can you turn your chairs around .. are you ready?
	P:	yes
	T:	turn your chair round . OK . no looking .
	T:	number one . hold
	P:	{ah
180	P:	{**anun sinih** <(K) *what's that*>
	T:	hold . I hold your hand . hold . **ngimet** <(K) *hold*>. hold . hold number two . touch .. touch . you know touch .
	P:	**sentuh** <*touch*>.
	T:	number one hold number two touch . . .
185	P:	number three?
	T:	number three . number three . shoulders shoul . ders . . . next one . arms . . . next one elbow
	Ps:	elbow
	T:	elbow . **iyuk** <(K) *elbow*> elbow . elbow .. OK next one .
190		wrist . . .
		next one finger .
	P:	finger
	T:	**bua' tidtu'** <(K) *finger*>
	Ps:	finger
195	T:	next one . thumb
	Ps:	thumb .
	T:	thumb . thumb . **bua' tidtu' rayeh** . <(K) *thumb*> thumb
	Ps:	thumb
	T:	thumb .. next one . fingernail . fingernail
200	P:	fingernail

T:	**ilun bua' tidtu'** <(K) *fingernail*)
Ps:	fingernail
T:	OK next one . face .
P:	face . **munong** <(K) *face*>
205	T:	face . **munong** <(K) *face*> .. next one . head . **uluh** <(K) *head*>
P:	**uluh** <(K) *head*>
T:	head .. next one .. forehead .. **mado** <(K) *forehead*>
P:	forehead
210	T:	next one . hair . hair
Ps:	hair
T:	**ebpuk** <(K) *hair*>
Ps:	hair

The extract shows that the teacher is testing the pupils' spelling of key lexical items that have been introduced in the earlier part of the lesson. As part of this, the teacher also provides the Kelabit meaning of the term (apart from item two, where the Malay term is given). As noted earlier, the teacher in this classroom came from another part of the country, but since coming to the area she had begun to learn Kelabit, and she had annotated her book with Kelabit glosses for key lexical items. The transcript shows how the teacher introduces the particular item, such as 'thumb' (line 195), which is then repeated by the pupils, then by the teacher, who also provides the Kelabit gloss **'bua' tidtu' rayeh'**. On one occasion, after the teacher introduces the term 'face', a pupil comes in, out of turn, so to speak, to repeat the term 'face', and to provide the Kelabit gloss, **'munong'**, before the teacher can do it.

Although Kelabit is not used to a large extent in this classroom, key lexical items are nevertheless provided in Kelabit, where known, by the teacher. More extended discourse, when not in English, is in Malay.

The final extract shows an activity towards the end of the lesson. The teacher instructs the pupils to turn to page 139 in the textbook where there are a series of questions about looking 'after your body'.

1. Do you look after your body?
2. Why should you stay healthy?
3. How can you stay healthy?

Extract 10 shows how the teacher unpacks the meaning of the text, and specifically these three questions in the text. For the first question, the teacher provides a complete translation in Malay (line 321). For the second question, the teacher establishes that the pupils do not know the meaning of the word 'healthy'. After repeating the word a number of times she provides the Malay equivalent, followed by a Kelabit approximation of the term. For the third question, the whole question is glossed in Malay, and then in Kelabit. What is of interest here is that use of these two languages is only to annotate the English text, and it does not appear to hand over any speaking rights to the pupils. In this short extract there are only five one-word responses from pupils and no meaningful discussion in response to the questions posed in the textbook.

Extract 10 (lines 315–336)

315	T:	OK turn to page one three nine . . . OK let's look at page one three nine . answer these questions .. one . 'do you look af ter your body?'
	P:	Yes
	T:	'do you look after your body?'
320	Ps:	yes
	T:	**adakah kamu jaga badan kamu?** . <_do you look after your body?_>'why should you stay healthy?' . 'why should you stay healthy?' .. know meaning of healthy?
	P:	no
325	T:	healthy . heal . thy .. healthy
	P:	healthy
	T:	healthy . **sihat** <_healthy_> . **rana'e** <(K) _condition_> .. now . number three . 'how can you stay healthy?' . ah . 'how can you stay healthy?' **bagaimana kamu boleh jadi sihat?**
330		<_how can you stay healthy?_> . **Tuda' iko kareb rana'e?** <(K) _how can you stay [in good]_ condition> ah . how can you stay . healthy . all right . reading . read this passage . now read this passage as far as you can and then answer the
335		questions .. number one. What is the passage about . from your reading . you know . what is it all about . yeh . number two . what is the title of the passage . what is the title of the passage . can you see?
	Ps:	yeh
	T:	what's the title? OK . who wants to read .

In this classroom, the teacher uses both Malay and Kelabit during the lesson. These languages are used simply to gloss words or statements that appear in the text, and not in any communicative or exploratory way. The brief analysis of the lesson shows that the classroom is a very tightly controlled environment, with the pupils positioned as recipients of teacher-mediated text. There is little active participation from the pupils. The interaction is orchestrated and managed by the teacher and, as I have pointed out above, and as others have noted in different multilingual contexts (Arthur, 1996; Chick, 1996), the participants appear to be going through the motions of the lesson. Although the pupils provide labels when requested, their own speaking rights are not clear, and there is certainly no exploratory use of Malay or Kelabit.

Tensions in Classroom Practices in the Local/Global Context

Having provided some brief glimpses of the discourses of two classrooms in rural interior schools in Malaysia, one primary and one secondary, I now want to refocus on some of the issues introduced in the early part of this chapter. In particular, it is my intention to focus on the tensions between classroom practice and language policy, and embed this discussion of these tensions within local, national and global contexts. Central to the discussion here is Pennycook's (2000: 90) notion of classrooms as 'sociopolitical spaces that exist in a complex relationship to the world outside', and Tollefson's (2000: 19) statement about the 'direct and powerful impact of social, political and economic forces' of English language education on classrooms and how students' lives are affected by such forces.

The clearest disengagement with language policy in the classrooms observed is that other linguistic resources are being used alongside the official language of the lessons. This is common practice in a large range of contexts, for example, Botswana (Arthur, 1996), Brunei (Martin, 1999, 2003), Kenya (Bunyi, this volume), and South Africa (Brock-Utne; Probyn, both this volume), to name but a few. The use of a local language alongside the 'official' language of the lesson is a well-known phenomenon and yet, for a variety of reasons, it is often lambasted as 'bad practice', blamed on teachers' lack of English-language competence, or put to one side and/or swept under the carpet. In a recent discussion of the impact of English as a global language on educational policies and practices in the Asia-Pacific region, for example, little mention is made of the way teachers switch between languages to accomplish lessons (Nunan, 2003). The prevailing rhetoric in the Malaysian context, as evidenced by the editorial from the major government-controlled English-medium newspaper, highlighted near the beginning of this chapter, is how use of the local language is 'sabotaging' the language policy rather than, for example, helping to bail it out.

Several authors have referred to the hegemony of English, specifically where English is the medium of instruction, and the inequalities that arise. Of particular relevance to this study is the unequal access to English-language education in Malaysia between urban and rural areas. As noted by Toh (1984: 260, cited in Pennycook, 1994: 203), 'the formal educational system in Malaysia has been utilised more as a mechanism for the intergenerational transmission of economic status by high-status families rather than as a vehicle for the social advancement of the poor'. These high-status families are generally found in the urban areas. According to Tollefson (2000: 18), these inequalities can result in 'classes that are not meaningful to most children'. Braighlinn (1992: 21), with reference to the Brunei situation, makes a similar point, suggesting that the 'majority of non-middle-class youth receive virtually no education at all, because the medium of instruction [English] cannot be understood'. While not arguing with the sentiments expressed here, I would suggest that such statements are only partially true, as they do not take into account the often creative, pragmatic and 'safe' practices of the classroom participants in such contexts. One of the most significant of these 'safe' practices is 'code-switching' between the official language of the lesson and a language which the classroom participants have a greater access to, usually a shared local language. In the classrooms in this study, the major language used to annotate the lessons is Malay, like English a language that is foreign to the two areas, albeit the official language of the nation, and a language in which the pupils have had the bulk of their education. I use the term 'safe' here after Chick (1996) and Hornberger and Chick (2001), but with my own slant, to refer to practices that allow the classroom participants to be seen to accomplish lessons. However, although the practices are 'safe' in that a language (or languages) in which the participants have greater access is used to annotate the lessons, there is little exploratory use of 'language' in the classroom.

The use of two or more languages, or 'code-switching', in the classroom creates its own tensions, particularly in the educational hierarchy outside the classroom. Language choice issues in the classroom are, in fact, much more complex than can be legislated for (cf. Merritt *et al.*, 1992). Several studies show how language planners, curriculum developers and school inspectors regard such bilingual practices as code-switching as a substandard form of communication in the classroom (for example, Lin, 1996; Martin, 2003). One reason for the lack of official recognition of or support for these practices might be the concern about the efficiency of a pedagogy that supports the switching between languages. But how much is actually known about this? This is a question I return to below. Another reason might be the pervasive influence of what Phillipson (1992: 185) has referred to as the 'monolingual fallacy', that is, the view that English is best taught monolingually (cf. Howatt, 1984).

Certainly, the tensions referred to above are felt by teachers. They are aware of this pervasive monolingual view, and the type of discourses expressed in, for example, the *The New Straits Times* editorial discussed previously, and of how the language policy is supposed to work. Within the South African context, for example, Setati *et al.* (2002: 147) make reference to the 'intentional but dilemma-filled' code-switching practices of teachers in their study of mathematics, science and English classrooms.

The dynamics of the interaction for learning and teaching bilingually are under-researched. And yet we need to question whether bilingual interaction strategies 'work' in the classroom context. For example, are bilingual exchanges of the type shown in Excerpt 3 in this study in Malaysian classrooms useful for the students and do they facilitate learning? Can classroom code-switching support communication, particularly the exploratory talk which is such an essential part of the learning process? A corollary to this is whether teacher-training programmes (both pre-service and in-service), in multilingual contexts take into account the realities and pragmatics of classroom language use in such contexts. Questions such as these are critical in view of the fact that an increasing number of governments 'are introducing English as a compulsory subject at younger and younger ages, often without adequate funding, [and] teacher education for elementary school teachers' (Nunan, 2003: 591).

It will be apparent from the discussion of classroom practices in this study that other tensions exist within the classroom. Textbooks, for example, are not neutral entities but, as pointed out by Pennycook (2000: 99), they carry 'cultural and ideological messages'. This is clearly seen in the textbook used in Lesson A in this study. Although the pictures and the lifestyles depicted are given a Malaysian flavour, they are nevertheless imbued with cultural content that is far removed from the cultural world of rural students.

The tensions in the classrooms need to be positioned within the world outside the classroom, at local, national and global levels. Unusually, perhaps, one specific event in the history of the communities in this study was responsible for bringing the 'world without' to these isolated Borneo communities, dubbed the 'world within' (Harrisson, 1984 [1959]). Early one morning in March 1945, Tom Harrisson and a small band of colleagues parachuted into the area as part of the war effort against the Japanese invasion forces in Borneo. This set off a chain of events, including the introduction of formal education to the area, which was the precursor of enormous change over the next half-century (Lian, 1979; Martin & Yen, 1994; see also Harrisson, 1984[1959]). Education brought with it two important and powerful languages, initially Malay and later English. These two languages have had, and continue to have, an increasingly significant effect on the language ecology in the two areas, although Kelabit and Sa'ben, the languages spoken indigenously in the area, are still the main languages passed down from one generation to another. Outside the village communities, however, particularly in the coastal towns of Sarawak where many villagers have settled, language shift is occurring and the younger generation is growing up learning Malay and English.

Neither Sa'ben nor Kelabit have a literate tradition, and there is no standard orthography for the two languages. Even up to the present time, messages between villages, and between villages and the coast, are conveyed through the traditional method of *metatad*, a process in which someone is asked to relay a message to someone else once they arrive at their destination (Harris *et al.*, 2000). However, it is just as common nowadays to contact relatives or friends living in or visiting the coastal towns through satellite telephone. Apart from the New Testament, *Bala Luk Do'* (Bible Society of Singapore and Malaysia, 1982), translated into Lun Bawang, a related language sharing approximately 70% of its vocabulary with Kelabit, and hymn booklets, there is little other reading material found in homes. *Bala Luk Do'*, though, has afforded some access to a limited literacy for any of the older generation who have learned to read, although the Malay version of the New Testament is actually more commonly used among the Sa'ben and Kelabit communities in this study. Outside the homes, in the schools, textbooks are available in Malay and English, although the amount of other reading materials is limited. Next to School B, a library has been set up, and it is stocked with a range of books in Malay and English. No material in Kelabit, Sa'ben or Penan is available in this library.

Outside the schools, there is very little access to literacy. Although people returning to the villages from the coast might bring in a newspaper (in English or Malay), they are not generally on sale. Other channels of communication include radio and satellite television, although in a survey of 140 residents in one of the areas under study, Harris *et al.* (2000) note that only 30% of those surveyed had a television set. Education has clearly resulted in a gradual change in the traditional patterns of communication within the community, although some of these patterns still persist. The oral tradition is still common, though literacy is becoming more important. However, what I am referring to here is literacy in Malay and, to a lesser extent, English. Kelabit literacy comes a very poor third.

One recent development in certain rural areas in Malaysia has been the development of Information and Communication Technology and Internet access. One such area is the community that is served by School B in this study. The government rationale is that those remote and marginalised communities that characterise rural life in Sarawak should be provided with equal access to ICTs as part of national development (http://www.unimas.my/ebario/overview.html). A computer laboratory with 16 computers has been established at the school, and an IT literacy programme is also in operation. In setting up the programme it was noted that the 'language barrier' was a problem and that manuals needed to be designed with this in mind. Although it has been suggested that the connectivity might help to ensure that the rich traditions of the Kelabit community are safeguarded, the emphasis on English for ICTs is likely to further reduce the role of Kelabit (and to a lesser extent Malay) in the school community. Although the government's attempt to provide access to ICTs for these remote communities should be applauded, as the provision is so inextricably linked to English as the language of modernisation and technology, it in effect lessens the opportunities for the younger generation of Kelabit speakers (and speakers of other languages in the area) to become literate in their own language. Kelabit, then, as with many smaller languages around the world, is being overtaken by the processes of globalisation.

At the national and global levels, as part of the former Malaysian Prime Minister's *Wawasan 2020*, a 'vision' that by the year 2020 Malaysia will have achieved the status of a developed and industrialised nation, former Prime Minister Mahathir Mohamad has called for a technologically literate workforce that is equipped to perform competently in a global environment. This 'vision', of course, and as noted above, is linked inextricably to the position of English as the language of the global environment. Running through the whole discussion here is the tension on the one hand between the local and national contexts, and the need to adapt to globalisation. The decision to emphasise English in education is the pragmatic response to the inevitable challenges of technological advances and globalisation, and linked to the fear in the falling standards of English. Mazrui (2002: 272–73) notes a similar 'English only ideology and policy in education' in Africa where there is what he calls an 'epistemological and intellectual dependency on the West' due to the fact that 'modern science and technology are part of the Western package of "modernity"'.

The point is made by Pennycook (1994: 201) that in Malaysia 'English [is no longer] tied to the discourses of colonial elitism', and instead it has become the 'language of development, modernization, capitalism, science, technology and even democracy'. Gill (2002), in tracing the change in language policy in Malaysia from post-independence to contemporary time, juxtaposes the two issues of nationalism, and pragmatism. English is now positioned as the language of nationalism as is clear in these two statements by former Prime Minister Mahathir Mohamad, both cited in Gill (2002: 41–42).

Learning the English language will reinforce the spirit of nationalism when it is used to bring about development and progress for the country. . . . True nationalism means doing everything possible for the country, even if it means learning the English language. (Mahathir Mohamad, *The Sun*, September 11, 1999)

We believe that a nationalist is someone who has acquired all the knowledge and mastered all the skills and is capable of contesting against the rest of the world. But they [some Malaysians] think that just being able to speak Malay makes you a nationalist, and that is wrong. (Mahathir Mohamad, *New Straits Times*, December 29, 2000)

A 'pragmatic nationalism', then, according to a separate newspaper report, argues 'for bringing back English into the classroom in order to improve the competitiveness of Malaysians, . . . amid relentless globalisation' (*New Straits Times*, 8 May 2002). There is no doubt that the term 'globalisation' 'pervades contemporary political rhetoric' (Block & Cameron, 2002: 1). This term, and its Malay cognate, *globalisasi*, do indeed pervade recent government rhetoric in Malaysia, bringing with it a new slant on the concept of nationalism.

In the current climate of globalisation, it appears that English will remain an important commodity in Malaysia. The statements quoted above are part of the former prime minister's justification for the change of the medium of instruction in science and mathematics from Malay to English, which was implemented in 2003. While some steps are being taken to facilitate the switch, for example, the 'ETeMS' (English for Teaching Mathematics and Science) initiative (http://www.tutor.my/tutor/etems/), 'an urgent interim measure to ensure that teachers of mathematics and science will have basic capacity to use English as the medium of instruction', there are other important issues that need to be faced, such as the student learning experience. Nunan (2003: 611), in a brief study of the Asia-Pacific region, which includes Malaysia, considers that 'English language policies and practices have been implemented, often at significant cost to other aspects of the curriculum, without a clearly articulated rationale and without a detailed consideration of the costs and benefits of such policies and practices'.

Conclusion

This chapter has attempted to show how teachers and learners implement a macro language policy in two micro contexts, through a discourse-analytic study of two classrooms in two rural schools in Malaysia. The study purposely gives emphasis to the actual language practices in the schools, as many studies that purport to consider policy and practice together actually give pre-eminence to the former and neglect the latter. And yet it is fundamental that planners and policy-makers need to be aware of what is happening in the classroom, and how the participants in the classroom are putting policy into practice. The language practices in the two classrooms are presented against a backdrop of the official policy, and the tensions inherent in the policy, as well as within a local, national and global framework. In their education, as well as in the global context, students in the two communities covered by the study are being given subtle and not so subtle messages about the status of languages. In education and literacy (including electronic literacy), English and Malay predominate, and their own languages are relegated to also-rans. The tensions between policy and practice in this study have led to what I refer to as 'safe' (but not necessarily pedagogically 'sound') practices in the classrooms. I conclude with the plea that as English is accepted as the contemporary global language, it is necessary to ensure that efforts are made to ensure equality of access to languages, including their own languages.

Notes

1. I acknowledge the support of a grant from the Southeast Asia Committee of the British Academy.
2. Kelabit is a language spoken by approximately 5000 people in around seven villages in eastern Sarawak, Malaysia. Sa'ben (also written as Saban and Sa'ban) is spoken in two villages in eastern Sarawak close to the border with Kalimantan. Varieties of Sa'ben are also found on the other side of the border, in Kalimantan (Indonesian Borneo).

Transcription conventions

T	:	Teacher
P	:	Pupil
Ps	:	Pupils
Plain font	:	English
Bold font	:	**Malay; (K) Kelabit**
<Italics>	:	<English glosses>
[UPPER CASE]	:	[COMMENTARY ON WHAT IS HAPPENING IN THE CLASSROOM]
{cat	:	Overlapping speech
{dog		
'Abu is ..'	:	Indicates reading from the textbook or other resource
underlining	:	Indicates raised intonation from the teacher where teacher expects pupils to orally 'fill in the blank'
/lif/	:	Phonological representation (where necessary)

All names that appear in the text are pseudonyms.

References

Arthur, J. (1996) Code-switching and collusion: Classroom interaction in Botswana primary schools. *Linguistics and Education* 8 (1), 17–33.

Asiah Abu Samah (1994) Language education policy planning in Malaysia: Concern for unity, reality and rationality. In Abdullah Hassan (ed.) *Language Planning in Southeast Asia* (pp. 52–65). Kuala Lumpur: Dewan Bahasa dan Pustaka.

Asmah Hj Omar (1994) Nationism and exoglossia: The case of English in Malaysia. In Abdullah Hassan (ed.) *Language Planning in Southeast Asia* (pp. 66–85). Kuala Lumpur: Dewan Bahasa dan Pustaka.

Bible Society of Singapore and Malaysia (1982) *Bala Luk Do'*. Singapore: Bible Society of Singapore and Malaysia.

Block, D. and Cameron, D. (2002) *Globalization and Language Teaching*. London: Routledge.

Braighlinn, G. (1992) *Ideological Innovation under Monarchy. Aspects of Legitimation Activity in Contemporary Brunei*. Amsterdam: VU University Press.

Brock-Utne, B. (this volume) Language-in-education policies and practices in Africa with a special focus on Tanzania and South Africa – Insights from research in progress.

Bunyi, G. (this volume) Language classroom practices in Kenya.

Chick, K. (1996) Safe-talk: Collusion in apartheid education. In H. Coleman (ed.) *Society and the Language Classroom* (pp. 21–39). Cambridge: Cambridge University Press.

Cleghorn, A. (1992) Primary level science in Kenya: Constructing meaning through English and indigenous languages. *International Journal of Qualitative Studies in Education* 5 (4), 311–23.

Eisemon, T.O., Prouty, R. and Schwille, J. (1989) What language should be used for teaching? Language policy and school reform in Burundi. *Journal of Multilingual and Multicultural Development* 10 (6), 473–97.

Gaudart, H. (1989) *KBSM English Form 2B*. Kuala Lumpur: Federal Publications.

Gaudart, H. (1992) *Bilingual Education in Malaysia*. Townsville: Centre for Southeast Asian Studies.

Gill, S.K. (2002) *International Communication. English Language Challenges for Malaysia*. Serdang: Universiti Putra Malaysia Press.

Harris, R., Bala, P., Songan, P., Khoo, E. and Trang, T. (2000) Challenges and opportunities in introducing information and communication technologies to the Kelabit Community of North Central Borneo. Paper presented at the 2nd International Conference on Cultural Attitudes Towards Technology and Communication, 12–15 July, Perth, Australia. (Available at: http://www.unimas.my/ebario/paperwork2.html)

Harrisson, T. (1984) *World Within. A Borneo Story*. Singapore: Oxford University Press. (1st edn, 1959, The Cresset Press.)

Heller, M. and Martin-Jones, M. (eds) (2001) *Voices of Authority. Education and Linguistic Difference*. Westport, CT: Ablex Publishers.

Hornberger, N. and Chick, K. (2001) Co-constructing school safetime: Safetalk practices in Peruvian and South African classrooms. In M. Heller and M. Martin-Jones (eds) *Voices of Authority. Education and Linguistic Difference* (pp. 31–56). Westport, CT: Ablex Publishers.

Howatt, A. (1984) *A History of English Language Teaching*. Oxford: Oxford University Press.

Lian, R.S. (1979) Kelabit ethnography: A brief report. *The Sarawak Museum Journal* XL (61). Special Issue 4, III.

Lin, A.M.Y. (1996) Bilingualism or linguistic segregation? Symbolic domination, resistance and code-switching in Hong Kong schools. *Linguistics and Education* 8 (1), 49–84.

Martin, P.W. (1999) Close encounters of a bilingual kind: Interactional practices in the primary classroom in Brunei. *International Journal of Educational Development* 19 (2), 127–40.

Martin, P.W. (2003) Bilingual encounters in the classroom. In J-M Dewaele, A. Housen and Li Wei (eds) *Bilingualism: Beyond Basic Principles.* (pp. 67–87). Clevedon: Multilingual Matters.

Martin, P.W. and Yen, E. (1994) Language use among the Kelabit living in urban centers. In P.W. Martin (ed.) *Shifting Patterns of Language Use in Borneo* (pp. 147–64). Williamsburg, VA: Borneo Research Council.

Mazrui, A.M. (2002) The English language in African education: Dependency and decolonization. In J.W. Tollefson (ed.) *Language Policies in Education: Critical Issues* (pp. 267–81). Mahwah, NJ: Lawrence Erlbaum.

Merritt, M., Cleghorn, A., Abagi, J.O. and Bunyi, G. (1992) Socialising multilingualism: Determinants of code-switching in Kenyan primary classrooms. *Journal of Multilingual and Multicultural Development* 13 (1 & 2), 103–22.

Mutiara Hj Mohamad and Azly Abdul Rahman (1996) *English Year 2.* Kuala Lumpur: Dewan Bahasa dan Pustaka.

Nunan, D. (2003) The impact of English as a global language on educational policies and practices in the Asia-Pacific region. *TESOL Quarterly* 37 (4), 589–613.

Ożóg, A.C.K. (1990) The English language in Malaysia and its relationship with the National Language. In R.B. Baldauf, Jr. and A. Luke (eds) *Language Planning and Education in Australasia and the South Pacific* (pp. 305–18). Clevedon: Multilingual Matters.

Ożóg, A.C.K. (1993) Bilingualism and national development in Malaysia. *Journal of Multilingual and Multicultural Development* 14 (1 & 2), 59–72.

Pennycook, A. (1994) *The Cultural Politics of English as an International Language.* London: Longman.

Pennycook, A. (2000) The social politics and cultural politics of language classrooms. In J.K. Hall and W. G. Eggington (eds) *The Sociopolitics of English Language Teaching* (pp. 89–103). Clevedon: Multilingual Matters.

Phillipson, R. (1992) *Linguistic Imperialism.* Oxford: Oxford University Press.

Probyn, M. (this volume) Language and the struggle to learn: The intersection of classroom realities, language policies and neo-colonial and globalisation discourses in South African schools.

Ricento, T. (ed.) (2000) *Ideology, Politics and Language Policies: Focus on English.* Amsterdam: John Benjamins.

Setati, M., Adler, J., Reed, Y. and Bapoo, A. (2002) Incomplete journeys: Codeswitching and other language practices in Mathematics, Science and English language classrooms in South Africa. *Language and Education* 16 (2), 128–49.

The New Straits Times (2000) 28 December, 2000.

The New Straits Times (2002) 8 May, 2002.

The New Straits Times (2003) Editorial. 23 April, 2003.

The Sun (1999) 11September, 1999.

Toh Kin Woon (1984) Education as a vehicle for reducing economic inequality. In S. Husin Ali (ed.) *Ethnicity, Class and Development: Malaysia* (pp. 224–64). Kuala Lumpur: Persatuan Sains Sosial Malaysia.

Tollefson, J. (2000) Policy and ideology in the spread of English. In J.K. Hall and W.G. Eggington (eds) *The Sociopolitics of English Language Teaching* (pp. 7–21). Clevedon: Multilingual Matters.

Tollefson, J. (2002) *Language Policies in Education: Critical Issues*. Mahwah, NJ: Lawrence Erlbaum.

Vavrus, F. (2002) Postcoloniality and English: Exploring language policy and the politics of development in Tanzania. *TESOL Quarterly* 36 (3), 373–97.

Watson, J.K.P. (1982) Education and colonialism in peninsula Malaysia. In K. Watson (ed.) *Education in the Third World* (pp. 88–107). London: Croom Helm.

Watson, J.K.P. (1983) Cultural pluralism, nation-building and educational policies in peninsular Malaysia. In C. Kennedy (ed.) *Language Planning and Language-in-Education* (pp. 132–45). London: George Allen & Unwin.

Wong, R.Y.L and James, J.E. (2000) Malaysia. In Ho Wah Kam and R.Y.L Wong (eds) *Language Policies and Language Education. The Impact in East Asian Countries in the Next Decade* (pp. 209–40). Singapore: Times Academic Press.

Chapter 6

The Four Language Stages in the History of Iran

ABDOLMEHDI RIAZI

[Courtesy of http://itrs.scu.edu/instructors/dlustig/lustig/student/
webpage/iran.htm]

A Brief History of Iran

The opening section of this chapter will briefly describe the history of
Iran from early times up to the present time, with reference to the ruling
powers at each of the periods in that history. The purpose of this section is
to outline the historical background of the country, and to identify major

stages in its history which have affected the use and the role of language in different aspects of the nation's development.[1]

The Persian Empire, the first of its kind, was founded in 550 BC by Cyrus the Great, who was followed by Darius. Cyrus was the first Achaemenian Emperor of Persia, and he issued a decree on his aims and policies, later hailed as his charter of the rights of nations. Inscribed on a clay cylinder in cuneiform, this is known to be the first declaration of human rights. It was discovered in 1879 and is now kept at the British Museum. A replica of this is also at the United Nations in New York.

The Persian Empire became the dominant world power for over two centuries. It made possible the first significant and continuous contact between East and West. It was the world's first religiously tolerant empire and consisted of a multitude of different languages, races, religions and cultures. Prior to the rise of the Roman Empire, it set a precedent for the importance of the rule of law and had a powerful centralized army and an efficient and systematic state administration. However, the greatest legacy of the Persian Empire was that it demonstrated for the first time how diverse peoples can flourish culturally and prosper economically under one central government.

The language of the Persian Empire was Old Persian, which was the language used in the cuneiform inscriptions of the Achaemenian dynasty and the vernacular of the Achaemenian elite. Old Persian was spoken in south-western Persia, an area known as Persis, and belongs to the Iranian branch of the Indo-European family of languages.

The Achaemenian dynasty was succeeded, after a period of Greek and Parthian rule, by the dynasty in the early 3rd century (around 211 AD). For about 400 years the Sassanids maintained Iran's independence against Roman and Byzantine encroachment, and under their benevolent rule the country prospered economically and socially. The Sassanids' control was ended when the Arabs defeated them in the 7th century (641 AD). With their takeover of Persia the Arabs brought Islam to the country and ruled for about two centuries. The Turks began their invasion in the 10th century and soon established several Turkish states. The Turks were followed by the Mongols, led by Chengiz Khan in the 13th century and Timur in the late 14th century.

The Safavid dynasty (1502–1736), founded by King Ismail, restored internal order in Iran and established the Shi'ite sect of Islam as the state religion; it reached its height during the reign (1587–1629) of King Abbas the first (Abbas the Great). He drove out the Portuguese, who had established colonies on the Persian Gulf early in the 16th century. King Abbas also established trade relations with Great Britain and reorganized the army. Religious differences led to frequent wars with the Ottoman Turks, whose interest in Iran was to continue well into the 20th century.

The fall of the Safavid dynasty was brought about by the Afghans, who overthrew the weak King Husein in 1722. An interval of Afghan rule followed until King expelled them and established the Afshar dynasty in 1736. The Afshar dynasty was followed by the Zand dynasty (1750–94), founded by Karim Khan, who established his capital at Shiraz and adorned that city with many fine buildings. His rule brought a period of peace and renewed prosperity. However, the country was soon again in turmoil, which lasted until the advent of the Qajar dynasty (1794–1925).

In 1921, Reza Khan, an army officer, established a military dictatorship following a coup. Reza Khan was subsequently elected hereditary king in 1925, thus ending the Qajar dynasty and founding the new Pahlavi dynasty (1925–1979). In 1941 the King abdicated in favor of his son.

Iran's pro-Western policies, which had started with the Qajar dynasty, continued into the 1970s. However, opposition to such growing Westernization and secularization was strongly denounced by the Islamic clergy, headed by the Ayatollah Ruhollah , who had been exiled from Iran in 1964. Khomeini's exile from Iran was the beginning of the opposition movement against the ruling government.

The Shah's (King's) autocratic rule and his extensive use of the secret police led to widespread popular unrest throughout the country in 1978. The religion-based protests were directed against the Shah's policies by the Ayatollah Ruhollah , who gained victory in 1979; this resulted in the establishment of the Islamic Republic of Iran (1979–present).

Iran's Language and Culture

The national language of Iran is Persian, also known as Farsi, which is an Indo-European language. The other main regional languages of the country are Azari (Turkish), Kurdish, Arabic and Lori. There are dozens of other Persian dialects and tongues throughout the 26 provinces, such as Gilaki, Baluchi and Turkmen. The major second or foreign languages taught and learned in schools across the country are English and Arabic and, to a lesser extent, French, German, Italian, and Russian. The Arabic script was adapted to Persian after the introduction of Islam, but there is no standard method of transliterating Persian into English.

Iranian culture has three components, originating from three cultural elements throughout its history. The first has been ancient Persian culture, which belonged to the Persian Empire and which is, in essence, the root of every Iranian thought. The second has been Islamic culture, introduced to Iran in the 7th century, and the third one has been Western thought, brought to the country in the 19th century. These three components have collectively and individually represented themselves in different aspects of the country's sociopolitical and cultural identity and movements at different times.

Iran's current population of more than 70 million people, which makes it one of the most populous countries in the Middle East, contains within itself sizable ethnic and religious minorities. The ethnic minorities include Azaris (the largest, by some estimates exceeding one quarter of the whole population, living mainly in the north-west of the country close to the newly independent state of Azerbaijan); Baluchis (several million, living in the remote south-east of the country bordering Afghanistan and Pakistan); Kurds (about 5 million, living in the west of the country); Arabs (about 1 million, living in the south-west of the country); Turkamen (living in the north-east of the country); and Lurs and other ethnic groups. Most Kurds, Baluchis and Turkamen are Sunni Muslims, making them a part of both religious and ethnic minority communities.

As in many countries, there is a considerable overlap between national and religious identity. The dominant Persian ethnic identity of Iran is well established. Shi'ism as the major and dominant religion of the country has also been a determining element in national identity. Since the time of the Safavid dynasty, founded by King Ismail the First in 1501, Iranian leaders have used Shi'ism as a central element of national identity, setting Iranians apart from the adherents of the dominant Sunni Muslim faith who form the majority in most neighbouring Islamic countries.

History of the Country: Four Stages Pertaining to Four Language Policies

We can think of four distinct stages in the history of Iran with regard to language. The first stage dates back to the formation of the Persian Empire and its continuation through the Sassanid dynasty up to the Arab conquest of the country and the exposure of the country to the Islamic religion. During this period, 'Old Persian' was the main and dominant language of the empire, used all over the territory for government communication and every aspect of people's life. The second stage is the introduction of Islam to Iran and the dissemination of Arabic language and culture, which resulted in a hybrid identity in the country's politics, culture, language, and social behaviour and activities. The Persian language welcomed and incorporated Arabic terms and the two languages mixed with each other to a great extent. The third stage dates back to about 150 years ago, during the Qajar dynasty, when the country was exposed to Western culture and language. Western culture and language in general, and English culture and language in particular, affected the indigenous language and culture to the extent that some believe that inclination toward Westernization became a main element in the country's identity. If Iran before Islam had a mainly 'Persian' identity and Iran after Islam had an 'Islamic-Iranian' identity, Iran after its exposure to the West found a triple identity, that of 'Islamic-Iranian-Western'. This represented itself in different aspects of the government's policies and people's sociocultural and economic lives. The fourth stage relates to the Islamic Revolution in 1979 and the aftermath of this historic event. The fact that the Western element of the country's identity was intruding into all corners of social life was not tolerable to the religious authorities and the public masses, who had a strong belief in Islamic principles. As conflict grew between people's Islamic thoughts and the practice of the government, the Islamic Revolution was initiated and gained victory with an outlook towards downplaying the penetration of Western thought and culture.

Language in Each Historical Stage

In each of these four episodes, language has played a crucial role in sustaining the status quo of the country in terms of sociopolitical as well as socioeconomic and sociocultural dimensions of the country's survival. In the first period the sole language for everyday communication, and also for education and bureaucratic communication, was Persian. In fact, Persian was the language of an empire, used by the ruling class and the elite to disseminate the culture of the empire. Given the lack of a nationwide system of schooling and the privilege of a restricted education for nobles to preserve the social strata in the country, only the noble class had the chance of being educated and using the language for higher levels of activity including politics and negotiations. One point, however, is that because the Persian Empire covered a vast territory with nations of different languages, multilingualism was a feature of the first historical period. During the Achaemenian dynasty, owing to the importance attached to the issue of education, especially for noble classes, learning and promoting the Persian language was of great significance. However, after the attack on Iran by Alexander the Great and the establishment of the Macedonian dynasty, the educational system in Iran was disrupted, thus bringing a halt to the promotion of the Persian language. When the Sassanid dynasty came to power, the teaching, learning and promotion of the Persian language once again came to the fore. One of the major cities during the Sassanid reign was Gondi Shapur (Ahwaz in present-day Iran). Many of the Roman texts were transferred to Gondi Shapur and translated into the Pahlavi language (Old Persian), and were kept in collections. In the 5th century AD, a university and a hospital were established in Gondi Shapur. In these institutions scientists and medical practitioners cultivated and used the knowledge and experience of, for example, Iranian, Indian, Greek, and Alexandrian medicine. In Anoushirvan's reign, research activities were fostered in Gondi Shapur and the city gained fame at that time. Medicine, philosophy, mathematics, theology, music, political sciences and agriculture were among the branches of learning practised at Gondi Shapur University. It is said that many scientists of Iranian and Indian nationality were employed there. Some medical texts were translated into Pahlavi and were taught at the university. These books were then translated into Arabic in later times. Crusaders then took these books to Europe, where they were translated again into Latin, and then, in the 15th to 20th centuries, into French and English to be taught partly in European universities. In Gondi Shapur Hospital Iranian, Indian and Greek medical treatments were applied, and it is said that the first medical symposium was held there in 550 AD.[2]

With the Arab conquest and the introduction of Islam to Iran in the 7th century, the whole political and social life in Iran changed, embracing and incorporating Islam in all aspects of life in the country. The Persian language was replaced by Arabic as the official language of the courts, and the Arabic script replaced the Pahlavi alphabet, although Persian remained the vernacular. Culture continued to flourish during this period. Men of Iranian origin served as administrators after the conquest, and Iranians contributed significantly to all branches of Islamic learning, including philology, literature, history, geography, jurisprudence, philosophy, medicine, and the sciences. Arabic as the official language of Islamic thought gained popularity in this period and the Islamic encouragement for seeking knowledge and promoting literacy among the masses resulted in a vast dissemination of the Arabic language, which was now mixed with Persian to a great extent. Persian writers did not try to coin new Persian words because of the availability of the Arabic terms. As a result, a considerable number of Arabic words and expressions were introduced and incorporated into the Persian language. This, in a sense, enriched the intellectuals' tool for meditation and scholarship as they were able to use Islamic sources including the holy Qur'an and other masterpieces by noble scholars in the Arab world. In fact, literate people were equipped with the resources and capabilities of the two languages, which led to the appearance of many famous Persian scholars, poets, and writers. These were able to benefit from the capabilities of the two languages and, thus, produce masterpieces in the form of treatises, scientific and literary books, books of poetry, and so on. These intellectual works are still considered to be masterpieces, not only at the national level but internationally. Although eminent scientists lived in Iran before Islam, science was a monopoly of the aristocratic class. Islamic culture and teachings encouraged people of all classes to seek knowledge in all areas. There is an Islamic saying that encouraged Muslims in the old days to seek knowledge even if they had to travel to China to get it. There is another saying attributed to Prophet Mohammed, which requires Muslims to seek knowledge from the cradle to the grave. There are many other such sayings, all encouraging Muslims to study sciences and become scholars to benefit their own societies and all the other nations. Inspired by such instructions, Muslims were able to build a strong civilization and develop a significant body of knowledge from the 9th to the 13th centuries, which affected scientific endeavours in Europe after the Middle Ages (Glubb, 1967). This wealth of scientific knowledge in the Islamic world led George Sarton (1952) to state in his book *History of Science* that Muslim scientists filled a period of about 500 years (from 700 AD to about 1200 AD) in the history of human scientific accomplishments with great achievements. In this glorious period, language played a very crucial role in knowledge production. Extensive contact with the Arabic language led to a large influx of Arabic vocabulary into the Persian language to enrich its own vocabulary. Eventually, however, the Persian language adopted the Arabic script. In fact, writers of Classical Persian had at their disposal the entire Arabic lexicon, and could use Arabic terms freely either for literary effect or to display erudition, all leading to Modern Persian that began to develop about 900 AD.

Coming in to Contact with the Western World

The exposure of Iranians to Western culture and language was initiated in the 19th century, during the Qajar dynasty, and continued and increased in the 20th century, especially during the Pahlavi dynasty. The practice of sending Iranian youth abroad for educational purposes goes back to the reign of King Fat'h-Ali, one of the Qajar kings, when Crown Prince Abbas Mirza decided to sponsor several students to go to Europe to become acquainted with new sciences and technology. With regard to the history of foreign-language instruction in Iran, Sadiq (1965, cited in Bagheri, 1994) mentioned that foreign-language instruction started in Iran in 1851 after the establishment of 'Dar-al-Fonoon' (The House of Techniques), the first organized institution of higher education in the country. In this school, teaching methods were based on the Western educational system, especially the French system of education. Communication was the main purpose of foreign-language instruction in The House of Techniques. The teaching staff wanted their students to learn the language so that they could communicate with them and understand the instruction. Because most of the teaching staff were not able to speak Persian, they used only the target languages (English and French) in their classes. However, as Farzinnia (1964) noted, foreign language instruction in Iran gradually shifted to English, for several reasons. Firstly, there was the establishment of the Iran-America Society to promote English language across the country. Secondly, Iranian students, teachers, and professors were dispatched to America and England for further study. Finally, there was the Iranians' increasing familiarity and contact with the American and British cultures.

Regarding the inclusion of English in the school curriculum, Azabdaftari (1975, cited in Bagheri, 1994) stated that English was taught in Iranian schools during the six years of secondary education in the period 1934 to 1970. After 1970, when the new system of education was put into practice, English was taught for seven years: three years in guidance and four years in high schools.

During the Pahlavi period, the idea of transforming social, economic, military, and cultural institutions in the country, and the shortage of an expert workforce to effect these changes, made it necessary for young people to revitalize the idea of going to other countries to pursue their education. As the first steps for effecting necessary changes had already been taken and only the required personnel were in short supply, action was taken inside the country, and schools were expanded at all levels, including higher education. The academic curricula were reformed and foreign experts were invited to teach in Iran, alongside Iranians. Nevertheless, Iranian statesmen still considered sending students to Europe a necessity owing to the lack of advanced teaching facilities and the limited number of qualified instructors in specialized fields. Eventually, a law was passed in Parliament which allowed 100 students to be sent abroad each year, at the expense of the state.

Transplanting a Western education system to the Iranian context was expected to contribute to development and solve the socioeconomic problems of the time. As such, during the Pahlavi era (1925–79), the government implemented a number of policies aimed at modernizing the country and expanding the education system. The Ministry of Education was given responsibility for regulating all public and private schools, and drafted a uniform curriculum for primary and for secondary education. The entire public system was secular and for many years remained based upon the French model. Its objective was to train Iranians for modern occupations in administration, management, science, and teaching. This education system was the single most important factor in the creation of the middle class in the country.

The goal of creating a nationwide education system was never achieved during the Pahlavi era. In 1940 only 10% of all elementary-age children were enrolled in schools, and less than 1% of youths between the ages of 12 and 20 were in secondary school. These statistics did not increase significantly until the early 1960s, when the government initiated programmes to improve and expand the public school system. By 1978 approximately 75% of all elementary-age children were enrolled in primary schools, while somewhat fewer than 50% of all teenagers were attending secondary schools.[3]

Modern college and university education was also developed under the Pahlavis; by the 1920s, the country had several institutes of higher education. In 1934 the institutes associated with government ministries were combined to form the University of Tehran, which was co-educational from its inception. The founding of the University of Tehran was a turning point in the contemporary cultural history of Iran. Its main achievements are, on the one hand, the teaching of the modern sciences and the training of specialists within the country (in humanities and natural and technical sciences) and, on the other, a decline in the number of students sent abroad, as well as a lesser reliance on non-Iranian specialists. The trend towards modernization made it a necessity to form such a centre for advanced education where various scientific and technical disciplines could be taught. The idea of setting up a university had been around for many years before the plan was actually carried out, but the lack of the necessary infrastructure delayed efforts in this direction. Finally, the need to train specialists to pursue various developmental activities that were already initiated, as well as the qualitative and quantitative limitations of the existing schools of higher education, and the return of Iranian graduates who were sent abroad between 1928 and 1933, provided the necessary impetus for the establishment of a centre for higher learning.

Following World War Two, universities were founded in other major cities, such as Tabriz, Esfahan, Mashhad, Shiraz, and Ahvaz. During the 1970s, these universities were expanded, and colleges and vocational institutes were set up in several cities. While most of the universities and institutes of higher education used Persian as the language of instruction, some universities (such as Shiraz University) offered all its programmes in English, and students were required to successfully pass a two-month intensive English course prior to starting their formal education. Some other universities used both Persian and English as the media of academic instruction. It can be said that the Persian language was the official first language all through these years, taught and learned in schools and universities. English was the major second language of the country and was included in the curriculum of both schools and universities.

The Islamic Revolution

After the Islamic Revolution in 1979, we witness a profound change in all aspects of educational planning and, accordingly, language planning and language in education policy in the country. The major impetus of the Revolution was to downplay the imposed Western norms in all aspects of the country's life, and to revitalize and boost Islamic and Iranian values. As such, the first targets of such a movement were the sociocultural issues that somehow represented Western thoughts and motives. The education system was the very first target. Curriculum change in order to eradicate elements of Western thought and to replace this with Islamic-Iranian values was the major agenda of the policy-makers and curriculum-developers.

Although the government reintroduced the study of religion into the public school curriculum from primary grades through to college, it did not act to alter the basic organization of the education system. The pattern prior to the Revolution was that students studied in primary schools for five years (Grades 1–5), beginning the first grade at about age seven. Then they spent three years, designated the guidance cycle, in a junior high school. In this cycle, the future training of students was determined by their aptitude as demonstrated in examinations. Having completed this cycle, students were then directed into one of three kinds of four-year senior high schools: the academic cycle, preparing for college; the science and mathematics cycle, preparing for university programmes in engineering and medicine; and the vocational technical cycle, preparing for more practical fields. About 20 million students are currently studying in different cycles in schools across the country.

Since the Revolution, higher education has experienced significantly more drastic changes than elementary and secondary education. The government closed all 200 institutes of higher learning in April 1980, to implement a Cultural Revolution. The universities were then purged of professors and students considered insufficiently Islamic, and they were not completely reopened until the fall of 1983. Over these years, a council called The Supreme Council for Cultural Revolution was in charge of developing new curricula and administration for the universities, with an agenda of moving toward the Islamization of the higher learning.

As regards the language policy for the country, Articles 15 and 16 in Chapter 2 of the Constitution (taken from Rasaenia, 1998: 32) clarify the issue:

> *Article 15:* The official language and script of Iran, the lingua franca of its people, is Persian. Official documents, correspondence, and texts, as well as textbooks, must be in this language and script. However, the

use of regional and ethnic languages in the press and mass media, as well as for teaching of their literature in schools, is allowed in addition to Persian.

Article 16: Since the language of the Qur'an and Islamic texts and teachings is Arabic, and since Persian literature is thoroughly permeated by this language, it must be taught after elementary level, in all classes of secondary school and in all areas of study.

These two articles clearly indicate the policy-makers' inclination toward a revitalization of Iranian-Islamic identity. In Article 15 the major focus and emphasis is on the recognition of Persian language as the lingua franca of the whole nation, to give it an official status. On the other hand, in Article 16, due attention has been given to the Arabic language as the language of Islamic thought and the necessity for its dissemination in the schooling system. Although the English language has more or less the same status (that is, it is taught after elementary level in all classes of secondary schools), it has not been given the status of being included in the constitution of the country. With regard to regional and ethnic languages, it can be said that the constitution has a liberal stance toward these languages, allowing their use in the mass media and for the sake of teaching the various literatures in schools.

The major problem after the Islamic Revolution, however, has been the lack of an official language-planning blueprint in the country to determine the status of available languages, as well as expectations from language teaching and learning curricula in the formal education system. Using Kloss's (1969) dichotomy of corpus and status in language planning, we can refer to language planning activities in the country as mostly directed toward the Persian language itself (corpus) rather than the social status of L1 and L2s and their role in the society. According to Sadeghi (2001), language planning in Iran has predominately aimed at the modernization of the Persian language through word coinage.

As regards teaching and learning language, a reductionist approach towards language instruction has been followed at all levels, from primary schools to postsecondary levels. Graduates of high schools, colleges and universities usually lack a 'functional' proficiency in their L2 and even they are unable to use their L1 with its total capacity. This is mostly a result of the language curriculum and teaching methods prescribed for the educational settings including schools and universities. Both L1 and L2 are introduced in the curricula of the secondary and tertiary levels as subjects. There is not a major difference in the teaching approach of the teachers teaching L1 or L2, and usually the same method (a form of grammar-translation) is followed in the language courses. Students in different levels of the schools, as well as those in colleges and universities, have to take some required L1 and L2 courses. In L1 courses some predetermined texts, which are usually a collection of prose and poetry passages, are used to teach language to students. In L2 courses, the major focus is on reading and grammar, which is materialized in textbooks containing such texts and activities. The methodology is mainly directed toward language 'usage' rather than language 'use'. Students have to learn words introduced in different lessons mainly through memorizing their meanings. After each lesson there is a list of new words with their meanings that students can use as a reference and criterion to master. Moreover, the grammatical points in each lesson (in both L1 and L2 courses) are illustrated in the textbooks and are explained by the teachers to the students. There are other exercise sections in the textbooks which do not usually receive enough attention, either from the teachers or from the students. The way language lessons are tested is mainly by testing students' recognition of the usage of the language. Rarely are students required to prepare for production tests, either oral or written. Multiple choice testing is very common in the country, even in language courses, with an emphasis on the knowledge of the words, grammatical points and reading comprehension. One might justify the present approach by saying that students do not have much opportunity to use their second language (English or Arabic or any other language) and, thus, do not need to invest in learning productive skills. For instance, some have tried to justify the present approach towards L2 instruction by stating that what are most needed in foreign contexts are reading skills, in order that students can read academic journals and books. However, this cannot by any means be justified when applied to students' L1.

The present approach toward language instruction (both L1 and L2) in Iran is not emancipatory and students do not become professional language-users. Learning has directly and indirectly been defined as the mastery of rules and words. We might describe the present approach towards teaching and learning in Iranian schools as fulfilling the features of a more quantitative approach rather than a qualitative one in which learners might come up with new visions and insights. The difference between learners and teachers is that of quantity rather than quality. Teachers are supposed to know more rules and a greater number of words than students, and students in their learning process should do their best to reduce this gap. Thus, the more rules and words they learn the closer they get to the experts. This is unfortunately the case with other subject matter courses, which signals a 'product'-oriented education system rather than a 'process'-oriented approach. The centralized system of education assigns

the same textbooks, the same teaching methods, and the same testing pro-
cedures to all parts of the country regardless of their geographical, social
and cultural differences. The educational outcome of the system is also
defined in terms of grades and scores, and students' achievements will be
compared using the same benchmarks. Students' professionalism in
language courses as well as in other courses is totally ignored, resulting in
the fact that graduates of the schools might have high grade average points
without being able to use their L1 and L2 communicatively and professionally in their lives. Oral and written language skills are only at the service of
memorizing course materials to reproduce them during the examinations.
If a student answers an examination question in an innovative way using
his/her own understanding of the materials covered in a course, the
response would be deemed wrong. This has created a very negative
backwash effect, which unfortunately has gone unnoticed by curriculum
developers and decision-making authorities, resulting in a superficial type
of literacy among school students and graduates.

With regard to language planning and language policy, besides the
Ministry of Education, there are other organizations that have been estab-
lished to promote language planning at a national and international level.
One of the most prominent organizations is the Academy of Persian
Language and Literature. The Academy of Persian Language and Literature was founded in 1991, with 25 permanent members and with a mandate
to promote the Persian language in all aspects. The Academy consists of
seven departments, namely Ancient Iranian Languages, Iranian Dialects,
Editing Classical Persian Texts, Persian Grammar and Writing System,
Compilation of a Comprehensive Persian Dictionary, Compilation of an
Encyclopedia for Persian Literature, and Word Coinage and Selection. Of
the seven departments of the Academy, the most active has been the
department of Word Coinage and Selection (Sadeghi, 2001). The main task
of this department is to find Persian equivalents for foreign words used
both in common language and in scientific writings. This department, as
Sadeghi (2001) states, encompasses committees for different disciplines,
which hold regular meetings in collaboration with members and researchers of the Iranian Academy of Sciences to select terms needed in different
branches of science. The main goal of the department of Persian Grammar
and Writing System is, in addition to the study of Persian grammar, to
study the Persian writing system in order to reform it. The amendments are
communicated to the Ministry of Education to be used in primary and
high-school textbooks.

As can be seen from the description of the organization of The Academy
of Persian Language and Literature, the major efforts in such organizations
concern the language itself (linguistics) rather than the planning of the use

of first, second, and minority languages in the society (sociolinguistics) and functional literacy (pragmatics). Language planning is seen as an activity concerned mainly with the internal aspects of the Persian language: preparing a normative orthography; grammar; word coinage; and a dictionary for the guidance of speakers and writers as well as an encyclopedic compilation of Persian literature. With respect to second and minority languages the situation is worse, as no organized body and institution attends systematically to the issues of language planning and teaching and learning. The major duty is left with the educational ministries – the Ministry of Education and Ministry of Science, Research, and Technology – to decide on the curriculum and instruction of second languages. As such, second languages (mainly English and Arabic and, in some instances, some European languages) are included in the school and university curricula, and students will take some courses to fulfill the requirements for their promotion to higher levels and graduation. As a required course from the second grade of junior high school, English is instructed with three to four hours of practice a week in schools. At the universities, students take 6–10 credits in English in the form of two to three courses in undergraduate programmes. The teaching and learning practices in these languages, especially English, as previously mentioned, are mostly directed towards knowledge of the language and its usage, rather than towards functional communication or use. With the increasing pace of globalization and the role that English language takes in this process, the need on the part of learners and their families for learning English in a communicative way is not being met by the formal curricula being practiced in schools and universities.

As Talebinezhad and Aliakbari (2002) state, there is an extended and still growing private sector in the country, a distinctive feature of which is introducing English at primary school and even pre-school levels. In almost all private schools functioning within the three levels of general education in Iran, namely, primary, junior and high schools, English receives particular attention. A crucial factor that determines choice of school is the quality of the English programme and the skill of the teacher or teachers working in each school.

It is generally believed that learning English facilitates access to science and technology. That is, the adoption of the English language as an international language is expected to promote modernization and participation in world trade and technology. As a result, in addition to formal private schools offering English language at different levels in their curricula, there are plenty of private and semi-private English-language institutes and centres that offer courses at different levels and for different purposes. Just in one city, Shiraz, there are 75 institutes offering English courses (*Nimnegah Newspaper*, 7 Oct., 2001). The largest of these institutes, which has branches all over the country, is the Iran Language Institute, which has its roots in the former Iran-America Society. As Farzin-nia (1964) reported, the first formal English language institute established in Iran in 1925 was the Iran-America Society, the main aim of which was teaching English. After the Islamic Revolution in 1979, this institute underwent some modifications. For instance, the name of the institute was changed to the Iran Language Institute (ILI). In addition, it underwent radical changes in management, objectives, and curriculum.

According to Talebinezhad and Aliakbari (2002), English seems to have smoothly found its way right to the heart of Iranian society, becoming an undeniable necessity, rather than a mere school subject. English is the dominant language of foreign trade, international conferences, air traffic in international airports and sea navigation. Our relations with the world are mainly in English. English dailies, weeklies and journals and other English periodicals produced and written by Iranians are issued and available throughout the country. The government's policy of promoting the export of non-oil products made companies and exporters take advantage of this medium to introduce their goods and products to the world market. Iranian national TV has started broadcasting programmes in English. The Internet, the use of which requires a proper English proficiency level and through which people enjoy global communication, has gained national recognition. Iran's cooperation with the UN, the Islamic Conference Organization, ECO, OPEC and other regional and world organizations makes English important. International book fairs and the trade exhibitions held annually in the country demonstrate the country's readiness to maintain its world relationship in English. The state policy towards the English curriculum is that learners should be able to read English texts and articles and to some extent write the language. However, the real demands in the society at large result from the active role of the country in the global socioeconomic environment. Despite the ideological stance of the state's policy towards English culture and language, which intends to keep it at a minimum level, there is nevertheless a strong need for the use of English language. This exemplifies the distinction suggested by Fishman (1972, cited in Daoust, 2000) between 'nationalism', characterized by feelings of uniqueness and the desire to develop culturally and otherwise, and 'nationism', which pertains to the more pragmatic problems of fulfilling these expectations.

Concluding Remarks

From a review of the language policy and practice over four historical stages in Iran, it has been shown that new political systems have necessitated changes in language use. Besides the teaching and learning activities and practices in the educational systems, recently two other factors have had and continue to have a strong impact on the status of languages in Iran. One of these is globalization. It was noted that although the state's policy towards the English language is not the vast dissemination of the language, the process of globalization has nevertheless exerted its own pressures to promote the learning of English as a hidden curriculum. This demand has been responded to in parallel formal and informal schools and language centres and, to a lesser extent, by the state-run education system. The economic power of the globalization process manifested in all aspects of people's lives has resulted in a social force which dictates English language use despite formal policies introduced in school curricula. If we subscribe to Labov's (1972) assertion that language use reflects social stratification and is a form of social behaviour, then in the near future we will witness social strata in the country with differing objectives and expectations that are not accounted for in the formal policies of the state.

The other important factor that relates more to the ethnic groups in the country is that of cultural and political survival. If learning one's own first language and one or two second languages is a basic tool for material survival, the learning and dissemination of minority languages are more about cultural and political survival.

In the present-day situation in Iran the two factors above exert their pressures strongly and thus there is a serious need for the policy- and decision-makers to pay attention to language planning and language-in-education policy as soon as possible from a sociolinguistic perspective, and to deal in a systematic way with an issue that so far has been almost ignored or, at least, attended to only partially.

Notes
1. The major part of the information in this section is taken, with permission, from the following source: Iran History. The *Columbia Electronic Encyclopedia*. Available at the following site: http://www.infoplease.com/ce6/world/A0858893.html
2. The information here is from the following site: http://www.cua.ac.ir/about/history.htm
3. The information here is from the following site: http://itrs.scu.edu/instructors/dlustig/lustig/student/webpage/iran.htm

References
Azabdaftari, B. (1975) A study of the problems of teaching English composition to Iranian senior high school students and suggestions for improving current practices. Unpublished PhD dissertation. Illinois: University of Illinois.

Bagheri, H. (1994) A profile of teaching English in pre-university schools of Sistan and Baluchestan Province: Problems and solutions. Unpublished master's thesis. Shiraz: Shiraz University.

Columbia Electronic Encyclopedia. Iran History. © 1994, 2000, 2001, 2002, 2003 on Infoplease.com. Available at http://www.infoplease.com/ce6/world/A0858893.html

Daoust, D. (2000) Language planning and language reform. In F. Coulmas (ed.) *The Handbook of Sociolinguistics* (pp. 436–52). Oxford: Blackwell Publishers.

Farzin-nia, S. (1964). French influences on the educational system of Iran. Unpublished master's thesis. Beirut: The American University of Beirut.

Fishman, J.A. (1972) The sociology of language: An interdisciplinary social science approach to language in society. Reprinted in T. Sebeok (ed.) (1974) *Current Trends in Linguistics* 12, 1629–784. The Hague: Mouton.

Glubb, J. (1967) *The Lost Centuries: From the Muslim Empires to the Renaissance of Europe*. Englewood Cliffs: Prentice Hall.

Kloss, H. (1969) *Research Possibilities on Group Bilingualism: A Report*. Quebec: Universite Laval, C.I.R.B.

Labov, W. (1972) *Sociolinguistic Patterns*. Philadelphia: University of Pennsylvania Press.

Nimnegah Newspaper, 7 Oct, 2001. Shiraz, Iran.

Rasaenia, N. (1998) *The Constitution of the Islamic Republic of Iran*. Tehran: Saman Publications.

Sadeghi, A.A. (2001) Language planning in Iran: A historical review. *International Journal of Sociology of Language* 148, 19–30.

Sadiq, I. (1965) *The History of Education in Tehran*. Tehran: Teacher College Press.

Sarton, G. (1952) *History of Science. Ancient Science Through the Golden Age of Greece*. Cambridge: Harvard University Press.

Talebinezhad, M.R. and Aliakbari, M. (2002) Evaluation and justification of a paradigm shift in the current ELT models in Iran. *Linguistik Online* 10 (1).

Chapter 7

Higher Education Language Policy and the Challenge of Linguistic Imperialism: A Turkish Case Study

TIMOTHY REAGAN and SANDRA SCHREFFLER

The increasing dominance of a small number of languages of wider communication (and of English in particular) in scholarly discourse has led to a common dilemma for many universities in the so-called developing world: whether to use English (or some other language of wider communication) as the principal medium of instruction, or to make provision for the use of an indigenous language. The former choice inevitably raises concerns about linguistic imperialism (see Holborow, 1999; Pennycook, 1994, 1998; Phillipson, 1992), as well as presenting a significant linguistic challenge to both students and many faculty and staff members (a challenge that is often disproportionately felt by individuals from lower socioeconomic backgrounds) (see Durand, 2001; Hall & Eggington, 2000). The latter choice entails the risk of cutting off students from the international scholarly community, placing potential barriers to further education, and often involves considerable commitments to corpus planning efforts and to publishing necessary works in the target language. Universities in societies whose dominant language is not a language of wider communication, in both the developing and the developed worlds, struggle with what is often perceived to be a 'no-win scenario'.

In this chapter, a third alternative will be explored. Specifically, the case of a major state university in Turkey will be examined. In this case, an institution with a long, well-established tradition of instruction in the national language is in the process of a significant status change with respect to language medium policy. Faced with growing competition from English-medium institutions in the private sector, this university is undertaking what is intended to be a middle path: in order to ensure that students have the necessary language skills to compete both nationally and internationally, all students

115

are now required to complete approximately one-third of their university courses in English. The policy is intended to ensure English language competence while at the same time maintaining a scholarly and academic context in which Turkish is a significant and necessary language. Given the historical significance of the Turkish language planning movement (see Doğançay-Aktuna, 1995; Gallagher, 1971; Hacieminoglu, 1972; Hazai, 1974), as well as issues related to nationalism and national pride, this policy should be an especially interesting one for language planners and for those interested in language-medium policy at the tertiary level.

The Dominance of English

A good place to begin our discussion is with the position of English internationally. English is not only a language of wider communication in the modern world, it is far more than that – it is, in a singularly powerful sense, *the* 'global language' of commerce, trade, culture, and research in the contemporary world. We offer this not as a normative claim, but rather as a descriptive one. While some writers have championed the ascendancy of English (see, for example, Barber, 1993: 234–261; Crystal, 1997; McArthur, 1998), others have been quite critical of the overwhelming dominance of English and the implications of such dominance (see Bruthiaux, 2002; Pennycook, 1994, 1998; Phillipson, 1992; Skutnabb-Kangas, 2000). While divided by many assumptions, what holds these two groups together is the common view of the *fact* of English ascendancy. As Ronald Wardhaugh has noted, 'English is now by far the most widespread of the world's languages . . . There is also no indication that English is in any way ceasing to spread; indeed it seems to be on the ascendant in the world with no serious competitor' (1987: 128).

Nowhere is the influence, power and dominance of English more clear than in the academic world, especially in such areas as science and technology (see Haas, 1995; Kaplan, 1993). As a language of international communication, English increasingly dominates academic and scientific publishing, discourse, and even instruction (see Burns & Coffin, 2001; Candlin & Mercer, 2001). In many academic disciplines, a knowledge of English is a necessary condition for even basic competence in the discipline. Students are expected to read much of the technical literature in their fields in English, and, in many settings, are expected to be able to function professionally in English. For instance, in describing the place and role of English in Thailand – which was never, unlike most of its neighbours, ever under English-speaking colonial rule – William Smalley notes that, '[a]lthough Thai universities are not English-medium institutions, students in . . . many scholarly fields do much of their technical reading in English . . . lecturers from abroad teach university classes in English . . . An occasional foreign lecturer will even require students to write or recite in English' (1994: 17).

The dominance of English in academic discourse is an important facet of the construction of professional discourse, and is also important with regard to issues of power and control in both English-dominant and other societies around the world (see Fairclough, 1989; Gunnarsson *et al.*, 1997; Hasan & Williams, 1996; Watts & Trudgill, 2002). For non-English speakers who wish to achieve a reasonable level of academic or professional success, especially internationally, competence in English has become something of a linguistic *sine qua non* – though second-language competence for English speakers is anything but necessary, a fact which serves to highlight the issues of linguistic inequality inherent in such discourse and communicative patterns (see Tollefson, 1991, 1995).

Although a case might be made for the advantages of a common intellectual language, on instrumental if not other grounds, often in practice one finds that the arguments for the use of English rather than other languages are in fact grounded in ideological assumptions and discourses – assumptions and discourses which are demonstrably misleading or simply wrong much of the time (see, for example, Benesch, 2001; Canagarajah, 1999).[1] For instance, Josef Schmied, writing about English in the African context, has argued that:

> English is believed, in many countries in Africa, and indeed in many parts of the Third World generally, to possess certain qualities. These are often characterized by adjectives like 'beautiful', 'rich', 'logical', 'sophisticated' or even 'pleasing to the ear' (although these words may have slightly different meanings in an African context!). English seems to enjoy high international prestige as an idealized world language. (1991: 165)

What is most interesting about these notions, though, is that they 'are largely irrational manifestations of a more general feeling which associates English with the modern, successful, educated upwardly mobile, or with a member of the cosmopolitan elite, and this creates an uncritical idealizing image of the world language' (Schmied, 1991: 167); needless to say, such positive views of English inevitably lead to negative views of other, and especially indigenous, languages.

Biases in favour of English go far beyond merely irrational preferences, however. As Pennycook has powerfully recounted:

> Other writers have claimed an even more fundamental role of English in the (re)production of global inequalities. Naysmith, for example, suggests that English language teaching 'has become part of the process whereby one part of the world has become politically, econom-

ically and culturally dominated by another'. The core of this process, he argues, is the 'central place the English language has taken as *the* language of international capitalism'. Such a position, which suggests that English is an integral part of the global structures of dependency, has been explored at length by Robert Phillipson. He argues that *linguicism* – 'the ideologies and structures which are used to legitimate, effectuate and reproduce an unequal division of power and resources (both material and non-material) between groups which are defined on the basis of their language (i.e. of their mother tongue)' – is best seen within the broader context of *linguistic imperialism,* 'an essential constituent of imperialism as a global phenomenon involving structural relations between rich and poor countries in a world characterised by inequality and injustice'. (1995: 43)

It should be noted that, while the dominance of English is indeed problematic in a variety of ways, for most national languages the challenge is not really one of survival; nor will this come to be the case. Although there is growing, and legitimate, concern about language death around the world (see Crystal, 2000; Dalby, 2003; Grenoble & Whaley, 1998; Nettle, 1999; Nettle & Romaine, 2000), for national languages the threat is not to their survival with respect to day-to-day usage, but rather to their use in technical spheres of discourse. In the Turkish case, for instance, there is no serious challenge to the Turkish language as the national language of daily use. In fact, with the collapse of the former Soviet Union, there is a very real potential for the spread of standard Turkish in the Turkic-speaking regions of central Asia (see Ahmed, 2001: 104–105, 200–204; Paksoy, 1994). What is potentially threatened, though, is the continued use of Turkish in various technical spheres of language use, such as in: engineering, medicine, the sciences, and so on, where ongoing lexical elaboration and use is essential.

Language Planning and Language Policy Efforts

The situation is by no means as clear-cut as this might suggest, however. Language planning and language policy formulation and implementation have been, and continue to be, important elements of national social and educational policy in many societies, and are often employed to protect, preserve and strengthen a national or indigenous language(s). This has been especially true in the so-called developing world, as efforts are made to address the legacy of colonialism and, in many cases, the ongoing presence of considerable cultural and linguistic diversity (see, for example, Weinstein, 1990). Questions of national and official language selection, orthographic selection and spelling standardisation, of language use in government, judicial and educational settings, and of language status and power, are rarely simple, and seldom avoid a considerable degree of controversy and conflict. As Philip Altbach has observed, '[l]anguage is a key to the intellectual situation in many Third World nations. Language also plays a role in the distribution of knowledge, since the medium through which material is communicated determines accessibility . . . [in] multilingual states . . . questions of language policy are often politically volatile' (1984: 234).

Such controversy is especially common where language policies are concerned with the provision of education, and this is understandable, since, as Kennedy has noted, '[t]he close relationship between use of a language and political power, socioeconomic development, national and local identity and cultural values has led to the increasing realization of the importance of language policies . . . in the life of a nation. Nowhere is this planning more crucial than in education . . .' (1983: iii).

The role of language planning as a component of more general educational planning and policy analysis is, in short, an important facet of understanding educational development in many developing societies. Language planning as an element of national development strategy can best be understood as the deliberate attempt to change or in some way alter existing language usage, and thus to resolve various types of language problems and controversies. As Eastman cogently asserted, '[l]anguage planning is the activity of manipulating language as a social resource in order to reach objectives set out by planning agencies which, in general, are an area's governmental, educational, economic, and linguistic authorities' (1983: 29).

Further, language planning activities can focus on issues of language status (status planning), on issues of internal development (corpus planning), or on combinations of these two types of language planning activities (see Cobarrubias, 1983; Williams, 1992: 123–47). Understood in this way, language planning activity can be seen as serving any of five different, although sometimes overlapping, functions: language purification, language revival, language reform, language standardisation and lexical modernisation (see Eastman, 1983: 28; Nahir, 1977).

Language purification is a prescriptive effort on the part of policy makers to delimit 'proper' or 'correct' linguistic usage, normally based on perceptions of the historically 'pure' variety of the language. Such efforts, which generally consist primarily of corpus planning, are often concerned with eliminating 'foreign' or 'alien' usages in both the spoken and written language, and are commonly tied to other manifestations of what might be termed purist ideologies, although they can also be outgrowths of anticolonialist sentiments and movements. An example of a call for language purification in language planning is provided in Abdallah

Khalid's *The Liberation of Swahili from European Appropriation*, published in Nairobi in 1977, in which a case is presented for the adoption of a pure variety of KiSwahili uncontaminated by European influences. As Khalid commented, '[o]nce our thinking has been freed from foreign domination, the reintroduction of the true Swahili language in the place of its colonialist falsification will follow as a matter of logic and self-respect' (1977: xiii).

Language revival takes place when a language which has lost official status is restored to that status, as well as to those somewhat rarer instances in which a language deemed to be 'dead' in some sense is brought back to life. Language revival is primarily an example of status planning, though elements of corpus planning (especially in terms of lexical expansion) are also likely to be involved. Examples of the former abound: KiSwahili in Tanzania is an obvious example, but other cases in the postcolonial world are common as colonial languages are replaced by (or asked to share official status with) previously dominant indigenous languages. The revival of 'dead' languages is considerably rarer, with the best case being offered by the revival of Hebrew as a modern spoken language in Israel.[2] Other instances of revival of nearly dead languages also exist, of course; the revival of Irish Gaelic is a well-documented, though arguably not a terribly successful, case in point here.[3]

Language reform takes place, both formally and informally, in many languages accorded official status in the modern world, and includes lexical and orthographic reform as well as occasional syntactic reform. Language reform as a type of language planning activity is, therefore, essentially corpus planning. The reform of written Chinese in the People's Republic of China provides an example of language reform (see Barnes, 1983; Tai, 1988), as do the reforms of Ibo and other indigenous languages in Nigeria (Emenanjo, 1990; Nwachukwu, 1983), and Norwegian (Gundersen, 1983/4; Haugen, 1966), among others. An especially interesting call for language reform along these lines has recently been made by the South African political activist Neville Alexander, who has advocated the creation of a 'Standardized Nguni' and a 'Standardized Sotho' to function as lingua francas in a postapartheid South Africa, as a way of addressing the dilemmas posed by both the risk of neocolonialism attached to the continued use of English and the risk of continuing tribalisation associated with current government policies of mandated linguistic pluralism, especially in the educational sphere (Alexander, 1989; see also Ndebele, 1987; Peirce, 1989; Reagan, 2001; Wright, 2002).[4]

Language standardisation involves both status planning, when it refers to the selection of a single variety of a language as the standard language, and corpus planning, when it refers to the codification of the language in a unified variety. Thus, the selection of Kiunguja, the Zanzibar dialect of KiSwahili, as the national linguistic norm in Tanzania, would constitute an example of language standardisation of the status-planning type (see Harries, 1983: 127–28), while efforts to create a standardised spelling and grammar for Indonesian constitute a corpus-planning approach to language standardisation (see Rubin, 1977). Language standardisation, it is important to note, can and often does overlap with both language reform and lexical modernisation in practice.

Lastly, lexical modernisation takes place as efforts are made to increase a language's lexicon to allow it to deal with new technological, political, economic, educational, and social developments and concepts. Lexical modernisation therefore constitutes a clear instance of corpus planning. All languages, of course, from time to time experience what can be termed lexical gaps; lexical modernisation refers specifically to controlled and directed attempts to expand a given language's lexicon in a systematic manner (see Eastman, 1983: 232–37; Nahir, 1977: 117). As Jernudd has noted, '[a] major activity of many language planning agencies . . . be they normal language academies, development boards or language commit-tees, is the development of terminologies, particularly in technical fields' (1977: 215). Examples of lexical modernisation abound; indeed, Fodor and Hagège's three-volume *Language Reform* includes studies of lexical (as well as orthographic and syntactic) modernisation efforts in more than 60 different languages (Fodor & Hagège, 1983/4). It should be noted here that while efforts at lexical modernisation are, then, quite common, the extent to which they are effective in mandating lexical usage is less clear (see, for example, Hinnebusch, 1979, for a discussion of the case of lexical moderni-sation in KiSwahili).

What holds all these approaches to language planning and language policy together is their focus on a single target language; rather than examining language in its ecological setting, they seek to deal with it as an essentially objectified entity (see Reagan, 2004). In fact, in order to adequately address issues of language, language oppression, and language dominance in the real world, what is required instead is to view language in its interactive and inevitably multilingual setting. Thus, effective language policies must address, *inter alia*, the over-whelming status of the languages of wider communication in general and of English in particular.

Implications for Higher Education

The countervailing pressures for the dominance of English on the one hand and for the protection of national languages on the other hand result in a number of challenges in education at all levels, but nowhere is the juxtaposition of English and national languages clearer or more significant than at the tertiary level. A functional knowledge of English has become one of the more important outcomes of a university education, not merely for practical reasons but for ideological and status-related reasons as well. At the same time, national languages develop technical lexicons and literatures largely in the university and professional contexts, and if English is the medium of communication in these contexts, then there will be little support for linguistic development of the national language. This fundamental tension has been addressed in different societies in a number of different ways (see Hall & Eggington, 2000; Shah, 1999; Smalley, 1994), but in most instances the choice has been seen as an 'either-or' one.

The Turkish Context

Although there had been earlier efforts to reform Ottoman Turkish, most notably during the Tanzimat Period of the late 19th century, it was with the establishment of the Turkish Republic in 1923 that the most significant, and lasting, language reforms took place. The language reforms were but one aspect of the social, political and cultural revolution in Turkish society which took place under Atatürk's leadership. König (1987) identified six ideologies that provided the framework and *raison d'être* for the new Turkish Republic in general, and for the sociolinguistic reforms in Turkey in particular: nationalism, secularism, populism, republicanism, modernism, and etatism. As Atatürk himself commented in 1930, '[t]he Turkish language will be free and independent, like the Turkish nation, and with it we shall enter the civilized world, at once and totally' (quoted in Doğançay-Aktuna, 1995: 231). Further, language reform in the Turkish context, which was ultimately aimed at making the Turkish language at once a 'symbol of external distinction and internal cohesion', can be best understood by recognizing that:

> Turkish language reform was centralized, government-sponsored language planning activity which was coordinated with the country's other plans and programs for national development . . . The reform essentially consisted of two undertakings: the change of the script from Arabic to Latin, and the modernization and renovation of the lexicon. (Doğançay-Aktuna, 1995: 227)

The primary responsibility for language planning in the Turkish context was given to the *Türk Dili Tetkik Cemiyeti* (the Association for Research on the Turkish Language), which later became the *Türk Dil Kurumu* (the Turkish Language Association). However, Turkish universities also played central roles in the development and promulgation of technical and professional terminology. Istanbul Technical University, for instance, proudly emphasises its own role in this process: 'ITU has educated its students in the Turkish language since 1773 and has thus played a significant role in the development of technical Turkish language and has been a leader in advanced-level technical publications' (ITU, 1997: 3).

The ITU Model

This is the context in which Istanbul Technical University began a challenging and controversial effort to develop an institutional language policy that would attempt to mediate between the countervailing pressures for English language competence (which had increased as a consequence of the emergence of a number of English-medium private universities in the country) and those for continued support of the Turkish language.

As early as 1983, as a part of the university's increased emphasis on graduate education, Istanbul Technical University developed a one-year preparatory English language course for students studying for advanced graduate degrees. A similar programme was developed in 1989 to allow undergraduate students to participate in a comparable preparatory English programme for one year before beginning their degree work. For undergraduates, this programme remained optional until the 1997–1998 academic year. With the 1997–1998 academic year, these two preparatory programmes were combined into a single, mandatory English preparatory programme. This decision was the result of consideration discussion and debate, and followed the election of a new rector, Prof. Gülsün Sağlamer, whose leadership and support in this matter proved essential. The new policy, adopted by the University Senate, required that:

> *beginning with the 1997 academic year, the university will be requiring all students to successfully complete English preparatory studies and 30% of each student's undergraduate studies will be conducted in English.* (ITU, 1997: 3, emphasis in original)

The guiding principle in this policy has been to ensure that students have the necessary competence in English to function professionally in an increasingly international, and increasingly English-dominant, world, while at the same time working to encourage the ongoing development of technical and professional language in Turkish, as well as technical and professional publications in Turkish. This policy, which is now well established and fully operational, has presented powerful challenges to the university community as a whole, and to the Department of Foreign Languages in particular.[5]

All students admitted to Istanbul Technical University must take an English language proficiency examination during the summer before their matriculation. This proficiency examination, although based in part on the TOEFL examination, is institution- and context-specific, and was designed to determine whether students had the necessary English-language skills to function in English-medium classes taught at Istanbul Technical University. This is an important point, since the kind of proficiency required is not identical with that needed by students studying in universities in the United States or Britain; rather, these Turkish students must be able to study in English-medium classes taught, primarily, by other native speakers of Turkish speaking English in a Turkish context. In addition, there is a strong emphasis on technical language use and vocabulary, as one would expect in a technical university setting. Approximately half of the students admitted to Istanbul Technical University each year pass the proficiency examination and are allowed to enter directly into their undergraduate programmes. The other half, roughly 1700 students per year, are required to complete the preparatory programme and to retake the proficiency examination before entering their faculties.

Some students in the preparatory programme come with extensive knowledge of English and need only limited review and practice to pass the proficiency examination, while others are novice or near-novice learners. Therefore, students required to participate in the preparatory programme are divided into four levels, based on prior study and knowledge of English:

A-Level   Upper-Intermediate Learners
B-Level   Intermediate Learners
C-Level   Pre-Intermediate Learners
D-Level   Beginners.

The A-level students are most typically graduates of private secondary schools, and are usually able to pass the proficiency examination at the end of the first semester. This group includes approximately 10% of all preparatory-programme students. The B-level students, who include about 35% of all preparatory-programme students, generally use the entire preparatory year to improve and hone the English language skills that they already possess. Finally, C-level and D-level students, roughly 55% of all preparatory-programme students, enter the preparatory-programme with little or no English, and for these students the preparatory year is an intensive exposure to the English language. Although the curricular objectives are the same for all three groups, the instruction is differentiated to allow for the often radically different levels of prior preparation of students.

In general, the preparatory programme involves a total of 18 to 30 hours a week of formal instruction, taught by a combination of instructors including both native and non-native speakers. The size and complexity of the preparatory programme has required a fairly centralised approach to both curriculum and evaluation, and this is facilitated by a number of administrative and support offices staffed by English-language teachers. There is a Testing Office, which is responsible for the production of weekly quizzes, cumulative examinations, and the proficiency examination. There are also offices responsible for the development of pedagogical materials for use in the classroom, for curriculum development and articulation, and, finally, for the professional development of staff. Computer and video labs are also available, both for independent student work and for classes, and there is a reasonably well-stocked library available for students and instructors in the Department of Foreign Languages.

Over the past five years, the success of completers of the preparatory programme has continued to show improvement, and on average, about 75% of all preparatory programme students pass the proficiency examination at the end of the preparatory year and continue their studies. Those who do not pass are provided with additional summer support activities, and allowed to take the proficiency test again. Given the nature of the population involved, we would argue that the pass rate for the proficiency examination is in fact quite impressive, although continuing efforts are underway to provide additional support for those students unable to pass the proficiency examination.

In addition to the preparatory programme, the Department of Foreign Languages also offers required advanced English language courses, and is currently in the process of developing an MA programme in the Teaching of English as a Foreign Language. Beginning in 1997, the Department has had a linkage relationship with the Neag School of Education at the University of Connecticut, which has provided ongoing technical and academic support for both the preparatory and the advanced programmes in the Department of Foreign Languages.

It would be both misleading and untrue to suggest that the implementation of the preparatory programme at Istanbul Technical University has been without challenges and problems. Istanbul Technical University has devoted considerable resources to the implementation of its language policy, and the Department of Foreign Languages has been able to utilise these resources fairly effectively. However, a number of essentially technical problems have plagued, and continue to affect, the preparatory programme. Among the more important of these problems, which are far from unique to the ITU context, have been the following:

- administrative and bureaucratic inertia;
- organisational complexity;
- faculty resistance to change;
- resource constraints on teaching and learning (including teacher shortages, large class sizes, limited pedagogical materials, etc.);
- lack of consensus about the purposes and nature of the proficiency examination;
- disagreements among teachers about the role and purpose of assessment;
- challenges related to student motivation (and the lack thereof);
- tensions between native English-speaking teachers and non-native teachers;
- over-reliance on the selected textbook series in curricular determination and in terms of the assessment processes;
- limited opportunities for teacher professional development, coupled with resistance to such opportunities among some teachers.

All these challenges and problems are common to those working in English language teaching contexts around the world, and there is no reason to believe that they are any more serious in the ITU case than is true elsewhere. In addition to these largely technical and resource-based issues, though, this is another set of challenges – the challenges related to issues of technicism, politics and ideology in English-language teaching and learning. Although the ITU preparatory program was designed and implemented as a way of addressing the challenge of English linguistic imperialism, it is not at all clear that the majority of either teachers or students involved in the programme are aware of this. The organisation and implementation of the programme have remained essentially technicist in nature, in large part because of the inevitable tension between the pragmatic needs of the institution, pre-existing student expectations about the nature and purposes of English language learning, and the assumptions commonly held by teachers of English (both native and non-native speakers) about their professional responsibilities. As Bill Johnson has recently argued, the challenge before us is the need to make clear to both teachers and students that 'language teaching and learning are shot through with values, and that language teaching is a profoundly value-laden activity' (2003: 1). Not only is English-language teaching value-laden, it is also profoundly and deeply political and ideological – and this must be recognised by students and teachers alike.

Conclusion

What the ITU case demonstrates, we believe, is how very difficult it is to implement this recognition of the value-laden nature of English-language teaching and learning, especially in institutional contexts. As an instance of English-language teaching at the tertiary level per se, the ITU experience would appear, in spite of some of the problems that have arisen in its implementation, to be operating reasonably successfully. Most students are learning English, and are doing so in a way appropriate for the contexts in which they are expected to use the language. What has not taken place thus far, though, is the political understanding that makes the ITU policy both unusual and promising. Neither students nor their teachers have been encouraged to explore the underlying rationale and justification for the programme, nor do they seem to recognise the political and ideological forces that have driven the policy. What makes the ITU model unique, in other words, has remained largely unarticulated and hence hidden from those most involved in its implementation – a fundamental dilemma for those interested in developing more critical approaches to English language teaching and learning.

Notes

1. We want to emphasise here that while we recognise that such a case *could* be made, and indeed has been made and may even have been widely accepted, it is not one that we accept. There are, in our view, powerful arguments in support of linguistic diversity in general and in academic discourse in particular, as well as incredible risks in linguistic uniformity.
2. The case of Hebrew is especially interesting, in that while it had long ceased to be a language of daily life, it was in fact maintained for religious and scholarly purposes. Thus, in an important sense, the revival of Hebrew was not so much the revival of a 'dead' language as it was the re-establishment of the language as a vernacular language. For further discussions of the Hebrew case, see Fellman (1973), Harshav (1993), Nahir (1987, 1988), and Sáenz-Badillos (1993).
3. For analyses of the Irish case, see Hindley (1990), Ó Raigáin (1997).
4. See Probyn's chapter in this volume.
5. The Department of Foreign Languages recently became the College of Foreign Languages, an indication of its increased status and importance in the university community.

References

Ahmed, A.S. (2001) *Islam Today: A Short Introduction to the Muslim World.* London: I.B. Tauris.

Alexander, N. (1989) *Language Policy and National Unity in South Africa/Azania.* Cape Town: Buchu Books.

Altbach, P. (1984) The distribution of knowledge in the third world: A case study in neocolonialism. In P. Altbach and G. Kelly (eds) *Education and the Colonial Experience* (2nd rev. edn) (pp. 229–51). New Brunswick, NJ: Transaction.

Barber, C. (1993) *The English Language: A Historical Introduction.* Cambridge: Cambridge University Press.

Barnes, D. (1983) The implementation of language planning in China. In J. Cobarrubias and J. Fishman (eds) *Progress in Language Planning* (pp. 291–308). Berlin: Mouton.

Benesch, S. (2001) *Critical English for Academic Purposes: Theory, Politics and Practice.* Mahwah, NJ: Lawrence Erlbaum Associates.

Bruthiaux, P. (2002) Predicting challenges to English as a global language in the 21st century. *Language Problems and Language Planning* 26, 129–57.

Burns, A. and Coffin, C. (eds) (2001) *Analysing English in a Global Context: A Reader.* London: Routledge.

Canagarajah, A.S. (1999) *Resisting Linguistic Imperialism in English Teaching.* Oxford: Oxford University Press.

Candlin, C. and Mercer, N. (eds) (2001) *English Language Teaching in its Social Context: A Reader.* London: Routledge.

Cobarrubias, J. (1983) Language planning: The state of the art. In J. Cobarrubias and J. Fishman (eds) *Progress in Language Planning* (pp. 3–26). Berlin: Mouton.

Crystal, D. (1997) *English as a Global Language.* Cambridge: Cambridge University Press.

Crystal, D. (2000) *Language Death.* Cambridge: Cambridge University Press.

Dalby, A. (2003) *Language in Danger: The Loss of Linguistic Diversity and the Threat to Our Future.* New York: Columbia University Press.

Doğançay-Aktuna, S. (1995) An evaluation of the Turkish language reform after 60 years. *Language Problems and Language Planning* 19, 223–49.

Durand, C. (2001) *La Mise en place des monopoles du savoir.* Paris: L'Harmattan.

Eastman, C. (1983) *Language Planning: An Introduction.* San Francisco: Chandler & Sharp.

Emenanjo, E. (ed.) (1990) *Multilingualism, Minority Languages and Language Policy in Nigeria.* Agbor, Nigeria: Center Books Ltd, in collaboration with the Linguistic Association of Nigeria.

Fairclough, N. (1989) *Language and Power.* London: Longman.

Fellman, J. (1973) *The Revival of a Classical Tongue: Eliezer Ben Yehuda and the Modern Hebrew Language.* The Hague: Mouton.

Fodor, I. and Hagège, C. (eds) (1983/4) *Language Reform: History and Future*, 3 vols. Hamburg: Buske Verlag.

Gallagher, C. (1971) Language reform and social modernization in Turkey. In J. Rubin and B. Jernudd (eds) *Can Language be Planned?* (pp. 159–78). Honolulu: University Press of Hawai'i.

Grenoble, L. and Whaley, L. (eds) (1998) *Endangered Languages: Current Issues and Future Prospects.* Cambridge: Cambridge University Press.

Gundersen, D. (1983/4) On the development of modern Norwegian. In I. Fodor and C. Hagège (eds) *Language Reform*, vol. 2 (pp. 157–74). Hamburg: Buske Verlag.

Gunnarsson, E., Linell, P. and Nordberg, B. (eds) (1997) *The Construction of Professional Discourse.* London: Longman.

Haas, G. (1995) 'English creep': English as *lingua franca* of corporate and technological globalization. *Geolinguistics* 21, 69–88.

Hacieminoglu, N. (1972) *Türkçenin Karanlik Gunleri* [Dark Days of Turkish]. Istanbul: Irfan Yayinevi.

Hall, J.K. and Eggington, W. (eds) (2000) *The Sociopolitics of English Language Teaching.* Clevedon: Multilingual Matters.

Harries, L. (1983) The nationalisation of Swahili in Kenya. In C. Kennedy (ed.) *Language Planning and Language Education* (pp. 118–28). London: George Allen & Unwin.

Harschav, B. (1993) *Language in Time of Revolution*. Berkeley: University of California Press.

Hasan, R. and Williams, G. (eds) (1996) *Literacy in Society*. London: Longman.

Haugen, E. (1966) *Language Conflict and Language Planning: The Case of Modern Norwegian*. Cambridge, MA: Harvard University Press.

Hazai, G. (1974) Linguistics and language issues in Turkey. In J. Fishman (ed.) *Advances in Language Planning* (pp. 127–61). The Hague: Mouton.

Hindley, R. (1990) *The Death of the Irish Language: A Qualified Obituary*. London: Routledge.

Hinnebusch, T. (1979) Swahili. In T. Shopen (ed.) *Languages and Their Status* (pp. 209–93). Philadelphia: University of Pennsylvania Press.

Holborow, M. (1999) *The Politics of English: A Marxist View of Language*. London: Sage.

ITU (Istanbul Technical University). (1997) *Istanbul Technical University: A Leader Through the Ages*. Maslak, Istanbul: Directorate of External Affairs and Information, Istanbul Technical University.

Jernudd, B. (1977) Linguistic sources for terminological innovation: Policy and opinion. In J. Rubin, B. Jernudd, J. Das Gupta, J. Fishman and C. Ferguson (eds) *Language Planning Processes* (pp. 215–36). The Hague: Mouton.

Johnson, B. (2003) *Values in English Language Teaching*. Mahwah, NJ: Lawrence Erlbaum Associates.

Kaplan, R. (1993) The hegemony of English in science and technology. *Journal of Multilingual and Multicultural Development* 14, 151–72.

Kennedy, C. (ed.) (1983) *Language Planning and Language Education*. London: George Allen & Unwin.

Khalid, A. (1977) *The Liberation of Swahili from European Appropriation*. Nairobi: East Africa Literature Bureau.

König, W. (1987) On some sociolinguistic aspects of language reform in Turkey. In E. Boeschoten and L. Verhoeven (eds) *Studies on Modern Turkish* (pp. 259–70). Tilburg: Tilburg University Press.

McArthur, T. (1998) *The English Languages*. Cambridge: Cambridge University Press.

Nahir, M. (1977) The five aspects of language planning. *Language Problems and Language Planning* 1, 107–24.

Nahir, M. (1987) L'aménagement de l'hébreu moderne. In J. Maurais (ed.) *Politique et aménagement linguistiques* (pp. 259–316). Quebec: Conseil de la langue française.

Nahir, M. (1988) Language planning and language acquisition: The 'great leap' in the Hebrew revival. In C. B. Paulston (ed.) *International Handbook of Bilingualism and Bilingual Education* (pp. 275–95). New York: Greenwood Press.

Ndebele, N. (1987) The English language and social change in South Africa. *The English Academy Review* 4, 1–16.

Nettle, D. (1999) *Linguistic Diversity*. Oxford: Oxford University Press.

Nettle, D. and Romaine, S. (2000) *Vanishing Voices: The Extinction of the World's Languages*. Oxford: Oxford University Press.

Nwachukwu, P. (1983) *Towards an Igbo Literary Standard*. London: Kegan Paul.

Ó Raigáin P. (1997) *Language Policy and Social Reproduction: Ireland, 1893–1993.* Oxford: Clarendon Press.

Paksoy, H.B. (ed.) (1994) *Central Asia Reader: The Rediscovery of History.* London: M.E. Sharpe.

Peirce, B. (1989) Toward a pedagogy of possibility in the teaching of English internationally: People's English in South Africa. *TESOL Quarterly* 23, 401–20.

Pennycook, A. (1994) *The Cultural Politics of English as an International Language.* London: Longman.

Pennycook, A. (1995) English in the world/The world in English. In J. Tollefson (ed.) *Power and Inequality in Language Education* (pp. 34–58). Cambridge: Cambridge University Press.

Pennycook, A. (1998) *English and the Discourses of Colonialism.* London: Routledge.

Phillipson, R. (1992) *Linguistic Imperialism.* Oxford: Oxford University Press.

Reagan, T. (2001) The promotion of linguistic diversity in multilingual settings: Policy and reality in post-apartheid South Africa. *Language Problems and Language Planning* 25, 51–72.

Reagan, T. (2004) Objectification, positivism and the teaching of languages: A reconsideration. *Critical Issues in Language Studies: An International Journal* 1, 41–60.

Rubin, J. (1977) Indonesian language planning and education. In J. Rubin, B. Jernudd, J. Das Gupta, J. Fishman and C. Ferguson (eds) *Language Planning Processes* (pp. 111–29). The Hague: Mouton.

Sáenz-Badillos, A. (1993) *A History of the Hebrew Language.* Cambridge: Cambridge University Press.

Schmied, J. (1991) *English in Africa: An Introduction.* London: Longman.

Shah, P. (1999) Perceptions of Malaysian ESL low achievers about English language learning. PhD dissertation, University of Connecticut, Storrs.

Skutnabb-Kangas, T. (2000) *Linguistic Genocide in Education – or Worldwide Diversity and Human Rights?* Mahwah, NJ: Lawrence Erlbaum Associates.

Smalley, W. (1994) *Linguistic Diversity and National Unity: Language Ecology in Thailand.* Chicago: University of Chicago Press.

Tai, J. (1988) Bilingualism and bilingual education in the People's Republic of China. In C. Paulston (ed.) *International Handbook of Bilingualism and Bilingual Education* (pp. 185–201). New York: Greenwood Press.

Tollefson, J. (1991) *Planning Language, Planning Inequality: Language Policy in the Community.* London: Longman.

Tollefson, J. (ed.) (1995) *Power and Inequality in Language Education.* Cambridge: Cambridge University Press.

Wardhaugh, R. (1987) *Languages in Competition: Dominance, Diversity and Decline.* Oxford: Basil Blackwell, in association with André Deutsch.

Watts, R. and Trudgill, P. (eds) (2002). *Alternative Histories of English.* London: Routledge.

Weinstein, B. (ed.) (1990) *Language Policy and Political Development.* Norwood, NJ: Ablex Publishing Corporation.

Williams, G. (1992) *Sociolinguistics: A Sociological Critique.* London: Routledge.

Wright, L. (2002). Why English dominates the central economy: An economic perspective on 'elite closure' and South African language policy. *Language Problems and Language Planning* 26, 159–77.

Chapter 8

Language Classroom Practices in Kenya

GRACE W. BUNYI

Introduction

As in virtually all African countries, the hegemony of the colonial language English in education has remained an enduring legacy of colonialism in Kenya. Current medium-of-instruction policy in Kenya is that in linguistically homogenous school neighbourhoods, the indigenous language of the area is to be used from Standard 1 to 3; in linguistically heterogeneous school neighbourhoods, such as is the case in urban areas, the national language Kiswahili or English is to be used. Where indigenous languages or Kiswahili are used as the medium of instruction from Standard 1 to 3 a switch to English is to be made at the beginning of Standard 4. While this policy may work well for the children of a small, dominant elite group who are well placed to acquire English-language skills early in their lives at home and in the community, it presents enormous challenges for the majority of Kenyan children and their teachers who live in rural areas in which English is rarely used. Similarly, children of the urban poor have little access to English outside the school, as Kiswahili is the language spoken in their communities (Bunyi, 2001).

On the other hand, in Kenya issues about language in education generally and the medium of instruction in particular seem to be of concern only to a few researchers. In her synthesis of five recent case studies on language policy and practices in Kenya, Muthwii (2002) reports that rural parents expressed the view that their children went to school to learn English, not their indigenous languages, which they already knew. However, urban parents assumed that English was the medium of instruction. Muthwii also reports that the March 15, 1976 three-page Ministry of Education circular to schools that articulated the language-in-education policy is stored in files which are by now closed and secured in archives.

She concluded that few teachers have ever read the policy. Most of the teachers the case-study researchers talked to seemed to think that since examinations are in English, they were expected to teach in it as early as possible, although they also felt that they could exercise flexibility and use as many languages as possible to make the children understand. The target language, however, remains English. All the same, in late 2002, the publication in the newspapers of the subjects of the new primary curriculum in which indigenous languages appeared as subjects and as media of instruction in Standards 1 to 3 sparked off some interest in language-in-education issues in the media.[1] Unaware of the fact that this had always been the policy, commentators criticised these proposals, observing that in the era of globalisation, school curricula should emphasise computer-based technology and English as the language of such technologies. Given the foregoing scenario, Mazrui's observation about the inseparable link between English and education in the colonial era – 'The command of the English language was often used as a criterion of one's level of education' (Mazrui, 1975: 55) – does not seem misplaced in Kenya even today.

In this chapter, I present ethnographic data from Standard 1 and Standard 4 classrooms in a marginalised rural primary school. I collected the data from May to December 1994, using participant observation methodologies.[2] Using this data, I demonstrate the dominant language practices in these two classrooms and by extrapolation in the majority of primary classrooms in Kenya,[3] and explore the hidden curriculum in these practices. I also try to explain where the language practices I identify come from and finally discuss the implications that these language practices have for ongoing educational reforms, policies and implementation in Kenya.

Gĩcagi School and the Two Classes

Gĩcagi was a three-stream school located in a marginalised rural community in Kĩambu District, which borders Nairobi – the capital city of Kenya. While those Gĩcagi people who have gone to school have learned to speak, read and write in English, Gĩkũyũ was the only language spoken there.[5] All the children and teachers in Gĩcagi school were Gĩkũyũ speakers, with all but a few teachers living within walking distance of the school. There were 45 girls and boys in the Standard 1 class I studied, and their ages ranged from six to eight years, while there were 47 girls and boys in the Standard 4 class. The Standard 1 children had attended a year or so of nursery school before joining Gĩcagi school, where they were taught all subjects by Mrs Wambaa who was a trained teacher with about 20 years' teaching experience in Standard 1–3. In Standard 4, different teachers taught different subjects.

In an effort to improve the children's competence in English, which is the medium of instruction from Standard 4, and thereby to attain better end-of-primary examination results, and also to improve their competence in Kiswahili, the national language and also a compulsory subject in the end of primary examination, there was a rule against children in Standard 4 and above speaking Gĩkũyũ in the school compound. However, the rule was only half-heartedly enforced, since the teachers were the first to break it by speaking Gĩkũyũ to the children. While admitting this failure to enforce the rule one teacher explained thus: **Onaithuĩ arimũ nĩtũremagwo nĩgwathĩkĩre watho ũcio. Onawe ũrĩ o mũndũ** ('We teachers too are unable to obey that rule. Even you [i.e. the teacher] are human.'). Such comments suggest that in the monolingual Gĩkũyũ environment, it was humanly impossible not to speak Gĩkũyũ.

In both Standard 1 and 4, the social organisation of the classrooms was regimented. The wooden forms on which the children sat and the long tables for writing on were arranged in three rows, all facing the blackboard at the front, where the teacher's table was and from where the teachers taught and controlled all classroom processes including assigning speaking rights.

The Major Features of Classroom Talk in the Two Classes

The dominance of the teacher in the highly structured classroom talk in Kenya and elsewhere in Africa has been noted (Arthur, 1994; Bunyi, 1997; Cleghorn et al., 1989; Rubagumya, 1994). In such classrooms, teacher explanations, questions and other talk take up most of the lesson time. The language practices I observed in the two classes in Gĩcagi school were no different. Teachers often engaged in lengthy explanations of lesson content, punctuated by episodes of teacher-controlled teacher/pupil interactions. In what follows, I will provide examples of the major language practices I found in the two classes. The language practices I focus on are linguistic routines, choral responses, strict Initiation-Response-Feedback (IRF) episodes (Mehan, 1979; Sinclair & Coulthard, 1975) and code-switching.

Linguistic routines

Greetings and end-of-the-morning prayers are the two uses of classroom talk in which what I categorise as linguistic routines were used. In Standard 1, when Mrs Wambaa entered the classroom in the morning, all the children stood up and greetings were exchanged, in English, as in the following excerpt:[6]

T: Good morning.
SS: Good morning, Mrs. Wambaa.
T: How are you?
SS: We are quite well, thank you..
T: Sit down.
SS: Thank you, teacher.

In the course of the day, if another teacher visited the classroom or when I entered, the children stopped whatever they were doing, stood up and waited to be greeted. At the end of each morning, Mrs Wambaa asked the children to gather their belongings and stand up to say two short prayers: 'Thank you, God, for your care from morning until now, Amen'; 'Bless us, O Lord, and our food, Amen'. These linguistic activities were 'routines' in the sense that they did not represent meaningful knowledge about how to greet (or pray) in English. This was clear from the fact that if I entered the classroom and did not initiate the greetings when the children stood up, they became confused and did not know how to proceed. However, the routines marked important points in the classroom lives of the children – the beginning and the end of formal curriculum activities and, in the case of the greetings, provided the children with an opportunity to display their English-language skills. As such, they were evidence of things that the children had learned in school. That they were performed in English underscored the importance of the language in the official knowledge of the school and hence the urgency for these Standard 1 Gĩcagi children to learn the language. In addition, the children were learning the language norm that English was the language for school-based knowledge.

The linguistic routine of greetings as a phenomenon of classroom language practices in Gĩcagi school was also found in Standard 4. Here, I found that the norm of using English for greetings (except during Kiswahili lessons, when Kiswahili was used) was very firmly established when, during one of my observations in the class, the science teacher came into the classroom and greeted the children in Kiswahili. The children were puzzled and did not answer, most probably because this use of Kiswahili for greetings was contrary to the 'English for greetings' norm. This prompted the teacher to comment in Gĩkũyũ: '**Rĩu ona mũtingĩenda kũgeithania?** ('Now you don't even want to greet?').

Choral responses (Language lessons)

A pervasive language practice in the two classes and especially in Standard 1 was the performance of what I refer to as choral responses. This involved pupils repeating individual letters, words or sentences after the teacher or even reading pieces of texts aloud. The teachers kept asking individual children, groups of children or the whole class to read aloud, repeat saying things they had said; or used some other means to elicit the choral responses, as in the description below of how Mrs Wambaa taught reading in Gĩkũyũ in Standard 1, using a pointing stick to initiate the choral responses.

There was a dearth of Gĩkũyũ reading resources in Standard 1. Available resources consisted of a chart above the blackboard. The chart contained lists of Gĩkũyũ three letter syllables such as **mba, mbe, mbi, mbĩ, mbo, mbũ, mbu; nda, nde, ndi, ndĩ, ndo, ndũ, ndu; and tha, the, thi, thĩ, tho, thũ, thu.** Each of three other charts on the back wall consisted of five or six pictures and the names of the objects in the pictures. On the blackboard itself, Mrs Wambaa always had seven Gĩkũyũ vowels: **a, e, i, ĩ, o, ũ, u,** and two- or three-letter syllables corresponding to each vowel as a permanent feature of the blackboard. During the entire period of my participant observation work in this class, all the reading activities were based on these materials. When teaching the reading of the syllables, Mrs Wambaa gave the following instructions: **Uthiĩ ũkĩheaga mĩgambo. Tũthondeke mĩgambo. Na tũkĩgwetaga ndemwa iria ithondekete mĩgambo ĩyo.** ('You give me the syllables. We make syllables and say the letters that make those syllables.')

Mrs. Wambaa directed the reading using a stick to point at what she wanted the children to read. When she pointed at **mba** for example, the whole class read 'mba'. Mrs Wambaa then pointed at each letter and the children read the letters thus: 'm **na** ('and') b **na** ('and') a'. After that, Mrs Wambaa pointed at the syllable **mba** again and the children read it again. The activity then moved to reading words. Mrs Wambaa wrote a word on the blackboard and the whole class proceeded to read the word in a chorus, as in the following example of the word **gĩkombe** ('cup'). Mrs Wambaa pointed at the initial syllable **gi** and the children read 'gĩ, g **na** ('and') ĩ gĩ'. Mrs. Wambaa then pointed at the syllable **mbe** and the children read 'mbe m **na** ('and') b **na** ('and') e **mbe**'. Lastly, Mrs Wambaa pointed at the whole word and the children read 'gĩ ko mbe', enunciating each syllable separately.

The most advanced Gĩkũyũ reading activity in Standard 1 was the reading of sentences. The children were asked to make short sentences. Once a child had produced an acceptable sentence, Mrs Wambaa wrote it on the blackboard. She then proceeded to direct the reading of the sentence letter by letter, syllable by syllable and word by word, as in the description above. Once all the words had been read, Mrs Wambaa read the sentence aloud and the children repeated after her. Mrs Wambaa insisted that the sentences had to be short and refused to accept sentences like '**Cũcũ njatũrĩra rwatũ rwa mũemba**' ('Grandmother, cut for me a piece of

mango'). The reason she gave was **'tondũ rĩu nĩwekĩra ciugo nyingĩ mũno.
Kau nĩkaraiha mũno'** ('because you have put too many words. That one is
too long'). These are the only ways I saw Mrs Wambaa teach reading in
Gĩkũyĩ. She explained to the children that they must learn to read the
syllables before they could read books, so that when it came to reading,
they would be able to read fluently. However, by the end of my fieldwork
(which was also very close to the end of the school year), the children had
not started reading books.

On the other hand, Mrs Wambaa taught reading in English and
Kiswahili using a 'pattern-and-drill' approach and making the children
repeat words and/or sentences found in the pupils' language textbooks
several times after her. For example, in one of the Kiswahili reading lessons
I observed, Mrs Wambaa made the children repeat the sentence 'HUYU NI
SIMBA' ('This is a lion') and all the other sentences five times each.
Similarly, in an English reading lesson I observed, the children had to
repeat the words 'riding' and 'bean bag' nine times each after Mrs Wambaa
(see Bunyi, 2001 for a detailed description). Similar language practices
were found in Standard 4, where Mrs Mũhoro, the English teacher, taught
reading by first reading the whole reading text aloud herself and then
asking the whole class to read the same text aloud.

When I asked Mrs Wambaa why she adopted these strategies, she told
me that Gĩcagi children did not learn easily and that therefore it was
necessary to get them to repeat the same thing over and over so that they
would know. Indeed, referring to reading in Gĩkũyũ, she told me that she
was happy, if by the end of the year, some children could read many Gĩkũyũ
words by sounding out the syllables. Mrs Mũhoro, on the other hand,
explained to me that many of the Standard 4 children had not mastered the
mechanics of reading and therefore were not able to read on their own.
However, whatever insights informed the two teachers' choices of
teaching-learning approaches, these approaches were not having the
desired effect: the children were not learning much reading. By the end of
their first year in school, most of the Standard 1 children had not learned
how to decode written symbols in any of the three languages they were
learning. By the end of their fourth year in school, many of the Standard 4
children had not learned how to read either.

My analysis of these reading lessons in Gĩcagi school is that, in addition
to their being tedious, boring and inefficient in the sense that the choral
responses were time-consuming and hence very little was covered in each
lesson, they carried negative hidden messages about reading. A possible
hidden message of these lessons in which the learners 'imitate' sounds and
focus on fragments of language was that reading is mere recitation – a game
that is unrelated to meaning. Indeed, the children often played the game.

For example, in Standard 1, before Mrs Wambaa entered the classroom in the morning, or even when she was in class but busy with something else at her table, the children could be heard imitating the Gĩkĩyũ reading lessons by chanting the letters and syllables. Sometimes, one self-appointed child would take the role of the teacher by taking Mrs Wambaa's stick and pointing to the syllables on the charts on the walls while she/he (and sometimes with the others joining in role) played the reading game. As in the Gĩkũyũ reading lessons, reading in the Kiswahili and English lessons was a performative activity. Many times, a good number of the children were not looking at what they were 'reading'. Only seven of the 45 children had Kiswahili textbooks of their own. Mrs Wambaa had another four books donated to the school. This meant that, on the best of days, there were 11 books to be shared by 45 children. The result was that many children 'read' without looking at the reading text. In one lesson, there were only 11 books and 65 children (a Standard 1 teacher for another class was absent and half her class had joined Mrs Wambaa's class). Mrs Wambaa tried to reorganise seating so that the children could share the books but soon gave up and announced the compromise: **Nĩ ngũkuonia mbica. No arĩa͂ mena mabuku nĩo tĩgũthoma nao no acio angĩ nĩ mbica ndĩrĩmonagia.** ('I will show you the pictures. We will read with those who have books, but I will be showing the others the pictures'). On another occasion, Wambui, one of the girls, had the wrong Kiswahili textbook, but had it open and was 'reading' from it, along with the others, until her neighbour noticed and reported the matter to Mrs Wambaa. In Standard 4, when Mrs Mũhoro asked the children to read aloud as a group, I observed that those who did not know how to read mumbled along with the others. On one occasion when Mrs Mũhoro was reading the text aloud, I observed a group of boys following Mrs Mũhoro read as one of them pointed at what was supposedly being read with a finger. I noticed he was pointing at the wrong lines. However, when Mrs Mũhoro finished reading, they pretended that they had also finished reading with the others even though they had not yet turned to the final page.

On the other hand, Mrs Wambaa actively discouraged the children's display of their knowledge of the Gĩkũyũ language in Gĩkũyũ lessons by rejecting their long sentences when she asked them to make sentences (see above). My interpretation of this phenomenon is that Mrs Wambaa was so focused on the performative aspects of the interactions that the learning it was expected to facilitate was sacrificed. The consequence was that rather than enhancing the children's Gĩkũyũ language development as a springboard to Kiswahili and English-language development (see Cummins, 1981), these Gĩkũyũ lessons actively constrained such development.

Choral responses (Non-language lessons)

Choral language practices were also adopted in teaching non-language areas of the curriculum in both classes. The teachers usually required the whole class to repeat what they considered important words or lesson content several times after them, in readiness to reproduce them in answer to examination questions. However, unlike in Standard 1 where the children had to repeat the same thing after the teacher, sometimes up to nine times, in Standard 4, they had to do so for only two to three times. As can be seen from the following examples, the teachers prompted the children to repeat after them either by explicitly instructing them to do so or by saying something and then looking at the class in a way that indicated he/she was listening.

In a Standard 4 Maths lesson:

T:	[Writes on the blackboard and then reads: 60 minutes = 1 hour]. Sixty minutes equals one hour. Read everybody.
SS:	Sixty minutes equals one hour.
T:	Again.
SS:	Sixty minutes equals one hour.

In a Standard 4 Science lesson:

T:	You place the patient on his back where there is fresh air.
SS:	You place the patient on his back where there is fresh air.
T:	You place the patient on his back where there is fresh air.
SS:	You place the patient on his back where there is fresh air.
T:	Again.
SS:	You place the patient on his back where there is fresh air.

Whether in language or non-language lessons, the choral responses were rhythmic and the children often adopted a playful attitude in performing them. The teachers sometimes increased the sense of performance by pretending not to have heard the children the first time, by using a rising voice to say things like 'ii?' and 'eh?' An extract from a Standard 1 English lesson will exemplify this.

T:	The plural of pencil is?
S:	Pencils.
T:	Ii?
SS:	Pencils.
T:	Eh?
SS:	Pencils.
T:	Eh?
SS:	Pencils.

The children responded by more of them joining in and progressively shouting more and more loudly.

Strict IRF episodes

Classroom discourse analysis researchers (for example, Lemke, 1990; Mehan, 1979; Sinclair and Coulthard, 1975) concur that where the teacher assumes a structured approach, discourse proceeds in three-part sequences, which Sinclair and Coulthard called 'moves'. According to these researchers, the teacher makes the first move, called 'initiation'; the second move, the 'response', is made by the pupil, and the third move, referred to as 'feedback', is made by the teacher. Thus we have the sequence Initiation-Response-Feedback (IRF). The teachers in the two Gĩcagi classes often fell back on a strictly IRF interaction pattern as a strategy to increase pupil participation in the lessons. The teacher's initiation move took different forms. Sometimes, it ended with a rise in voice indicating a blank to be filled using information just given.

In a Standard 4 lesson in Agriculture:

T: We said they have four officials. They have four . . . ?
SS: Officials.
T: Four officials. We have the chairman. We have the . . . ?
SS: Chairman.
T: Chairman. We have the treasurer. We have the?
SS: Treasurer

Sometimes all the children were required to do was to complete a word, a task which the teacher sometimes assisted them with as in the following example, in which the response and feedback moves overlap.

In a Standard 4 lesson in Agriculture:

T: HAYA. **Wĩra wa** officials **aya nĩguo tũrenda kũrora**. . . . including
       the officials. Including the offi . . . ?
       (Okay. We want to know the work of these officials.)
T: {Officials.
SS: {Officials

Sometimes, the teacher initiated by asking a question that only required the pupils to repeat information just given, as in the following example:

In a Standard 4 lesson in Agriculture:

T: **Haha hena** official **ũngĩ na nĩ** very important. . . . **Hena** official **ũngĩ**
       very important **wĩtagwo** patron. **Wĩtagwo**?
       (Here there is another official and who is very important . . . There
       is another very important official called patron. Called?)

SS:	Patron
T:	Patron. Can you say patron
SS:	Patron
T:	Patron

Other times, the teachers asked one-word answer questions, as in the following examples:

In a Standard 1 Maths lesson:

T:	Three times two is equal to?
SS:	Six.
T:	Six. Four times five equal to?
SS:	Twenty.

In a Standard 1 English lesson:

T:	Tomato **nĩ kĩĩ?**
	(Tomato is what?)
S:	**Nĩ waru.**
	(It is potato)
T:	**Ihĩ ti waru.**
	(No. It is not potato)
S:	**Nĩ nyanya.**
	(It is tomato)
T:	Very good. **Nĩ nyanya.**
	(Very good. It is tomato).

In a Standard 4 GHC (Geography, History and Civics) lesson:

T:	What is the name of our province?
S:	Central province.
T:	Central province. Good.

The foregoing examples illustrate how linguistically and intellectually undemanding the strict IRF episodes were for the pupils. Often, the pupils did not have to think at all to participate successfully as the required information was provided by the teacher only a fraction of a second before. Most of the questions posed by the teachers were of the closed type requiring only one-word answers creating the impression that knowledge is little bits and pieces of information and that knowing is reproducing from memory. Consequently, the pupils were learning that they did not need to engage meaningfully in what was going on and a game like atmosphere persisted.

Code-switching

As already indicated, Gĩcagi was a multilingual school. It was located in a Gĩkũyũ-speaking community and Kiswahili and English were taught from Standard 1 to Standard 8, while Gĩkũyũ was taught in Standards 1 to 3 only. Teachers used Gĩkũyũ with these children both in and out of the classrooms. In formal out-of-class activities involving the whole school, such as the school assembly held on Monday morning and Friday morning and evening, messages, targeted to children in these classes, were in Gĩkũyũ.

In spite of the 'no Gĩkũyũ in the school compound' rule mentioned earlier, which was only half heartedly applied to children in Standards 4 to 8, I heard these children speak only Gĩkũyũ among themselves. However, for fear of breaking the rule, in the little talk there was between teachers and the children outside the classroom, the children normally waited for the teachers to initiate talk and then responded in the language the teacher had initiated in. In the school assembly, messages targeted at Standard 4 to 8 children were in English with code-switching into Gĩkũyũ and Kiswahili.

Inside the Standard 4 classroom, pupil-pupil talk was in Gĩkũyũ. On the other hand, although language choice varied from one teacher to another during lesson time, there was a definite attempt to use English (except in the Kiswahili lessons, when efforts to use Kiswahili were made) as the medium of instruction by all the teachers I observed. The result was that there was constant code-switching between English, Gĩkũyũ and Kiswahili. In the discussion below, I present data to exemplify some of the functions code-switching served and/or the forms it took.

Organisational and classroom management tasks

There was a tendency for the teachers to use code-switching to carry out organisational classroom management tasks. For example, outside the Kiswahili lessons, Mrs Wambaa carried out organisational and classroom management tasks through code-switching into Kiswahili. In carrying out these tasks, Mrs Wambaa made one-word or short-phrase switches into Kiswahili as follows: 'NGOJA, NGOJA' ('Wait, wait') to the children when they tried to go on with whatever activity before she was satisfied. Often, when a child got the right answer, Mrs Wambaa would say: 'MPIGIE MAKOFI' ('Clap for him/her') or 'MPIGIE MAKOFI KIDOGO' ('Clap for him/her a few claps'). Other Kiswahili words and phrases that Mrs Wambaa codeswitched into were: 'MWINGINE' ('Another person'); 'KUJA HAPA' ('Come here'); 'SOMA' ('Read').

Mrs Wambaa's occasional code-switching into Kiswahili outside the Kiswahili lesson had to do with classroom management concerns rather than with the teaching of lesson content. Since the students did not know Kiswahili, Mrs Wambaa could not have been code-switching into Kiswahili for the purpose of being understood better. Her use of Kiswahili in these instances can be seen as representing a multilingual's behaviour of drawing on different linguistic resources for the accomplishment of different tasks.

Interestingly, although Mrs Wambaa used some Kiswahili in other lessons for classroom management tasks, she used a lot of Gĩkũyũ for the same tasks in the Kiswahili lessons. In this case one can argue that Mrs Wambaa was already doing a lot in keeping some of the lesson content in Kiswahili, and therefore felt at liberty to use some Gĩkũyũ for non-lesson content purposes. An alternative explanation is to see code-switching as a framing device that separates official classroom tasks from organisational tasks. In a Kiswahili lesson, Kiswahili is the language of official tasks and therefore there is a need for another language for carrying out the organisational tasks; hence the use of Gĩkũyũ for these tasks. Conversely, in Gĩkũyũ language and other lessons, Gĩkũyũ and English were the languages of official tasks and this led to the use of Kiswahili for organisational and classroom management tasks. The use of code-switching for framing purposes remains the same, but the form it takes varies.

Code-switching for organisational and classroom management purposes was also observed in Standard 4, where the English teacher Mrs Mũhoro used English only when teaching. However, she often used Gĩkũyũ or code-switched between English and Gĩkũyũ in these lessons to admonish the children and to keep order in the class, especially when, after assigning seatwork, she walked round the class checking on the work. The following exemplify instances of such code-switching:

T: **Rĩrĩ nĩ ibuku Wangarĩ? Nĩ tũratathi tũigana?**
      (Is this a book Wangari? How many papers?)
T: What is the noise for? **Nũũ ũcio ũtoĩ ũrĩa agĩrĩirwo nĩ gwĩka?**
      (What is the noise for? Who doesn't know what he/she is sup-
      posed to do?)
T: Where was this book when the . . . **Rĩrĩa mabuku mararehetwo**
      waregire kũrehe wĩra ũyũ nĩkĩ? Ta rũgama.
      (Where was this book when the . . . Why did you not bring this
      work when the books were brought? Stand up).

Official content tasks

In both Standard 1 and Standard 4, official curriculum content (or those bits and pieces of information the teachers considered to constitute the lesson content and which the children therefore needed to remember) were put in English. Often, the children were asked to repeat the words or sentences after the teacher in English several times, as in the examples of choral responses presented earlier on in this chapter. In fact, all the choral responses in the non-language lessons were always in English. Examples of this linguistic practice abound in the data. In a Maths lesson, Mrs Wambaa was teaching how to tell the time, and she got the children to repeat the words 'clock face' ten times and the words 'hands of the clock' five times. Also, each time Mrs Wambaa pointed at a certain time, say two o'clock, the children had to repeat the statement, 'The time is two o'clock' several times. In a Science lesson on 'air', the points that received emphasis were: 'We cannot live without air', 'We breathe in fresh air' and 'Moving air is called wind'. The children had to repeat these statements several times in the course of the lesson. These are also the statements that they wrote in their exercise books as a record of what they had learned. Clearly, as these Gĩcagi children were learning the official content knowledge of the curriculum, they were also learning language norms and internalising the high value bestowed on English in Kenya.

Sometimes, the teachers taught the children language norms explicitly in different classes, as in the following examples.

In a Standard 4 Kiswahili lesson:

S: **Nĩ ndoiga**, KIFARANGA
        (I have said a chick)
T: WEE SEMA KWA KISWAHILI BWANA. HAYA SEMA VILE UNASEMA KWA KISWAHILI
        (You say in Kiswahili mister. Okay. Say what you are saying in Kiswahili)
S: NIMESEMA KIFARANGA
        (I have said chick).

In a Standard 1 Kiswahili lesson:

T: KETI
        (Sit)
SS: Thank you teacher
T: **Nĩ Gĩthũngũ? Ndamwĩrĩre werwo ũndũ na Gĩthweri ũkaria na Gĩthweri. Werwo na Gĩthũngũ ũkaria na Gĩthũngũ.**
        (Is it English? I told you that when you are told something in Kiswahili you speak in Kiswahili. When you are told in English you speak in English).

In a GHC lesson in Standard 4:

T: What do we mean by the word to communicate?
S: **Gũkinyia ũhoro.**
        (To pass a message).
T: Why can't you put that in English?
S: To pass messages.
T: Good. To pass messages.

In a Standard 1 Kiswahili lesson:

T: MKALI KWA NINI? KWA NINI SIMBA NI MKALI?
        (Why fierce? Why is the lion fierce?)
S: **Niyũragaga mũndũ**
        (It kills a person)
T: NDIYO. KWA SABABU INAUA
        (Yes. Because it kills)

Other times the teacher gave the children permission to use the 'wrong' language.
In a Standard 1 Kiswahili lesson:

T: NDOVU NI MUNYAMA GANI? KWA KIKIKUYU NI MNYAMA
        GANI? **Nĩnyamũ ĩrĩkũ ĩyo?**
        (What animal is elephant? What animal is it in Gĩkũyũ? What animal is it?)
S: **Njogu.**
        (Elephant).
T: **Ndiyo.**
        (Yes).

From the above examples, it appears that learning the appropriate language in Gĩcagi school is not a simple matter. Teachers often translated difficult English and Kiswahili lexical items into Gĩkũyũ (see below). However, when the student in the Standard 4 GHC lesson above adopted the same strategy, his answer was not accepted as correct until he put it in English. Again, when the student in the first Standard 1 Kiswahili lesson example adopted the same strategy, although the teacher accepted his answer, she indicated it was only partially acceptable since she went on to put it into Kiswahili – the 'right' language in the Kiswahili lessons.

Giving meanings of lexical items

During the Kiswahili and the English language lessons, and also as teachers taught other areas of the curriculum, they often code-switched into Gĩkũyũ to give the meaning of lexical items they considered to be unfamiliar to the children, as in the following examples.

In a Standard 1 Kiswahili lesson:

T: MKALI **nĩ gũthũka.**
    (MKALI is to be fierce)

and

T: MADOADOA **nĩ maroro**
    (MADOADOA are spots)

In a Standard 4 Science lesson:

T: **Tũkiuga atĩ twĩna** artificial sources of light. Artificial **nĩ iria mũndũ ethondekeire.**
    (We said we have artificial sources of light. Artificial are the ones a person makes for him/herself).

In a Standard 4 lesson in Agriculture:

T: We have another official who is the secretary. Secretary **na Gĩkũyũ etagwo mwandĩki.**
    (We have another official who is the secretary. The secretary in Gĩkũyũ is called the writer).

Giving meanings of whole sentences or questions

Often, in both Standard 1 and 4, the teachers gave direct translations of whole sentences or questions that they had just produced. Some examples of this practice follow.

In a Standard 1 Maths lesson:

T: Okay. What you are going to do is to count eight then from eight you take away six so as to get the missing number. **Atĩ ũrĩa ũgwĩka ũgũtara inyanya. Watara inyanya wambe weherie ithathatũ. Kĩrĩa gĩgũtigara nĩyo** missing? Number. (What you are going to do is to count eight. When you have counted eight you first remove three. What will be left is the missing number).

and

T: Now, we are getting the story of ten. **Tũracaria rũgano rwa ikũmi.**
    (We are looking for the story of ten).

In a Maths lesson in Standard 4:

T: How can we know a year is a leap year?

T: **Tũngĩmenya nakĩ atĩ mwaka nĩ** leap year?
         (How can we know that a year is a leap year?)

Socialising the elite

Myers-Scotton (1993) has identified the insertion of English lexical items in indigenous language sentences as a mark of the education based elite in East Africa. Writing about the code-switching behaviour of members of the academic staff in the University of Dar Es Salam in Tanzania, Blommaert (1992) concurs. However, I believe that in Kenya today an adequate linguistic characterisation of the elites would include the ability to embed English and Kiswahili lexical items in indigenous language speech, since Kiswahili is also an important language in education coming second after English.[7] The classroom language data in this chapter shows this use of the three languages in the same move by teachers.

In a Standard 4 Agriculture lesson:

T: Chairman **nĩwe ũrũgamagĩrĩra kũngikorwo** MKUTANO **kana** a
         Meeting. The Chairman is the one who is supposed to chair. **Nĩwe**
         wagĩrĩĩrwo gũkorwo akĩrora andũ acio ũrĩa mekwaria. Akahota
         kuona atĩ . . . na a ga control that meeting.
         (The chairman is the one who oversees when there is a meeting
         or a meeting . . . He is the one who should be watching how the
         people will speak. He tries to ensure . . . And controls that meet-
         ing).

Given the discussion in this chapter so far, it is unlikely that many of the Standard 1 and 4 Gĩcagi children would do so well in school as to join the group of education-based elites in Kenya. Even their teachers did not expect them to achieve this feat. However, given the data I have, one can argue that on entering school in Kenya, all children become candidates for 'elitedom' and are socialised thus. Those who achieve high levels of competence in English and accompanying academic success among other things (Bunyi, 2001) become the real elites (people with good jobs and good incomes), while those who achieve low levels of competence in English and fail to attain academic success become pseudo-elites.

From the foregoing examples of the code-switching behaviour in Standards 1 and 4 in Gĩcagi school, it can be seen that teachers' language choice in these classes was fluid. As regards the educational value of the code-switching in these lessons, one could view it as helping to improve communication between the teacher and the students, and hence enhancing students' understanding of lesson content. However, because most of it involved direct translation, the children could very well soon learn that there was no need to struggle with English as the teacher would provide the same information in Gĩkũyũ. Therefore, in terms of learning English – the language the children require to learn other subjects in the code-switching could be seen as working against the English-language development of these students.

Discussion

Where do these language practices come from?

Other classroom ethnographers in Kenya and elsewhere in Africa (Arthur, 1994; Cleghorn *et al.*, 1989; Ndayipfukamiye, 2001) have reported on linguistic practices similar to the ones I have described and analysed in this chapter. Indeed, similar findings have been reported from other postcolonial contexts where children are schooled through languages that are not their own (Hornberger & Chick, 2001; Martin, 1999). Explanations as to why these practices predominate are varied. Cleghorn *et al.* (1989), for example, suggested that these practices could be a reflection of existing and traditionally rooted interaction patterns. On the other hand, Hornberger and Chick (2001) refer to these practices as 'safe talk' and argue that teachers and learners engage in such talk to achieve a sense of purpose and accomplishment despite the fact that little learning is taking place. By so doing, both the teachers and the students avoid losing face owing to lack of competence. This seems to be a reasonable explanation when one thinks of the lessons taught in English in Kenya. Eisemon *et al.* (1989) reported that science instruction in the primary classes they studied in Kenya was characterised by imprecise and incoherent discourse due to teachers' insecurity in both the science content and the English language. In her report that I have referred to previously, Muthwii (2002) indicates that the Standard 6 students who were interviewed confessed that they had problems following instructions in English, but that when they do not understand they 'leave it alone', suggesting that they let things ride and thus create the impression that all is well. My data reveals similar instances. A good example is when Mrs Mũhoro (the Standard 6 English teacher) kept asking whether the class had finished reading assigned texts and accepting the chorus answer 'Yes' although she knew and had even told me that some of the students could not read.

However, there is still a need to explain why lessons taught in the teachers' and children's own language, such as the Gĩkũyũ reading lessons described in this chapter, adopt these language practices. I have elsewhere argued that this could be the result of existing teacher education programmes that do not develop the teachers' classroom interaction skills in order to maximise the use of classroom talk (Bunyi, 1997). My further hypothesis is that these language practices have to do with the missionary education roots of modern education in Kenya and elsewhere in Africa. A central part of the missionary education curriculum was the learning of Christian literature such as the catechism, which had to be committed to memory; hence the need for the teacher to engage the learners in repeating the same text over and over.

Implications of the classroom language practices for ongoing educational reforms and policies

Following the National Rainbow Coalition (NARC) party's victory over the Kenya African National Union (KANU) – the ruling party since independence in 1963 – in the general election of 27 December 2002, the NARC government started implementing a free primary education (FPE) policy in January 2003. FPE is now seen as part of the worldwide Education for All (EFA) goal first articulated in Jomtien, Thailand in 1990 and reaffirmed in Dakar in April 2000. The EFA goal poses both quantitative and qualitative challenges for education in Kenya, the attainment of which can be adversely affected by the existing classroom language practices discussed in this chapter.

As regards the quantitative aspect, the objective is that all primary-school-age children should enrol in school and complete the full eight years of primary education. It is estimated that more than 3 million such children were out of school before FPE and that FPE has now brought into the schools 1.5 million of these children. However, even if the government can somehow find the required resources and make primary education compulsory, thus enabling all children to enrol, there will still be the question of keeping them in school. Currently, the drop out rate from the primary education level is high, standing at 44% (Obura *et al.*, 1999). This means that over 50% of the children who enter Standard 1 drop out of school before finishing Standard 8. Government policy documents such as the Education Master Plan (Republic of Kenya, 1998) and the Poverty Reduction Strategy Paper (Ministry of Finance and Planning, 2001) blame these high school drop-out rates on existing high levels of poverty. My hypothesis is that the language practices discussed in this chapter could be playing a considerable role in pushing marginalised children out of school. If these children fail to find meaning in what they are learning in school, as I have argued in this chapter, they are likely to intellectually disengage from their lessons and subsequently drift out of school.

I believe that there is a need for in-depth interpretive research that will help us understand how poverty interacts with school processes such as the classroom language practices described in this chapter, and with what consequences, in order to better guide educational policy and implementation.

The qualitative aspects of the EFA goal refer to the quality of school processes and the outcomes of education. The classroom language practice data I have presented and discussed in this chapter clearly show that primary school classroom processes in Kenya are of poor quality. Most of the activities the children are subjected to are boring, and intellectually uninspiring and unchallenging. The outcomes in Gĩcagi school were that the children were not learning much that is of value. Indeed, many of them were not even acquiring basic literacy. These poor primary education outcomes evident in Gĩcagi school are clear at the national level. A regional English language reading test administered to Standard 6 children in 1998 as part of the Southern Africa Consortium for Monitoring Educational Quality (SACMEQ) learning assessment revealed unacceptable results. It was found that 35% of Kenyan Standard 6 pupils failed to achieve the minimum English reading mastery, defined as the ability to recognise the alphabet and simple English words. Further, it was found that 77% of Standard 6 pupils have not achieved the desirable level of mastery defined as the mastery necessary for successful learning in Standard 7 (UNESCO, 2001).

Currently, the view that these poor outcomes are mainly a result of lack of teaching/learning materials and facilities seems to hold sway in the Ministry of Education corridors. 5.5 billion Kenya Shillings of the 7.9[8] billion Kenya Shillings FPE budget has been allocated to textbooks and related school supplies. However, any basic textbook on curriculum implementation stresses that the teacher is the most critical participant in an educational reform, particularly in one that touches on what goes on in classrooms. The data presented in this chapter has shown that trained teachers like Mrs Wambaa, Mrs Muhoro and others in Gĩcagi school lacked the competence to provide meaningful teaching/ learning activities for their regular classes. This is not surprising, given primary school teacher-recruitment policies and practices and the quality of teacher education and teacher professional support services in Kenya. Primary-school teacher trainees are not always the academically superior. They are recruited from secondary-school graduates who may have attained as low a grade as D- in their secondary leaving examination.[9] On the other hand, the primary-teacher education curriculum is overburdened. In a two-year programme, teacher trainees have to take all 13 primary school subjects plus professional studies, as well as doing teaching practice. Thus there is little time for them to adequately acquire the competencies they need to provide meaningful learning activities for their pupils. Further, there is little professional support available to teachers. Some of the school inspectors who are expected to provide curriculum support to teachers see their role as one of 'policing' (Bunyi, 2002).

On the other hand, FPE has radically changed the number and composition of pupils in primary school classrooms for the marginalised. There are now more students in class (even more than a hundred in some cases), over-age children and greater variability in abilities due to new students who may never have gone to school before and some who might have dropped out earlier but have now re-entered the system. Yet, within the FPE programme, in-service teacher education has been allocated only 500 million Kenya Shillings at a time when teachers are already disgruntled owing to the previous government's failure to pay them increments agreed upon in 1997. While I agree that teaching/learning resources are very important, there is a need to rethink the proportions of the FPE budget that go to materials and to teacher in-service programmes. At the same time, I believe that the goals (quantitative and qualitative) of a major reform such as FPE and of language policies and classroom language practices should be conceptualised holistically since they intersect, as this chapter has shown.

Notes

1. A new curriculum was implemented in January 2003 following many years of criticism of the previous 8-4-4 vocational education-oriented curriculum, which was introduced in 1985. The 8-4-4 curriculum was part of an educational reform that changed the structure of education in Kenya from the 7-4-2-3 structure – seven years of primary education, four of secondary, two of advanced secondary and three of university to the 8-4-4 structure: eight years of primary, four of secondary, and four of university education.
2. The research within which the data used in this chapter was conducted was part of my doctoral studies at the Ontario Institute for Studies in Education, University of Toronto, Canada. It was supported by a full scholarship awarded by the International Development Research Centre.
3. More than 50% of Kenyans of whom 75% live in the rural areas live below the poverty line of one United States dollar per day (Ministry of Finance and Planning, 2001).
4. For the sake of anonymity, Gĩcagi and all proper names in this chapter are pseudonyms.
5. One of the more than 40 indigenous languages in Kenya and the language with the most speakers.
6. Transcription conventions are: bold for all Gĩkũyũ words and particles; capital letters for all Kiswahili words and regular typeface for all English words. Translations are within ( ) brackets; T = teacher; S = student; SS = students and SS&T = students and teacher. Overlapping speech represented by {.
7. Kiswahili has been gaining status nationally since the 8:4:4 curriculum reforms introduced in 1985 made it a compulsory and examinable subject at both the end of primary and secondary education examinations.
8. 75 Kenya Shillings are approximately equal to one US dollar.
9. A mean score is the average grade for a candidate in the secondary leaving examination. The scores range from A to E.

References

Arthur, J. (1994) Talking like teachers: teacher and pupil discourse in Botswana primary classrooms. *Language, Culture and Curriculum* 7 (1), 29–40.

Blommaert, J. (1992) Code-switching and exclusivity of social identities: Some data from campus Kiswahili. *Journal of Multilingual and Multicultural Development* 13, 57–70.

Bunyi, G.W. (1997) Multilingualism and discourse in primary mathematics in Kenya. *Language, Culture and Curriculum* 10 (1), 52–65.

Bunyi, G.W. (2001) Language and education inequalities in Kenya. In M. Martin-Jones and M. Heller (eds) *Voices of Authority: Education and Linguistic Difference* (pp. 77–100). London: Ablex.

Bunyi, G.W. (2002) Theory and practice in providing an all round primary education in Kenya: Implications for initiatives to develop improved approaches. In L. Stewart and P. Mutunga (eds). *Life Skills, Menstruation and Sanitation. What's (Not) Happening in Our Schools?* (pp. 74–102). Harare: WLC.

Cleghorn, A., Merritt, M and Abagi, J.O. (1989) Language policy and science instruction in Kenyan primary schools. *Comparative Review* 33 (1), 21–39.

Cummins, J. (1981) The role of primary language development in promoting educational success for language minority students. In California State Department of Education (ed.) *Schooling and Language Minority Students: A Theoretical Framework.* Evaluation, Dissemination and Assessment and Pedagogy. Los Angeles: California State University;

Eisemon, T., Cleghorn, A. and Nyamate, A. (1989) A note on language of instruction, teaching and cognitive outcomes of science instruction in primary schools in Kisii and Kwale districts of Kenya. *Kenya Journal of Education* 4, 153–65.

Hornberger, H. and Chick, J. K. (2001) Co-constructing school safetime: Safetalk practices in Peruvian and South African classrooms. In M. Martin-Jones and M. Heller (eds) *Voices of Authority: Education and Linguistic Difference* (pp. 31–56). London: Ablex.

Lemke, J.L. (1990) *Talking Science: Language Learning and Values.* New Jersey: Ablex.

Martin, P.W. (1999) Close encounters of a bilingual kind: Interactional practices in the primary classroom in Brunei. *International Journal of Educational Development* 19, 127–40.

Mazrui, A. (1975) *The Political Sociology of the English Language. An African Perspective.* The Hague: Mouton.

Mehan, H. (1979) *Learning Lessons.* Cambridge: Harvard University Press.

Myers-Scotton, C. (1993) Elite closure as a powerful language strategy: The African case. *International Journal of the Sociology of Language* 103, 149–63.

Ministry of Finance and Planning. (2001) Poverty reduction strategy paper for the period 2001–2004. Nairobi: Ministry of Finance and Planning.

Muthwii, M. (2002) *Language Policy and Practices in Education in Kenya and Uganda.* Nairobi: Phoenix

Ndayipfukamiye, L. (2001) The contradictions of teaching bilingually in postcolonial Burundi: from *nyakatsi* to *maisons en étage.* In M. Martin-Jones and M. Heller (eds) *Voices of Authority: Education and Linguistic Difference* (pp. 101–16). London: Ablex.

Obura, A., Spring, K.A. and Cristofoli, V. (1999) *Indicators III on Primary Education in Eastern and Southern Africa.* Nairobi: UNICEF.

Republic of Kenya, (1998) *Master Plan on Education and Training 1997–2010.* Nairobi: Jomo Kenyatta Foundation.

Rubagumya, C.M. (1994) Language values and bilingual classroom discourse in Tanzanian secondary schools. *Language, Culture and Curriculum* 7 (1), 41–53.

Sinclair, J.M. and Coulthard, R.M. (1975) *Towards an Analysis of Discourse: The English Used By Teachers and Pupils*. London: Oxford University Press.

UNESCO (2001) The quality of education: Some policy suggestions based on a survey of schools. Kenya. Paris: UNESCO.

Chapter 9

Language and the Struggle to Learn: The Intersection of Classroom Realities, Language Policy, and Neocolonial and Globalisation Discourses in South African Schools

MARGIE PROBYN

'*Englis open my breans*' wrote Mzuvumile, a Grade 8 learner in a South African township school, justifying his preference for English as a medium of instruction. Whether English medium of instruction does in fact open opportunities for meaningful education, or in fact serves to constrain such possibilities, is part of the debate about school language policies in South Africa. However, such a debate needs to be placed within an historical-political context: language-in-education polices have been closely inter-twined with South Africa's political history and continue to be hotly contested.

Historical-political Context

Like many African countries, South Africa's colonial history has imprinted itself on the linguistic ecology. Dutch settlers introduced their language and political control from 1652 until they were succeeded by the British in 1795. The anglicisation policies of the British colonial government (1854–1909) included making state funding of public schools dependent on their use of English as the sole medium of instruction. These efforts were stepped up in the wake of Britain's defeat of the two Afrikaner Boer republics in 1902 and provoked fierce resistance amongst Afrikaners,[1] making the use of Afrikaans[2] for education a rallying point for Afrikaner politics (Hartshorne, 1995: 308–09).

When the Afrikaner Nationalist government came to power in 1948, it in turn used language-in-education policies to further its particular political aims. In 1953 it extended mother tongue education for African learners from the first four years to the first eight years of schooling, as part of its separatist and discriminatory Bantu Education[3] package. Although this was consistent with the recommendations of the 1953 UNESCO report supporting the use of mother tongue for initial education, the purpose of the apartheid[4] government was political rather than educational – to separate and suppress African education (Heugh, 1995: 42). This aim was made perfectly clear by H.F. Verwoerd, Minister of Native Affairs in 1953 and later Minister of Bantu Education:

> When I have control over native education, I will reform it so that natives will be taught from childhood that equality with Europeans is not for them. (Christie, 1991: 12)

Consequently, current perceptions of mother-tongue education are tainted by this link to the apartheid education system of the past.

In 1976, it was the same government's attempts to impose Afrikaans as the medium of instruction for 50% of school subjects in African secondary schools, that sparked the Soweto student uprising. This quickly spread throughout the country, and marked the beginning of two decades of political resistance, much of it based in schools. These protests against Afrikaans and in favour of English as a medium of instruction, together with the use of English as the lingua franca for resistance politics by the educated African elite, served to establish English as the language of political liberation (Heugh, 1995: 342) as has been the case in other parts of anglophone Africa[5] (Pennycook, 1994: 262).

From 1979 until the introduction of the new Language-in-Education Policy in 1997 (Department of Education, 1997a), the language-in-education policy for African learners (approximately 80% of the population) reverted to mother tongue instruction until Grade 4 with a switch to English-medium instruction in Grade 5. By contrast, the majority of white and 'coloured' learners learned though the medium of their mother tongues, English or Afrikaans – the two official languages until 1996. Thus, unequal access to the curriculum though language combined with vast inequalities in resourcing and teacher-training requirements[6] to create a system of education for African learners that was grossly inferior to that of their white and even that of their 'coloured'[7] counterparts.

The unbanning of the ANC[8] in January 1990 and the moves towards the first democratic elections in 1994 marked a break with the colonial and apartheid past and the re-entry of South Africa into the global mainstream after two decades of political and economic isolation. The new government set about dismantling apartheid institutions and embarked on an ambitious programme of political, economic and social transformation aimed at redressing the injustices and inequalities of the apartheid past and preparing the country for active participation in the global economy. This included the transformation of education and the development of a clutch of policies to direct that process, including a new outcomes-based curriculum: Curriculum 2005 (Department of Education, 1997b, c, d), and a new Language-in-Education Policy – both introduced in 1997. However, there is a tension between the government's stated goals of equity, redress, democracy, access and participation on the one hand, and that of participation in the global marketplace on the other. Economic stringency resulting from policies of structural adjustment has meant reduced funding for social spending. This, combined with a range of factors including administrative inexperience in the provincial governments responsible for policy implementation, has resulted in real problems of policy delivery (Kgobe, 1999).

The principles of redress and social justice extend to the language provisions in the Constitution (1996), which recognises eleven official languages: nine indigenous 'previously marginalised' languages in addition to English and Afrikaans, the two former official languages (see Table 9.1).

However, thus far these provisions have not had the effect of boosting the role of indigenous languages in public affairs. Instead, the dominance

Table 9.1 Official languages in South Africa

Official languages	Home language speakers
Zulu	22.9%
Xhosa	17.9%
Afrikaans	14.4%
Sepdi	9.2%
English	8.6%
Setswana	8.2%
SeSotho	7.7%
Xitsonga	4.4%
SiSwati	2.5%
Tshivenda	2.2%
IsiNdebele	1.5%
Other	0.6%

Source: Statistics South Africa (Census 1996), 2000

of English has increased at the cost of Afrikaans, despite the fact that it is the home language of less than 9% of the population. Wright (2002: 8) notes the decline in the demand for African language courses at universities and that 'the central fact of the South African linguistic ecology is the magnetic pull of the formal economy' where English has the greatest economic value at a national level. It has been suggested that the constitutional recognition of eleven official languages in South Africa is largely 'intended and perceived as a symbolic statement and that for instrumental purposes, English remains the dominant language in South Africa' (McLean & McCormick 1996: 329 cited in Mazrui, 2002: 269).

These tensions between the post-apartheid policies of redress for indigenous languages and the pull of the market economy and the global dominance of English are played out in the Language-in-Education Policy, in its formulation and implementation.

In addition to the political-historical context, the Language-in-Education Policy needs to be considered in relation to the linguistic contexts of schools.

Linguistic Contexts of Schools

The different linguistic profiles of schools reflect their apartheid origins as well as the post-1990 political changes and demographic shifts. Schools that were previously reserved for white or 'coloured' or Indian learners and teachers, with either English or Afrikaans (usually the learners' home language) as the medium of instruction, have now become racially mixed, frequently with learners from a range of different home language backgrounds, while the teachers' linguistic and racial profiles have remained largely unchanged (Macfarlane, 2003). These schools have been able to preserve their relatively privileged positions by charging school fees to supplement state teacher quotas and provision of resources. However they provide for a minority of approximately 20% of learners in South Africa.

The majority of learners in South Africa (approximately 80%) are in township and rural schools that were previously reserved for African learners and have remained racially and linguistically unchanged. The movement of learners has been away from these poorly resourced schools to better-resourced formerly white, 'coloured' or Indian schools, by parents who can afford the higher fees. Therefore the old divisions in schooling along racial lines are increasingly being replaced by class stratifications, and historic inequalities in the material conditions at schools remain unchanged as many working class or unemployed[9] parents cannot afford anything but minimal school fees.

In most parts of South Africa, particularly in rural areas, African schools[10] are relatively homogenous, linguistically as well as racially, with teachers and learners sharing a common home language (Heugh, 2002: 185). In the vast majority of such schools, English is the official language of learning and teaching (LoLT) from at least the beginning of the 4th grade – the start of the Intermediate Phase in Curriculum 2005. This is despite the fact that there are very limited opportunities for learners to acquire English outside the classroom. By contrast, in metropolitan areas such as around Johannesburg in the centre of the country, African schools reflect the mix of indigenous home languages in their communities and so have tended to introduce English medium instruction even earlier, from Grade 1, to accommodate the wide range of home languages in the classroom.

Research confirms that learners in African schools use their home language in family and community contexts (PANSALB, 2000; Probyn *et al.*, 2002; Strauss, 1999: 22) In urban townships, an additional informal language of broader communication is 'tsotsitaal'[11] – a mixture of indigenous languages and Afrikaans and English – and in fact many urban township learners do not have a good command of the formal variety of their home language that is taught in schools. Demographics limit opportunities for interaction with mother tongue speakers of English and although learners may have some exposure to oral English through television and popular music, indications are that there are few reading materials at home. In a national survey of Grade 4 learners[12] (where the average performance by learners on the literacy task was only 48%), only 10% of parents indicated they bought newspapers and magazines and more than 50% indicated they had access to fewer than 10 books (Strauss, 1999: 25). There is also a shortage of reading material in schools, as 83% of schools have no libraries (Bot & Shindler, 1997: 80–81) and there are chronic shortages of textbooks. In addition, 57% of learners are in rural schools (Gordon, 1999: 41), where opportunities for the informal acquisition of English are even further reduced.

Research studies indicate that in African schools, the lingua franca for informal interaction among teachers and learners outside the classroom tends to be in their common home language (Probyn *et al.*, 2002). Inside the classroom, there are suggestions that teachers' limited proficiency in English may reduce opportunities for language development, and research indicates that relatively little reading and writing takes place during lessons (Taylor & Vinjevold, 1999: 151–53). Yet it is proficiency in reading and writing in English, where it is the medium of teaching and learning, that is a necessary condition for learners' academic success. In a number of research studies teachers referred to the language medium as posing a problem for learners' understanding and academic success (NCCRD, 2000;

Probyn, 1995, 2001; Strauss, 1999). Thus it is not surprising that the TIMMS-R[13] study found:

> The majority of South African pupils cannot communicate their scientific conclusions in the languages used for the test (i.e. English and Afrikaans which were the medium of instruction and are the languages currently used for matriculation examinations). In particular, pupils who study mathematics and science in their second language tend to have difficulty articulating their answers to open-ended questions and apparently had trouble comprehending several of the questions. (Howie, 2001)

These problems are not unique to South Africa, as Rubagumya (1994: 1) notes with regard to the medium of instruction in different countries in Africa that it 'acts to varying degrees as a barrier to effective learning'.

The Language-in-Education Policy clearly sets out to address some of the problems outlined.

Language-in-Education Policy (LiEP)

The Language-in-Education Policy (LiEP) (1997) has been informed by three main discourses. Like other education polices, it is informed by the competing discourses of transformation and the market economy – in this case, creating a tension between redress and equality for indigenous languages on the one hand, and the instrumental need to acquire English for participation in national and global affairs on the other.

In addition, it is informed by the academic discourse of Second Language Acquisition theory, largely through the ANC-led National Education Policy Initiative (NEPI, 1992) and through the advocacy of non-governmental organisations such as the Project for the Study of Alternative Education in South Africa (PRAESA). These initiatives have drawn on research evidence from South African classrooms, notably that of Macdonald (1990), who found that Grade 5 learners in African schools were not able to engage with the curriculum effectively through the medium of English, after learning English as a subject for four years. They have also drawn on notions of 'additive' and 'subtractive' bilingualism, advocating an increased use of learners' home languages as media of instruction as the approach most likely to promote cognitive development and improved L2 learning (Heugh, 1995; Luckett, 1995). Although these ideas are current in academic circles, they have not been widely communicated and understood by parents and teachers or even politicians. Some commentators, such as Makoni (1994), have cautioned against a simplistic adoption of theories of 'additive and 'subtractive' bilingualism, which were developed in linguistic contexts in Europe and North America – very different to the South African linguistic context.

The LiEP thus reflects the constitutional commitment to the redress of historically disadvantaged indigenous languages. It values cultural diversity, and multilingualism as a means to intercultural communication and nation-building, and national and international communication. It recognises individual language rights and the right for learners to be taught in their home language, and aims to provide learners with equitable access to the education system. To this end it advocates polices that will promote additive multilingualism, which it claims are most supportive of general conceptual growth among learners, with the underlying principle of maintaining home languages while 'providing access to and effective acquisition of additional languages' (DoE, 1997a).

The responsibility for developing school language policies is devolved to School Governing Bodies (SGBs), made up of teacher, parent and learner representatives. Each SGB has to stipulate how it will promote multilingualism 'through using more than one language for learning and teaching and/or by offering additional languages as subjects and/or applying special immersion or maintenance programmes' (DoE, 1997a: 8). In addition, Curriculum 2005 requires that learners take their home language and at least one other official language (one of which must be the LoLT) as subjects from Grade 1 through to Grade 12 – a continuation of language provisions in the previous curriculum. Thus the controversial aspect of the LiEP is not the requirement that learners should learn more than one language – bilingualism is the norm in the country – but rather the proposal that this should be achieved through using more than one language as LoLT, and that indigenous languages should be used as LoLT beyond the Foundation Phase. However, the LiEP stops short of a directive for bilingual languages of learning and teaching, and the proviso that any policy should be subject to 'practicability', leaves the way open for schools to maintain the status quo by teaching through the medium of English and offering other languages as subjects, particularly where introducing further languages as subjects or media of instruction would involve additional teaching staff (NCCRD, 2000). This proviso appears to reflect a certain lack of conviction or political will on the part of some policy-makers, and the kinds of compromises made.

Responses to the Language-in-Education Policy

A view of policy as a dynamic process, which is contested and changing as it interacts with different role players at different stages and levels in the education system (Ball, 1994; Dale, 1992; Kgobe, 1999), frames the discussion on responses to the LiEP.

Formal language policies

Evidence from a number of small-scale research studies indicates that in fact the majority of schools have not drawn up formal school language policies in line with the required processes and policy recommendations of the Language-in-Education Policy (Brown, 1998; NCCRD, 2000; Probyn *et al.*, 2002; Taylor & Vinjevold, 1999). These studies suggest a number of reasons for this, which have to do with timing, capacity, and linguistic attitudes and contexts.

Ball (1994: 19) notes that policies are introduced into contexts where other policies are in circulation, and that the enactment of one may inhibit or contradict or influence the possibility of enactment of others. The timing of the launch of the LiEP in 1997 coincided with and was overshadowed by the introduction of Curriculum 2005. The lack of capacity on the part of the provincial education departments responsible for policy dissemination and implementation contributed to poor communication of the LiEP. Consequently, many teachers and principals said in interviews that they had not received information about the LiEP, or they confused it with the constitutional recognition of eleven official languages, or the Languages, Literacy and Communication learning area in Curriculum 2005.

The requirement in the LiEP for SGBs to draw up school language policies provides for democratic participation and responsiveness to local contexts. However, research evidence indicates that, in the majority of schools, School Governing Bodies are not functioning effectively, particularly in communities where the parent bodies are poor and illiterate[14] (NCCRD, 2000; Probyn *et al.*, 2002). In addition, the lack of resources in many schools constrains their capacity for effective engagement with new policies. The School Register of Needs Survey conducted in 1996 revealed that many schools lacked basic facilities: for example 57% of schools had no electricity and 59% had no telephones (Bot, 2001). Although there has been a steady improvement in provision since then,[15] lack of basic resources remains a limiting factor in policy development by SGBs.

Teacher morale has been sapped by a far-reaching process of redeployment, introduced in 1997 as part of the process of transformation in education and in order to equalise spending across the previously segregated public school sectors. This process, which was contested by teachers who did not wish to be moved away from their families and homes to rural areas, was only concluded in 2002, and has had a destabilising effect on schools, with negative consequences for teachers' possible engagement with new policies (NCCRD, 2000). What energy and enthusi-asm teachers were able to muster under the circumstances were absorbed by the challenges of getting to grips with a radically changed national curriculum.

Informal school language policies

Despite the lack of formal language policies in schools in line with the Language-in-Education Policy, all schools have informal or generally understood language policies that 'exist in the tacit practices of their teachers and administrators, and can be inferred from their interactions with students' (Corson, 1999: 3).

Where changes have been made in response to changing demographics and other contextual factors, these have generally been to extend the use of English as the medium of instruction, contrary to the recommendations of the LiEP (NCCRD, 2000; Vinjevold, 1999). Formerly white, 'coloured' or Indian schools have tended to accommodate African learners through introducing African languages as subjects, and providing English medium classes for African learners when the main language of the school is Afrikaans. Few of these schools embraced the opportunity for English speaking learners to learn an African language. They have tended to be assimilationist, with little commitment to multilingualism, and with both African language and Afrikaans learners shifting towards English (De Klerk, 2002; NCCRD, 2000; Probyn *et al.*, 2002).

In these multilingual schools, it would appear that there is a fairly close fit between intended language policy (formal or informal) and enacted language policy. Teachers are very often not proficient in the home languages of African learners and so do not have recourse to those languages when there is a communication breakdown. Therefore, for better or worse, the language medium is adhered to. African learners are immersed in an English only environment in the classroom and interact with English first-language speakers and so generally acquire the English-language skills necessary to cope. However, the relatively small number of home-language speakers of English (8.6%) does not make this a viable model for English acquisition nationally (De Klerk, 2000), and such schools at present cater mainly for a middle-class elite of African learners.

In African schools indications are that where changes to the language policy have been made, they have generally been to introduce English as LoLT earlier (NCCRD, 2000; Probyn *et al.*, 2002; Taylor and Vinjevold, 1999) and the recommendations of the LiEP to use the learners' home language as the medium of instruction for as long as possible, in order to promote 'additive bilingualism', have largely been ignored.

However, in such schools, the language proficiency of the learners moulds the classroom practice of the teachers (Macdonald, 1990: 44) and the linguistic constraints are such that there is frequently a breakdown between the intended and the enacted language policy.

Teachers claim that learners do not understand the textbooks (Langhan, 1993: 94). This is hardly surprising, considering that Macdonald found that learners who had been learning English as a second language for four years would have, at best, an English vocabulary of 800 words whereas the vocabulary requirements for the Grade 5 textbooks when they switched to English medium instruction were at least 5000 words (Macdonald & Burroughs, 1991). As a result, it is common practice for teachers to provide notes for learners to learn off by heart and reproduce for tests and exams (Langhan, 1993; Probyn, 1995), thus locking learners into dependency on the teacher and limiting opportunities for independent reading and learning.

Teachers have noted that teaching and learning through the medium of a poorly-acquired additional language is time consuming, and as a result they frequently do not complete the syllabus. In addition, it is stressful for learners as well as teachers, who feel helpless in the face of such problems. It has been suggested that learners may feel alienated from the subject content when it cannot be expressed in their own language because the corpus has not been developed to express subject specific terminology (Probyn, 2001).

In most cases teachers share or at least can communicate in the learners' home language (Heugh, 2002: 185). Thus the most common strategy used by teachers is that of code-switching to the learners' home language for a range of communicative, affective and management purposes:

- to communicate aspects of the lesson content, for example new concepts and vocabulary;
- to draw learners' attention to a new idea or word;
- to clarify a difficult English grammatical construction (for example the sentence 'I want you to compare the brightness of the bulbs now with the brightness of the bulbs before' is translated for clarity);
- as an attention check (for example, using a home language question tag);
- to encourage learners to participate in classroom discussion;
- to create a relaxed atmosphere in the classroom;
- when joking to relieve the stress of learning though a second language;

- when relating aspects of the lesson to the learners' own lives and contexts;
- to appropriate unfamiliar terminology by adding home language prefixes to English words (for example, using the Xhosa prefix 'i-' as in i-battery or i-cell);
- for classroom management and discipline.

Small-scale research studies have shown that there is a wide range of practice in terms of teachers' code-switching, and how much of the learners' home language is actually used by the teachers in class. Some teachers conduct the lesson entirely in the learners' home language with the only English being chunks of text read from the textbook, whereas others stick to English as far as possible and use the learners' home language, as a resource to scaffold understanding (Probyn, 2001; 2002). However, research indicates that many teachers regard code-switching as illicit, a lack of proficiency in the LoLT, rather than as a valid linguistic strategy (Adendorff , 1996; NEPI: 1992: 49; Setati *et al.*, 2002). A teacher referred to 'smuggling the vernacular into the classroom' (Probyn, 2001), and several teachers participating in a research project admitted to using far less of the learners' home language in lessons when they were being observed (Probyn, 2002). These attitudes seem to stem from teachers' training, where it was assumed that tuition would be in English and no concessions were made for learners' lack of proficiency.

The new outcomes-based curriculum advocates a learner-centred approach with a strong emphasis on group work. Research indicates that learners use their home language in group discussions but generally are required to report back to the class in English. As the writing in preparation for reporting back is usually done by one learner per group, as is the oral reporting back, opportunities for developing English skills are not always widely shared.

There appears to be a wide range of practice regarding language use for teacher-led question-and-answer sessions – in some cases teachers insist learners attempt to use English, but others allow learners to use their home language, to encourage their participation, or when learners find it difficult to express their ideas in English. However, it appears that generally the language spoken by learners at school, both outside and inside the classroom, is mainly their home language, whereas the language of reading and writing and assessment is English (Probyn, 1995, 2002; Probyn *et al.*, 2002), with many learners experiencing problems in bridging the gap between the two modes and few resources available to support literacy development.

Despite all these difficulties of teaching and learning in English in African schools, and the apparent gap between language policy intentions and classroom practice, in several small scale research studies all the teachers and the majority of learners still preferred that the language medium should remain English (Barkhuizen, 2001; NCCRD, 2000; Probyn, 1995, 2001, 2002; Probyn *et al.*, 2002).

Opting for English Medium or 'the Necessity of Limited Options'

Given the difficulties described, it may appear contradictory that African schools should prefer to stick to English medium of instruction, if only in name, and ignore the recommendations of the LiEP for increased use of the learners' home language for teaching and learning. The same research studies and one by De Klerk (2000) revealed a cluster of perceptions and attitudes on the part of parents, teachers and learners that underpin such choices. As the NCCRD report notes:

> Language attitudes have played a significant role in relation to the Language-in-Education Policy. . . . The attitudes of teachers and learners, as well as of parents, seem to have a strong impact on the choice of language and language practices in schools. (NCCRD, 2000: 49)

The reality is that, as in many parts of anglophone Africa, 'English has become the language of power and prestige . . . thus acting as a crucial gate-keeper to social and economic progress' (Pennycook, 1994: 13). Thus a strongly expressed view was the need for learners to acquire English for instrumental purposes: for access to the formal economy. In the words of a teacher, 'English puts bread on the table' (Probyn *et al.*, 2002). In addition, the perception is that English is a lingua franca within the country and internationally, with the assumption that the onus is on non-English speakers to learn English rather than for English speakers to learn other languages. English is perceived to be the language of education and its historic role as such appears to be hardly questioned. As Pennycook notes:

> As English spread into Africa through trade, missionary work and education, it developed close ties with religion, intellectual work and politics. As the definition of what it meant to be 'educated' came to be seen increasingly in terms of Western education, and, therefore, in terms of ability in English . . . , speaking English and being an intellectual came to be almost synonymous. (Pennycook, 1994: 261)

Coupled with these attitudes is the perception that the instrumental need to acquire English is best served by a pedagogy of 'time on task' or 'maximum exposure'. The theory underpinning the notion of 'additive multilingualism' – that learners should strongly maintain their home language by using it as the LoLT and learn additional languages as subjects, and that time spent developing academic language proficiency in their home language will impact positively on the development of their proficiency in additional languages – is somewhat counter-intuitive, not widely understood and thus not seriously considered (NEPI, 1992). Neither is the apparent paradox that the language that learners so desperately desire for access to jobs, further education and upward social mobility in fact in many cases limits their opportunities for academic success.

As mentioned before, the notion of the use of indigenous languages for learning and linguistically homogenous schools is fatally tainted by its link with apartheid education, despite the fact that this is indeed the reality for the majority of African learners outside metropolitan areas. Another argument frequently offered in favour of English, particularly by teachers, is that indigenous languages do not have the necessary subject terminology. However, in South Africa there is a very obvious precedent of corpus planning that enabled the necessary subject terminology to be developed for Afrikaans in order for it to be used as a LoLT to tertiary level, and current constraints have more to do with resources and political will.

Although the research studies indicated that parents, teachers and learners opted overwhelmingly for English as their preferred LoLT, the same studies revealed that the respondents' valued their home language highly for cultural expression and for communication at home and in their communities. They expressed concern that the widespread use of English might pose a threat to their language and culture and therefore felt strongly that their home language should be studied as a subject at school (Barkhuizen, 2001; De Klerk, 2000; Probyn, 1995, 2002).

Certain practical contextual issues have also affected decisions regarding languages in schools and have contributed to the trend to introduce English as a LoLT earlier. Teachers interviewed in township schools were of the opinion that the reason parents were moving their children to formerly white and 'coloured' schools was that they wanted them to be educated in English (Probyn *et al.*, 2002; Vinjevold, 1999). In fact, as research has indicated (De Klerk, 2000), the LoLT was an important consideration for such parents but so were better resources and an ordered learning environment. Nevertheless, township teachers felt it was important to introduce English as a LoLT earlier in order to counter the haemorrhage of learners from their schools and the possibility of learner numbers falling so low that teachers would lose jobs. In addition, it would be very difficult for any one school to introduce a language policy that deviated materially from those in the area, as policies would need to be aligned to ensure coherence in the learners' progress through the system.

Textbooks also play an important role in constraining language choices. The new curriculum has grouped grades into broad three-year phases. Publishers have produced textbooks in indigenous languages for the first three years, for the Foundation Phase. However, all textbooks for the next 'Intermediate Phase' are in English, and this has contributed to an earlier introduction of English as the medium of instruction in Grade 4 rather than in Grade 5, as was previously the norm. Publishers, on the other hand, are unlikely to extend their production of learning materials in indigenous languages beyond the Foundation Phase unless they are guaranteed a market and this would in turn require a more interventionist approach from government.

Thus it appears that strongly-held perceptions and attitudes on the part of those responsible for making decisions about school language policies combine with practical contextual conditions in schools to mitigate against take-up of the recommendations of the LiEP – a choice resulting from what Ndebele (1987) describes as 'a necessity of limited options'.

Looking Forward

Academic debates about the Language-in-Education Policy, and in particular the language of learning and teaching, continue to be hotly contested between those advocating an increased role for home languages as media of instruction (see for example Heugh, 2002) and those who pragmatically opt for English (see Vinjevold, 1999).

The aims in the LiEP of equity, access to the curriculum, redress for previously marginalised languages and national multilingualism as a means to reconciliation and nation-building, appear to have come up against entrenched neocolonial perceptions of English as the language of education, as well as the realities of globalisation – its impact on economic policies and consequent reduced resources for policy implementation, and the perceived need for learners to access English as the language of global social, political and economic power. These factors combine to maintain the hegemony of English in the curriculum and appear to override the classroom difficulties of teaching through the medium of English for the majority of learners in African schools and the consequent breakdown between policy and practice. In formerly white, 'coloured' and Indian schools, it appears that the support for previously marginalised languages and the requirement to promote multilingualism is not taken seriously, and instead African-language speakers are assimilated into an English ethos.

The much-publicised TIMSS-R results and the finding that performance in mathematics, science and technology – widely regarded as essential for economic success in the global marketplace – is negatively affected by the language medium, has provided a much-needed wake-up call to the problems of language and learning for the majority of teachers and learners. This appears to have prompted several government initiatives to address problems in schools concerning the language medium, including a programme intended to address the lack of implementation of the LiEP (DoE, 2002b). Although this retains the long term aim of promoting indigenous languages as languages of learning and teaching, there is an apparent acceptance that in the short term English is likely to remain the language medium of choice after the Foundation Phase (Grades 1–3), and so efforts are being focused on improving the English-language skills of teachers and learners.

Given the current scenario, it seems that even if attempts to extend the use of indigenous languages as languages of learning and teaching in a 50/50 bilingual system succeed, English is likely to be retained as the LoLT for part of the curriculum at least. Teachers in African schools are therefore likely to continue to be faced with the challenge of teaching both content and language, and, as noted by Wong Fillmore (1986), these objectives are for practical purposes, in conflict. She suggests that it is possible to accomplish both goals at the same time, but in order to do so the competition between these two objectives needs to be recognised and resolved. The majority of teachers in South Africa have received no training or support in this regard and this is an issue that needs urgent attention. There is much that could be learned from the skilled practice of some experienced teachers in terms of their use of the learners' home language as a resource and a bridge to understanding content, and as a support for the acquisition of an additional language (Probyn, 2001, 2002). Teachers' code-switching skills need to be recognised as legitimate classroom strategies, and to be woven into effective classroom practice that plans for the strategic and coherent use of both the learners' home language and the LoLT.

It appears that the capacity of School Governing Bodies to develop policy has been seriously overestimated by policy-makers. The Minister of Education has acknowledged that the voluntary approach that allowed parents and SGBs to decide on the language medium had 'not really worked on the ground' and noted that some parents chose English for their children 'irrespective of their children's competencies or the value of the maintenance of the home language and culture' (Lewis, 2001: 9). Whether the state will be prepared to take a more directive line in deciding on appropriate school language policies remains to be seen. Jansen (2001: 286) has criticised education policies in South Africa for an over-investment in political symbolism to mark the break with apartheid, at the expense of practical considerations. If parents, teachers and learners are to be convinced of the advantages of additive bilingualism and an expanded role for indigenous languages as media of instruction, a massive education programme will be needed to popularise the pedagogical advantages and theoretical underpinnings. As noted by the PEI Report (Vinjevold, 1999: 217), there is a need for systematic, longitudinal research into various additive bilingual models, particularly in the context of African schools, to find what works best for content-learning and language acquisition. But school communities are unlikely to be convinced of the value of indigenous languages over English for learning while only lip service is paid to increasing the status of indigenous languages politically and economically.

For the majority of learners like Mzuvumile, the daily struggle to learn through the medium of an unfamiliar language continues. It contributes to poor pass rates in African schools and is a major source of inequality and a block to equitable access to the curriculum. Such learners and their teachers are caught at the intersection of local and classroom linguistic realities on the one hand, and neocolonial attitudes and the pressures of globalisation combining to maintain the power of English on the other. If school language policies are to mean anything to the majority of teachers and learners in classrooms, they will need to take into account these tensions and contradictions, to confront linguistic realities and to balance these carefully against dominant neocolonial attitudes and the demands of globalisation.

Notes
1. Descendants of Dutch colonists who arrived in South Africa in 1652.
2. An indigenous language derived from Dutch.
3. Bantu Education refers to the separate and deliberately inferior system of education for Africans introduced by the Nationalist government.
4. 'Apartheid' was the system of government based on legislated racial segregation in every aspect of social, economic and political life, with privileges reserved for 'whites'.
5. Former British colonies in Africa include South Africa, Tanzania, Malawi, Kenya, Uganda, Zimbabwe, Nigeria, Ghana.
6. There were separate and unequal training institutions and qualification requirements for teachers: for example, an African teacher could teach at an African secondary school with a matric (school-leaving qualification) and two years' training at a teacher-training college, whereas a white teacher needed a university degree and a year's post-graduate teaching diploma. There were separate schools and education departments and educational provision was on the basis of race. For example, in 1984 the per capita expenditure on white students was R1926 and for African students R294. By 1994 the gap had reduced, but the spending on students in African schools was still only 44% of that on students in formerly white schools (SAIRR, 1995).

7. 'Coloured' is a term used as a racial classification under apartheid and refers to people of mixed racial ancestry.
8. African National Congress – the liberation movement that was banned for 30 years and led the first democratically elected government in 1994.
9. Unemployment levels in South Africa are currently estimated at an average of 34%, although in some rural areas they are as high as 82% (Bot *et al.*, 2000)
10. In this chapter, 'African' schools refers for convenience to schools that were previously reserved for African learners in township and rural areas, and which now, although legally non-racial, for reasons of demographics and economics, remain racially homogenous.
11. 'Tsotsitaal' – literally 'gangster language'.
12. The Monitoring Learning Achievement (MLA) survey (Strauss, 1999) tested the literacy, numeracy and life skills proficiency of Grade 4 learners in 400 schools in all nine provinces and collected baseline indicators of the learners' socioeconomic backgrounds.
13. Third International Mathematics and Science Study-Repeat was an international survey of the mathematics and science proficiency of Grade 8 learners. South African learners came last out of the 38 participating countries (Howie, 2001).
14. 41% of the adult population (20 years and older) is considered illiterate (with seven years of schooling or less) (Bot *et al.*, 2000).
15. The 2000 School Register of Needs update showed for example a 12% improvement in electricity provision and a 24% improvement in access to telephone communication – although this is mainly through the privately owned cell phones of teachers (DoE, 2002a).

References

Adendorff, R.D. (1996) The functions of code switching among high-school teachers and students in Kwazulu and implications for teacher education. In K.M. Bailey and D. Nunan (eds) *Voices from the Language Classroom: Qualitative Research in Second Language Education* (pp. 338–406). Cambridge: Cambridge University Press.

Ball, S.J. (1994) *Education Reform: A Critical and Post-structural Approach.* Buckingham: Open University Press.

Barkhuizen, G. (2001) *Learners' perceptions of the teaching and learning of Xhosa first language in Eastern and Western Cape high schools. Summary report.* PANSALB Occasional Papers No. 3.

Bot, M. (2001) School Register of Needs 2000: An update. *Edusource* 35, 1–5. Houghton, The Education Foundation.

Bot, M. and Shindler, J. (1997) *Baseline Study: Macro Indicators 1991–1996.* Braamfontein: Centre for Policy Development , Evaluation and Management.

Bot, M., Dove, S. and Wilson, D. (2000) *The Education Atlas of South Africa 2000.* Houghton: The Education Foundation.

Brown, D. (1998) *Educational Policy and the Choice of Language in Linguistically Complex South African Schools.* Durban: Education Policy Unit, University of Natal.

Christie, P. (1991) *The Right to Learn.* Johannesburg: Raven Press.

Corson, D. (1999) *Language Policy in Schools.* Mahwah, NJ: Lawrence Erlbaum Associates.

Dale, R. (1992) Whither the state and education policy? Recent work in Australia and New Zealand. *British Journal of Sociology in Education* 13 (3), 387–95.

De Klerk, V. (2000) To be Xhosa or not to be Xhosa . . . that is the question. *Journal of Multilingual and Multicultural Development* 21 (3), 198–215.

De Klerk, V. (2002) Part 2: The teachers speak. *Perspectives in Education* 20 (1), 15–27.

Department of National Education (1997a) *Language-in-Education Policy*. Government Gazette, Vol. 17997, No. 383. Pretoria: Department of Education.

Department of National Education (1997b) Curriculum 2005 Foundation Phase (Grade 1 –3) document.

Department of National Education (1997c) Curriculum 2005 Intermediate Phase (Grades 4 – 6) document.

Department of National Education (1997d) Curriculum 2005 Senior Phase (Grades 7 – 9) document.

Department of National Education (2002a) 'Brochure for the 2000 School Register of Needs Report.' At http://education.pwv.gov.za/Policies%20and%20Reports/2001_Report/SRN/srn.htm

Department of National Education (2002b). Unpublished position paper.

Gordon, A. (1999) Rural schools: Are the new policies bearing fruit? In J. Hofmeyr and H. Perold (eds) *Education Africa Forum*. (3rd edn) (pp. 40–45). Pinegowrie: Education Africa.

Hartshorne, K. (1995) Language policy in African education: A background to the future. In Mesthrie, R. (ed.) *Language and Social History: Studies in South African Sociolinguistics* (pp. 306–18). Cape Town: David Philip.

Heugh, K. (1995) From unequal education to the real thing. In K. Heugh, A. Siegruhn and P. Pluddermann (eds) *Multilingual Education for South Africa* (pp. 42–52). Johannesburg: Heinemann.

Heugh, K. (2002) The case against bilingual and multilingual education in South Africa: Laying bare the myths. *Perspectives in Education* 20 (1), 171–96.

Howie, S.J. (2001) *Mathematics and Science Performance in Grade 8 in South Africa 1998/1999*. Pretoria: Human Sciences Research Council.

Jansen, J. (2001) Explaining non-change in education reform after apartheid: Political symbolism and the problem of policy implementation. In Y. Sayed and J. Jansen (eds) *Implementing Education Policies: The South African Experience* (pp. 271–92). Cape Town: University of Cape Town Press.

Kgobe, P. (1999) Monitoring and evaluating policy implementation and transformation: An overview of the project. Paper given at Education 2000 Plus Conference, August 1999.

Langhan, D. P. (1993) *The Textbook as a Source of Difficulty in Teaching and Learning*. Pretoria: HSRC Publishers.

Lewis, C. (2001) Provincialisation of education: A review (January–June 2001). *Edusource* 34, 1–20. Houghton: The Education Foundation.

Luckett, K. (1995) National additive multilingualism: Towards a language plan for South African education. In K. Heugh, A. Siegruhn and P. Pluddermann (eds) *Multilingual Education for South Africa* (pp. 73–78). Johannesburg: Heinemann.

Macdonald, C.A. (1990) *English Language Skills Evaluation: A Final Report of the Threshold Project*. Pretoria: Human Sciences Research Council.

Macdonald, C. and Burroughs, E. (1991) *Eager to Talk and Learn and Think: Bilingual Primary Education in South Africa*. Cape Town: Maskew Miller Longman.

Macfarlane, D. (2003) Schools not yet melting pots. *Mail and Guardian*, May 2–8 2003.

Makoni, S.B. (1994) Mother-tongue education: A literature review. *ELTIC Reporter* 18 (1&2), 18–26.

Mazrui, A.A. (2002) The English language in African education. In J.W.Tollefson (ed.) *Language Policies in Education: Critical Issues.* New Jersey: Lawrence Erlbaum Associates, Publishers.

McLean, D. and McCormick, K. (1996) English in South Africa: 1940–1996. In J.A. Fishman, A.D. Conrad and A. Rubal-Lopez (eds) *Post-Imperial English: Status Change in Former British and American Colonies, 1940–1990* (pp. 307–37). Berlin: Mouton de Gruyter.

National Centre for Curriculum Research and Development (2000) *Language in the classroom: Towards a framework for intervention.* Research report. Pretoria: Department of Education.

National Education Policy Investigation (1992) *Language.* Cape Town: Oxford University Press/National Education Co-ordinating Committee.

Ndebele, N. (1987) The English language and social change in South Africa. English *Academy Review* 4, 1–16.

PANSALB (2000) *Language Use and Language Interaction in South Africa: A Sociolinguistic Survey.* Pretoria, PANSALB.

Pennycook, A. (1994) *The Cultural Politics of English as an International Language.* London: Longman.

Probyn, M.J. (1995) Exploring a myth. Unpublished paper, submitted in part-requirement for BEd degree, University of Cape Town.

Probyn, M.J. (2001) Teachers' voices: Teachers' reflections on learning and teaching through the medium of English as a second language. *International Journal of Bilingual Education and Bilingualism* 4 (4), 249–66.

Probyn, M.J., Murray, S., Botha, L., Botya, P., Brooks M. and Westphal, V. (2002) Minding the gaps – An investigation into language policy and practice in four Eastern Cape districts. *Perspectives in Education* 20 (1), 29–46.

Probyn, M.J. (2002) Language and learning in some Eastern Cape science classrooms. Paper presented at the SAALA/LSSA Conference. Pietermaritzburg, 8–10 July 2002.

Rubagumya, C. (1994) Introduction. In C. Rubagumya (ed.) *Teaching and Researching Language in African Classrooms* (pp.1–5). Clevedon: Multilingual Matters.

SAIRR (1995) *Race Relations Survey 1994/95.* Johannesburg: South African Institute of Race Relations.

Setati, M., Adler, J., Reed, Y. and Bapoo, A. (2002) Code-switching and other language practices in mathematics, science and English language classrooms in South Africa. In J. Adler and Y. Reed (eds) *Challenges of Teacher Development: An Investigation of Take-up in South Africa* (pp. 73–93). Pretoria: Schaik Publishers.

Statistics South Africa (2000) *Stats in Brief.* Pretoria: Statistics South Africa.

Strauss, J.P. (Nov 1999) *Monitoring Learning Achievement (MLA) Project.* Research Institute for Education Planning, University of Orange Free State. Online www.education.pwv.gov.za

Taylor, N. and Vinjevold, P. (1999) Teaching and learning in South African schools. In N. Taylor and P. Vinjevold (eds) *Getting Learning Right: Report of the President's Education Initiative Research Project* (pp. 131–62). Witwatersrand: The Joint EducationTrust.

Vinjevold, P. (1999) Language issues in South African classrooms. In N. Taylor and P. Vinjevold (eds) *Getting Learning Right: Report of the President's Education Initiative Research Project* (pp. 205–26). Witwatersrand: The Joint Education Trust.

Wong Fillmore, L. with Valadez, C. (1986) Teaching bilingual learners. In M.C. Wittrock (ed.) *Handbook of Research on Teaching* (pp. 648–85). New York: Macmillan.

Wright, L. (2002) Mother tongue, other tongue: Law, learning and literature. Keynote address presented at the 14th Conference of the English Academy of Southern Africa. Pretoria, 4–6 April 2002.

Chapter 10

Language-in-Education Policies and Practices in Africa with a Special Focus on Tanzania and South Africa – Insights from Research in Progress

BIRGIT BROCK-UTNE

Introduction

> It has always been felt by African educationists that the African child's major learning problem is linguistic. Instruction is given in a language that is not normally used in his immediate environment, a language which neither the learner nor the teacher understands and uses well enough. (Obanya, 1980: 88)

If the African child's major learning problem is linguistic, then all the attention of African policy-makers and aid to the education sector from donors should be devoted to a strengthening of the African languages as languages of instruction, especially in basic education. My own experience after having taught in Africa for four years and having visited hundreds of classrooms both in east and west Africa is that Obanya is completely right; the African child's major learning problem *is* linguistic. Children are being stamped as dumb when they just lack knowledge of the language used in instruction, a language they often hardly hear and seldom use outside the classroom. The aim of 'education for all' becomes a completely empty concept if the linguistic environment of the basic learners is not taken into account (Brock-Utne, 2000, 2001; Klaus, 2001).

Yet there is scarcely one other sociocultural topic you can start discussing with Africans that leads to such heated debates and stirs up so many emotions as the language of instruction in African schools. It is difficult to discuss this topic as a strictly educational question, phrased perhaps as follows: 'through which medium of instruction would children learn subject matter best?'; 'if the aim is to master a 'world' language, would it be better to have that language as a language of instruction at the earliest time possible or to develop the vernacular or a commonly spoken national language further first?'; or 'what does it mean for the learning potential, the development of self-respect and identity, that the language one normally communicates in does not seem to be deemed fit for a language of instruction in school?'

When it comes to the choice of language of instruction in African schools, sociocultural politics, economic interests, sociolinguistics and education are so closely interrelated that it is difficult to sort out the arguments. It is an area with strong donor pressure, mostly from the former colonial masters, who want to retain and strengthen their own languages. There are strong economic interests from publishing companies overseas, who see that they will have easier access to the African textbook market when the European languages are used. There are also faulty, but widely held, beliefs among lay people when it comes to the language of instruction. In a five-year research project, LOITASA[1] (Language of Instruction in Tanzania and South Africa), which I am conducting together with partners in Tanzania and South Africa, we come across many of these beliefs.

Last year I was sitting for several hours at the back of a classroom in a secondary school in Tanzania. I observed students who did not understand what the teacher was saying when he spoke English, who had to ask each other what the teacher said and sometimes ask the teacher to express himself in Kiswahili, a language they all commanded very well. When I spoke in Kiswahili to one of these students afterwards and mentioned that I had noticed that he did not understand the language of instruction, he admitted that my observation was correct. He did have great difficulties following the teacher, especially if the teacher did not switch to Kiswahili during the lesson when he saw that the students did not understand. I asked the student if it would not have been much better for him had the lesson been given in Kiswahili throughout. He admitted that it certainly would have been much easier. Then he would be able to understand what the teacher was saying. When I then asked him, did he not think one should change the language of instruction, he said no, he did not think so, because English was the language of technology and modernisation. English was the global language without which one could not get a good job. He had to learn English and could not see any other way than having it as a language of instruction.

We shall return to this argument. In this chapter I want to revisit and critically discuss some of the commonly heard arguments against the strengthening of the African languages as languages of instruction. Some of these arguments are promoted by Western donors and Western academics, others by Africans. One argument often heard is that there is such a multitude of languages in Africa that it would be impossible to choose which language to use. It is therefore better to retain the colonial languages. Another argument frequently heard is that it is too costly to publish textbooks in these languages. Some African parents, schoolchildren and lay public claim that children need to study in an ex-colonial language as early as possible in order to get the best possible command of that language. This is supposed to further the personal development and the earning potential of the child, and the development of his family, society and country. There is a tendency that, even in a country like Tanzania, where more than 95% of the population are fluent in the national language, Kiswahili, and where Kiswahili is the official medium of education all through primary school, the new private schools in Dar es Salaam advertise that they are English-medium primary schools. These are schools where parents who are somewhat better off send their children, and where school fees are charged. These schools are better resourced and their teachers are better paid (Rubagumya, 2003). Towards the end of the chapter I shall discuss the coping strategies African teachers use in their classrooms.

The Myth of the Many Languages of Africa

At the end of May and the beginning of June 2001 I had the pleasure of being invited to a conference to mark the creation of a centre for African languages in Bamako, Mali. I was one of just three researchers from outside Africa, all knowledgeable in African languages. The rest of the participants were sociolinguists and linguists from all over Africa, east and west, north and south. One of the main speakers was the renowned sociolinguist and sociologist Kwesi Kwaa Prah. Prah is originally from Ghana, but has for many years worked as a professor at the University of Western Cape in South Africa. He is now the Director of the Centre for Advanced Studies of African Society (CASAS) in Cape Town.

Professor Prah started his impressive keynote speech by quoting some of the Western linguists with their different estimates of the numbers of African languages. While for instance David Westley (1992) claims that at least 1400 languages are spoken in Africa in 51 countries, Barbara Grimes (1992) assesses the number of languages in Africa to be 1995.[2] He asked: What is this? Don't we know how many languages we have in Africa? Who has classified them? Who has put them into writing, for what purpose? According to what system? To what effect? He went on to say that he would now read aloud a list of African languages and he wanted everybody present to raise their hand if they heard a language mentioned by him that they could communicate comfortably in. This language did not need to be our first language, but a language we understood well and felt comfortable using. When he had read out a list of 12–15 core languages (by core language is meant clusters of mutually intelligible speech forms which in essence constitute dialects of the same language) *all* of the participants in the conference had their hands up. These core languages included Nguni; Sesotho/Setswana; Kiswahili; Dholuo; Eastern Inter-Lacustrine; Runyakitara; Somali/Rendile/ Oromo/Borana; Fulful; Mandenkan; Hausa; Yoruba; Ibo and Amharic. These languages he characterised as the first order languages of prominence. Below these, there might be about six which are not so large, in terms of speakers, but which have significant numbers of users. The work of the Centre for Advanced Studies of African Society (CASAS) over the past five years has revealed that as first, second and third language speakers about 85% of Africans speak no more than 12–15 core languages. (See, for example, Prah, 2000, 2002). This is actually fewer languages than the number of core languages spoken in the much smaller continent of Europe.

The truth is that the demographics of language and linguistic diversity in Africa are not really different from what obtains in other parts of the world. The myth of the multitude of languages seems to fit well into a description of Africa as the dark and backward continent. It is also a convenient excuse for donors backed by strong publishing interests in the West to use when they insist that one of the colonial languages has to be used as the language of instruction.

What may be different in Africa from in other parts of the world is that the identification of linguistic units in Africa tends to be loose. The identification of language communities in Africa has been approached in a way which favours the recognition of practically all dialects, and phonological variations as separate languages. When in 1995 I made a study for the Namibian Ministry of Education on the situation of the African languages after independence (Brock-Utne, 1995, 1997), to my great surprise I discovered that the two main 'languages' in the north of Namibia, Oshindonga and Oshikwanyama, are actually the same language. The reason why there are two written forms of the language has to do with rivalry between Finnish and German missionaries and later the creation of separate language committees, which suited the divide and rule policy of the apartheid government.

Roy-Campbell (1998) describes how faulty transcriptions, some arising from inaccurate associations by missionaries, occurred across the African continent, resulting in a multitude of dialects of the same language and different languages being created from what was one language. The difficulty of putting a definite figure on the number of African languages on the continent can be attributed to this process, as contention has arisen over whether certain language forms are indeed languages or dialects. Sinfree Makoni (2000) likewise writes about the crucial role of missionaries in the specification of speech forms subsequently regarded as African languages. African missionary converts played the role of laboratory assistants. They provided the vocabulary and the missionaries the orthography and the grammar. Makoni claims that the grammar books made did not aid any meaningful communication between English and Shona speakers in Zimbabwe. The phrases for translation and the vocabulary used reflected settler and missionary ideology. The phrases were useful for talking about Africans but not for engaging with them in any egalitarian communication. He further writes about the way in which different missionary stations magnified differences between dialects, obscuring the homogeneity of the real situation. To quote him: 'Missionaries were not sin-free in their creation of African vernaculars' (Makoni, 2000: 158). He concludes a chapter on the Missionary influence on African vernaculars in general and on Shona in particular with these words:

> It is generally well known that the spread of 'European languages' was one of the consequences of European imperialism. What is less well known, however, is the effect of the work of missionaries in the construction of African languages. The written African languages which they created were 'new' in many respects. (Makoni, 2000: 164)

Kwesi Kwaa Prah (2003), in a keynote speech he gave at the opening of the LOITASA project, also talked about the harm done to African languages through the missionary settlements, missionary rivalry and evangelical zeal. Missionaries without a proper understanding of the language transcribed any speech form they heard into a written language resembling the way similar sounds were transcribed in their own indigenous language. By this approach, dialects such as Cockney, Tyneside and broad Yorkshire, in Britain, could easily be made into languages in themselves. This fragmentation approach is still popular with the Summer Institute of Linguistics (SIL), a leading group in the field of rendering African languages into script, in order to translate the Bible into African languages. I agree entirely with Kwesi Kwaa Prah when he claims that the rendition of African languages into scripts for the purposes of the development of Africa cannot proceed at the same time as the fragmentation of languages that is being conducted by the SIL. In effect, the SIL is building and destroying at the same time. To quote Prah (2002: 13):

When one asks why this is the case, the reason that comes easily to the fore is that the object of such endeavours at rendering African languages into script is not in the first instance to help in the development of Africa, but rather simply to translate the Bible into African speech forms and to evangelise and convert Africans into Christians. Unless one assumes that converting Africans to Christianity represents development. All other considerations are for such purposes insignificant.

Kwesi Kwaa Prah (2002) notes that those who write about the multitude of languages in Africa have, in most instances, never looked at African societies outside the framework of colonial boundaries. It is necessary for African linguists to work across national boundaries because practically all African languages are cross-border speech forms which defy the colonially inherited borders. When the colonial powers divided up Africa between themselves in Berlin in 1884 they never considered the language borders of Africa. Working within the framework of African neocolonial borders creates many more problems than working across borders.

Prah claims that the sentimental glories of neocolonial flags and national anthems maintain the fragmentation process of African languages. For the sake of flag and so-called national identity, Kamuzu Banda of Malawi refused to accept the reality of the fact that ciNyanja and ciCerwa are the same language. Sometimes these tensions are perceptible in the same country and represent attempts to own and control linguistic turf. In Ghana, 25 years after the harmonisation of Akan to produce a unified Akan orthography, writers still persisted in using the pre-unification orthography that separated mutually intelligible dialects like Akuapim, Asante, Fanti, Akim and Brong.

The approach of the Centre for Advanced Studies of African Society (CASAS) is to organise the technical work on the harmonisation of orthography and the development of common spelling systems of African languages. When this has been successfully done, workshops are organised so that the new system can be taught to writers and teachers, who then produce materials using the new orthographies. Many such workshops have already been organised by CASAS. The target of CASAS in the short run is to complete work within the next few years on the 12–15 core languages. The logic of this work is that once this approach runs its course, it should be possible to produce materials for formal education, adult literacy and everyday media usage for large readerships, which on the economies of scale make it possible to produce and work in these languages. According to Prah (2002: 15), 'it is the empowerment of Africans with the use of their native languages, which would make the difference between whether Africa develops, or not'.

The argument about the many languages in Africa is often being used to strengthen the ex-colonial languages. The claim is made that if, for instance, the majority African language of the area were chosen as the language of instruction it would disadvantage children speaking a minority language, therefore everybody should instead use an ex-colonial language. If one looks more closely into this claim, one will often find that children from minority groups will find the African majority language much easier to use as a language of instruction than the ex-colonial language. For instance, in Zambia research carried out by Robert Serpell (1980) demonstrated that children from Bemba-speaking families showed greater communicative competence in Nyanja than in English. Likewise, children from Nyanja-speaking families showed greater communicative competence in Bemba than in English.

It is Too Expensive to Publish in African Languages

This is another argument that we often hear and which is being used to promote the ex-colonial languages and publishing companies in the West. When it comes to Africa, it certainly would be too expensive to publish textbooks all through primary and secondary school, as well as in tertiary and adult education, in between one thousand and two thousand languages, which is, as mentioned, the number some Western linguists give for the number of languages in Africa. But through inexpensive desk top publishing techniques it should be possible in Africa, as it has been in Papua New Guinea (Klaus, 2001), to have African children study through their mother-tongue in the first years of schooling. At the same time they should be taught a regional, cross-border African language which comes close to their mother tongue which they can use as the language of instruction at higher levels of learning. Through the harmonisation process that, for example, CASAS is working on it should be possible to concentrate on 12–15 languages that are understood by at least 85% of the African population and to have these languages being used as languages of instruction at the highest level of teaching. This would also mean an intellectual revival of Africa, since it is only when textbooks are published on a large scale that publishing companies have money to publish fictional and especially non-fictional books.

When economists try to figure out how much it will cost to publish textbooks in African languages, they also have to figure out how much it costs to have African children sit year after year in school, often repeating a class, without learning anything. The African continent abounds with examples of the low pass rate and high attrition rate in schools. I concur with the sociolinguist Roy-Campbell (2000: 124), who has done extensive work in Tanzania and Zimbabwe, when she writes:

> What is often ignored is the cost to the nation of the continued use of European languages which contributes to the marginalisation of the majority of the population. One cannot overstate the damage being effected upon the psyche of African children being forced to access knowledge through a language in which they lack adequate proficiency and upon the nation which produces a majority of semi-literates who are competent neither in their own language nor in the educational language.

The Camerunian sociolinguist Maurice Tadadjeu (1989), in his well-argued and interesting book *Voie Africaine*, argues for a three language model for Africa whereby everybody first learns to master his/her mother tongue, then learns a regional African language that can be used as a language of instruction in secondary and tertiary education, and then learns an international language as a subject, a foreign language.

The Ex-Colonial Languages as the Languages of Modernisation and of Science and Technology

We shall return to the argument from the secondary-school student I interviewed in Tanzania. He viewed English as a language he had to master to get anywhere in the world. In actual fact there are not many Tanzanians who need English in their daily lives, as all communication outside the classroom is either in vernacular languages or in Kiswahili. Kiswahili is the language spoken in Parliament, in the lower courts, on the radio and on television, in the banks and the post office, and in the Ministries. There are more newspapers in Kiswahili than in English and they sell much better. But let us assume that this student needs a good command of English in his future career. I shall argue here that it would be better both for his knowledge acquisition in general and for his learning of English if the normal language of instruction were Kiswahili and he learned English as a subject, as a foreign language. For the latter, the teachers would need a good command of English, know the children's first language, and have knowledge of English-teaching methodology and of language acquisition. One of the Tanzanian participants in the LOITASA project group, Martha Qorro (2002), is herself a Senior Lecturer in English in the Department of Linguistics and Foreign Languages at the University of Dar es Salaam. The reason why she is a great promoter of the use of Kiswahili as the language of instruction in Tanzanian secondary schools has to do with the fact that she, as an English teacher, has seen that children learn neither English (they learn bad and incorrect English) nor subject matter. The English language has become a barrier to knowledge.

In the English language newspaper the *Guardian* in Tanzania, the editors started a Kiswahili medium debate in the spring of 2002. In an editorial of 30 April 2002 the editor openly warned Kiswahili medium advocates. On 29th May Martha Qorro gave a substantial answer to the editor based on her own observations and research, part of which is reproduced below:

> In terms of language use in public secondary schools in Tanzania most students and the majority of teachers do not understand English. For example, the headmaster of one of the secondary schools once admitted that, of the 45 teachers in his school, only 3 understood English well and used it correctly. This in effect means that the other 42 teachers used incorrect English in their teaching. This is not an isolated case. Those who have been working closely with secondary school classroom situations will agree with me that this situation prevails in most public secondary schools in Tanzania. (Qorro, 2002)

Qorro claims that it is the prevailing situation in the secondary schools in Tanzania, where most teachers teach in incorrect English, that forces her to argue for the change of medium of instruction to Kiswahili. She feels confident that students can, in fact, learn English better than is currently the case when it is taught well as a subject, and eliminated as the medium of instruction. In her own words:

> The use of English as a medium actually defeats the whole purpose of teaching English language. For example, let us suppose that, in the school mentioned above, the 3 teachers who use English correctly are the teachers of English language, and the other 42 are teachers of subjects other than English. Is it not the case that the efforts of the 3 teachers of English are likely to be eroded by the 42 teachers who use incorrect English in teaching their subjects? If we want to improve the teaching and learning of English in Tanzania secondary schools, I believe, that has to include the elimination of incorrect English to which students have been exposed from the time they began learning it. (Qorro, 2002)

In her article, Martha Qorro argues for the elimination of incorrect English by not using it as a medium of instruction. She knows that many people are put off by this suggestion because of the belief that using it as a medium of instruction means that students master English better. Though she agrees that mastering English is important, she feels that the best way to do this is through improved teaching of the English language as a subject, and not by the use of English as a medium.

And then she adds:

> Not everyone who recommends a change of medium of instruction to
> Kiswahili is a Kiswahili Professor. I for one am *not* a Kiswahili
> Professor, I have been teaching English for the last 25 years, and to me a
> change to Kiswahili medium means:
>
> - Eliminating the huge amount of incorrect English to which our sec-
>   ondary school students are exposed.
> - Enhancing students' understanding of the contents of their subjects
>   and hence creating grounds on which they can build their learning
>   of English and other languages.
> - Eliminating the false dependence on English medium as a way of
>   teaching/learning English, addressing and evaluating the problems
>   of teaching English.
> - Impressing on all those concerned that English language teaching is
>   a specialized field just like History, Geography, Physics, Mathemat-
>   ics, etc. It is thus unreasonable and sometimes insulting to teachers
>   of English when it is assumed that teachers of all subjects can assist
>   in the teaching of English.

To the young secondary-school student I met in Tanzania it would be
correct to reply, yes, it is important for you to learn English and learn it well,
but there is reason to believe that you will learn the language better if you
study it as a foreign language, as a subject. Using Kiswahili as the language
of instruction will help you learn science and other subjects better than you
do now.

Ferguson (2000) points to several research studies showing that those
students who learn in their own language do better in school. He refers to a
study by Prophet and Dow (1994) from Botswana. A set of science concepts
was taught to an experimental group in Setswana and to a control group in
English. They then tested understanding of these concepts and found that
Form I students taught in Setswana had developed a significantly better
understanding of the concepts than those taught in English. A similar study
with the same results was recently carried out in Tanzania. Secondary-
school students taught science concepts in Kiswahili did far better than those
who had been taught in English (Mwinsheikhe, 2001, 2002).

Inside the African classroom

How do African teachers, who often do not master the language of
instruction themselves very well, behave in the classroom? What teaching
methods do they use? What coping strategies do they employ? The chorus

teaching often heard in African classrooms owes much to the fact that the teacher does not have a vocabulary large enough to employ an interactive teaching method. It is difficult to use an interactive teaching strategy when you do not command the language well. Observations that I have made in Tanzania both in secondary-school classrooms and when I have taught university students show that if a teacher attempts to engage her/his students in group work or group discussions the groups will immediately switch into Kiswahili. Most of the time the teacher will either use what Heller and Martin-Jones (2001: 13), have called 'safe talk' or will code-mix or code-switch in the classroom.

Safe talk

The term 'safe talk', originally coined by Chick (1996), has been defined by Heller and Martin-Jones (2001: 13) as:

> Classroom talk that allows participation without any risk of loss of face for the teacher and the learners and maintains an appearance of 'doing the lesson', while in fact little learning is actually taking place . . . This particular style of interaction arises from teachers' attempts to cope with the problem of using a former colonial language, which is remote from the learners' experiences outside school, as the main medium of instruction.

Rubagumya (2003) found in a study he made of the new English medium primary schools in Tanzania that the main manifestation of 'safe talk' is in an encouragement of chorus answers from pupils, repeating phrases or words after the teacher and copying notes from the blackboard. He found very little encouragement of pupils to freely express their ideas without the teacher's control.

The two examples below are taken from Rubagumya's (2003: 162) research, and illustrate 'safe talk' as observed in many classrooms of the sample schools.

T: So you have positive fifty-five plus positive what now?
PP: (chorus) ten
T: Positive ten. What do you get then?
P: (one student answers) Positive sixty-five
T: Sixty-five positive. How many got that? Only one . . . any question? . . . no question. Do this exercise [Mathematics, Standard 3, School D2]

In this example, the teacher is going through the exercise he had given pupils earlier. After making the corrections, he asks how many pupils got the right answer. Only one out of a class of 35 pupils had the right answer. The teacher then asks whether pupils have any questions. After a very brief moment (about two seconds) he decides that pupils have understood, and he proceeds to give them another exercise. Here both the teacher and the pupils are practising 'safe talk'. Since only one pupil got the right answer, we would have expected several pupils to ask some questions. But they hesitate because they do not want to lose face. The teacher on his part waits for only about two seconds and proceeds with the next task. He does not want to encourage pupils to ask questions, either because this might expose his lack of fluency in English, or because he is trying to cover the syllabus. Either way, this is 'safe talk'.

T: number twelve . . . let us go together . . . one two three
PP: (chorus) The doctor and his wife has gone out
T: The doctor and his wife *has* gone out . . . Kevin?
Kevin: The doctor and his wife *have* gone out
T: The doctor and his wife *have* gone out . . . is he correct?
PP: (Chorus) YEES!
[English, Standard 2, School A3] (Rubagumya, 2003: 163)

Here the teacher is trying to correct the pupils when they say 'the doctor and his wife *has*'. Kevin gets the right answer 'the doctor and his wife *have*'. Once the other pupils confirm this as correct in a chorus, the teacher does not care to explain why the right form of the verb is *have* and not *has*. There is no way he can find out from the chorus answer whether every pupil understands the difference between *have* and *has*, but accepting the chorus answer is 'safe' both for him and for his pupils.

Code-mixing and Code-switching in the African Classroom

The young student I talked to in Tanzania told me about the difficulties he had in understanding the lesson if his teacher did not translate the English words for him from time to time. This is what most Tanzanian teachers teaching in secondary schools do. In their classrooms they use strategies we term code-mixing, code-switching or regular translations.

In the research project sponsored by the Norwegian Research Council, my research assistant / collaborator and I have decided to use the following definitions of code-switching and code-mixing:

> Code-switching refers to a switch in language that takes place *between* sentences, also called an *intersentential change*, code-mixing refers to a switch in language that takes place *within* the same sentence also called an *intrasentential change*. (Brock-Utne & Holmarsdottir, 2003: 88)

Code-mixing is generally looked at more negatively than code-switching. Code-mixing may often indicate a lack of language competence in either language concerned. Code-switching does not necessarily indicate a deficiency on the part of the speaker, but may result from complex bilingual skills (Myers-Scotton, 1993). Code-switching is a strategy that even a teacher with a good command of English (if that is the language of instruction) may use when s/he sees that his/her students do not understand. It is a strategy often used by teachers who are knowledgeable in the first language of their students. From observations I have made so far and by analysing observations made by other researchers it seems to me that the strategy of code-mixing is mostly being used by teachers who are not language teachers and who do not have a good command of the language of instruction.

Examples of code-mixing

In the example below, the geography teacher mixes in English words in his sentences but lets the important words be said in Kiswahili. The following excerpt is taken from classroom observations made in a Form I geography lesson:

T: These are used for grinding materials. It looks like what?
S: **Kinu** (mortar)
T: **Kinu** and what?
S: **Mtwangio** (pestle)
T: It looks like **kinu** and **mtwangio** and it works like **kinu** and **mtwangio.**
(Rubagumya *et al.*, 1999:18)

In this example the teacher is satisfied with the answer from the student, which shows that the student has the right concepts. The fact that these concepts are expressed in Kiswahili does not seem to bother the subject-matter teacher, who does nothing to expand the vocabulary of the student within the English language. From the excerpt we do not even know whether the teacher knows the correct terms in English. Even if s/he does, s/he does not bother to make his/her students partake of this knowledge. Had the teacher insisted on an answer in English, s/he would most likely have been met by silence.

Observations that Osaki made in science teaching in secondary schools in Tanzania have made him reach the following conclusion:

> Students either talk very little in class and copy textual information from the chalkboard, or attempt discussion in a mixed language (i.e.

English and Kiswahili) and then copy notes on the chalkboard in English . . . teachers who insist on using English only end up talking to themselves with very little student input. (Osaki, 1991)

As all educators know, student input is essential for learning. As part of the research on the project to which I have previously referred, Halima Mwinsheikhe (2001, 2002) had teachers teach some biology lessons solely through the medium of English, and later had the same teachers teach some other biology lessons solely through the medium of Kiswahili. She reports that during the experimental lessons one could easily see that teachers who taught by using English only were exerting a great effort not to succumb to the temptation of code-mixing or -switching. They seemed to be very tense and their verbal expressions were rather 'dry'. Those who taught in Kiswahili were much more relaxed and confident. Those who taught through the medium of Kiswahili also seemed to enjoy teaching. They found it easy to make the lessons lively by introducing some jokes.

It is not only when teachers are to teach students that the language of communication becomes a problem. Halima Mwinsheikhe (2003) tells that after completing her studies and on her return to Tanzania she felt compelled to probe further into the issue of Kiswahili/English as LOI for science in secondary schools. Whenever she found herself among teachers and/or students, she observed and sought information/opinions regarding this matter. She tells how in May 2002 she co-facilitated a training workshop for science teachers of the SESS (Science Education in Secondary Schools) project, together with an American Peace Corp. The main objective was to train the teachers in the use of participatory methods to teach/learn some topics on Reproductive Health. She relates:

> The intention was to conduct the workshop in English. However, it became evident that the low level of participation, and the dull workshop atmosphere prevailing was partly due to teachers' problem with the English language. This is not a very shocking observation considering that some of these teachers were students some four years ago. The workshop co-ordinator and I agreed to use both Kiswahili and English. The problem was immediately solved. Since we started with this mixture, the working atmosphere was good, lively and conducive to learning. The other workshop co-ordinator was well aware of the language problem in secondary classrooms in Tanzania. . . . An interesting observation is that my co-facilitator, an American, who had been in Tanzania for only 18 months, used Kiswahili rather well in teaching a science subject intended for secondary schools! (Mwinsheikhe, 2003: 145)

Halima Mwinsheikhe sees the observations made during this particular workshop as a cause for concern, because in the final analysis the language problem of the teachers involved will have an impact on students during teaching/learning experiences. The implication is that teachers will most likely opt to use Kiswahili to surmount the existing language barrier. And yet eventually students will be required to write their test/examinations in English.

Examples of code-switching

The examples of code-switching reported here are taken from Tanzania and South Africa, the countries in which the research project is located. The same practice has, however, been observed in classrooms in Uganda, Swaziland, Namibia and Burundi (see, for example, Ndayipfukamiye, 1993). In Tanzania, Kiswahili is used as the language of instruction in primary school while English is supposed to be the language of instruction in secondary school and institutions of higher learning (except in some training colleges for primary-school teachers, where the language of instruction is Kiswahili). Despite what may be regarded as a very progressive language in education policy in South Africa, which in principle enables learners or their guardians to choose any of the 11 official languages as the language of instruction, English is used as the medium of instruction from Grade 4 in primary school onwards. The transition to English is only a policy decided by individual schools, and reflects the actual 1979 apartheid language policy. When one reads the official government policy carefully, one sees that this policy does *not* state that a change of language of instruction needs to take place in the fourth or fifth grade in primary school or, for that matter, at all. According to this policy, the whole of primary school and indeed secondary school could be conducted in African languages as the languages of instruction (Brock-Utne & Holmarsdottir, 2003).

In connection with the South African part of the research project, a reading comprehension task was given to 278 students in six different classrooms in three schools in Cape Town. The overall results showed that students who received instruction only in isiXhosa and did the task in isiXhosa performed far better than those who received the same task in English only. In addition, the isiXhosa group also outperformed the group that was given the task in English, but where instruction was given in both English and isiXhosa, that is, using 'a code-switching method'. All sessions were videotaped and are currently being analysed as part of the doctoral thesis written by Holmarsdottir.

Teachers in African classrooms know that they are not allowed to code-mix or code-switch, yet most of them still do. Halima Mwinsheikhe, who has worked as a biology teacher in Tanzanian secondary schools for many years, admits:

> I personally was compelled to switch to Kiswahili by a sense of help-lessness born of the inability to make students understand the subject matter by using English. (Mwinsheikhe, 2001:16)

In the following passage the science teacher changes languages completely as he sees that his students do not understand (taken from Rubagumya *et al.*, 1999: 17). His own English is not easy to understand. He expresses himself more clearly and much better in Kiswahili. For him the important thing is to get the subject matter across. He is a teacher of science, not of English.

T:	When you go home put some water in a jar, leave it direct on sun rays and observe the decrease of the amount of water, have you understood?
Ss:	(silence)
T:	**Nasema, chukua chombo, uweke maji na kiache kwenye jua, maji yatakuaje?** (I say take a container with water and leave it out in the sun, what will happen to the water?)
Ss:	**Yatapungua** (it will decrease)
T:	**Kwa nini?** (Why?)
Ss:	**Yatafyonzwa na mionzi ya jua** (it will evaporate by the sun's rays)

In the example above, the teacher, after his initial try in English and the ensuing silence from the students, switches completely to Kiswahili.

In South Africa it is also assumed that by using English in all content subjects students will in turn become more proficient in English. Also here teachers of students from the black majority population generally code-switch or code-mix during most lessons. In this case research shows that, although officially the language of instruction is English, the actual language used most in the upper-primary-school classrooms in the western Cape where our research was conducted is isiXhosa. The following example highlights the use of both English and isiXhosa (code-switching) in a South African classroom.

During a mathematics[3] lesson at the grade four level the teacher was explaining to the students the sum 20 + 19, which she had written on the board. At first the teacher made an attempt to explain the lesson in English, but quickly switched to isiXhosa after realising that the students were not following along. During the explanation of this lesson the teacher proceeded as follows:[4]

T: We are now going to do the addition together and I will explain and you will follow along. We are breaking up the numbers. Do you understand?

Ss: (Silence, no one responds).

T: **Siyacalula ngoku, siyawaqhekeza la manani. Sithatha bani phaya** (We are simplifying now, we are breaking these numbers. What do we take from there)?

Ss: **Utwo** (two).

T: **Sithathe bani phaya** (And what do we take from there)?

Ss: **Uone** (one).

T: **Utwo ujika abe ngubani** (two changes into what number)?

Ss: **Abe ngu**–20 (becomes 20).

T: Right, **u**–1 **lo ujika abe ngubani** (Right, this 1 becomes what)?

Ss: **Abe ngu**–10 (becomes 10).

The entire lesson was carried out in isiXhosa except for the initial attempt to use English only. The teacher switched languages after receiving no response from the students when she initially used English only. The remaining mathematics lesson then continued in isiXhosa with only some minor code-mixing taking place, like the insertion of words such as 'right', 'okay', 'understand'. The book the teacher was working from was in English. The mathematics lesson described above is not an isolated case and in fact many of the lessons observed during the fieldwork in the South African part of the project were conducted mainly through the medium of isiXhosa. However, at the end of the day students are expected to use English for all the writing that is done in the subjects, except for the subject isiXhosa. They are also expected to answer all examination questions in English.

National examiners working for the National Examination Board of Tanzania have told me of the many times they have seen students answer examination questions correctly, but in Kiswahili. The examiners were instructed to give such students zero points because the answers were supposed to be in English.

Conclusion

The situation that African teachers are forced into is tragic. Their own limited command of the language of instruction, plus the great difficulties their students have in understanding what the teacher is saying when s/he expresses him or herself in the ex-colonial language, force them to use teaching strategies I have here characterised as safe talk, code-mixing and code-switching. This gives the teachers a bad conscience, since they know that they are not supposed to code-switch or code-mix but to use the ex-colonial language throughout the lesson. They also know that on examination day students who code-switch will be punished.

To me, the ideal situation when it comes to classroom learning in Africa seems to be the three-language model so well argued for by Maurice Tadadjeu (1989). As mentioned, this language model for Africa would mean that the students first learn to master their mother tongue, then learn a regional African language that can be used as a language of instruction in secondary and tertiary education, and then learn an international language as a subject, a foreign language. This would mean that the local language would be used as a language of instruction during the first grades while lessons in the regional language would also be given. The regional language would gradually become the language of instruction throughout secondary and tertiary education. The so-called international language would be taught as a subject from the time the regional language takes over as the language of instruction.

While we are waiting for the ideal situation to happen, teachers must be allowed to code-switch because this speech behaviour is sometimes the only possible communicative resource there is for the management of learning. Learners should be awarded full points for a correct answer in exam questions whether they express themselves in the local, the regional or a foreign language.

Notes

1. The LOITASA project was planned together with partners in South Africa and Tanzania in Bagamoyo, Tanzania in January 2000 to be a five-year project with NUFU (Norwegian University Fund – co-operation between Norwegian universities and universities in developing countries) funding from Norway. When I returned to Norway, however, I learnt that the money for 2001 had been frozen and I decided that while waiting for the NUFU funding I could start part of the project with money from the Norwegian Research Council. This project is a four year project (1.1.2001 – 31.12.2004) entitled: An analysis of policies and practices concerning language in education in primary schools in South Africa and secondary schools in Tanzania. For the first three years of the project period I have employed an assistant, Halla Holmarsdottir, who works on the South African part of the project gathering data which will be analysed as part of her PhD thesis. Several master's students from Tanzania are working, under my guidance, on the Tanzanian part of the project, gathering data which have been or will be analysed in connection with their master's theses. From January 2002 I also received NUFU funding for the project called LOITASA (Language of Instruction in Tanzania and South Africa). This project works in close co-operation with the Norwegian Research Council-funded project. The LOITASA project, which started on 1 January 2002 and is going to run until 31 December 2006, contains two different research components and also a staff development component. The first research component is rather similar to the project sponsored by the Norwegian Research Council. The second research component of

LOITASA involves an action component where we plan an experiment where we shall let some Form I and Form II classes in secondary school in Tanzania and fourth-, fifth- and sixth-grade classes in primary school in South Africa be taught in mother tongue or at least in a language that is familiar to them (isiXhosa in the western Cape region of South Africa, Kiswahili in Tanzania) in some subjects for two more years. We have used 2002 to translate material and get the necessary permissions to carry out the experiment. We have just started the experimental phase in South Africa. The NUFU funding was not sufficient for our experimental phase and we have secured some extra funding from a Norway–South Africa research programme.

2. A number of bibliographies have been published on the subject 'education and language in Africa'. Stafford Kaye and Bradley Nystrom (1971) have in their extensive bibliography covered the colonial period, while *Sprachpolitik in Afrika* by Mechthild Reh and Bernd Heine (1982) contains a vast bibliography with especially good coverage of the period from independence to 1980. David Westley (1992) has made an updated bibliography on the period 1980–1990.
3. Officially, the policy of this particular school states that English is the LOI from Grade 4 onwards. Mathematics is therefore supposed to be taught through this language. The reality is, however, far different.
4. The data below have been gathered by Halla Holmarsdottir as part of her PhD research on the project.

References

Brock-Utne, B. (1995) The teaching of Namibian languages in the formal education system of Namibia. National Institute for Educational Development (NIED), Ministry of Basic Education and Culture, Namibia.

Brock-Utne, B. (1997) Language of instruction in Namibian schools. *International Review of Education* 43 (2/3), 241–60.

Brock-Utne, B. (2000) *Whose Education for All? Recolonization of the African Mind.* New York: Falmer Press.

Brock-Utne, B. (2001) Education for all – In whose language? *Oxford Review of Education* 27 (1), 15–134.

Brock-Utne, B. and Holmarsdottir, H.B. (2003) Language policies and practices in Africa – some preliminary results from a research project in Tanzania and South Africa. In B. Brock-Utne, Z. Desai and M. Qorro (eds) (pp. 80–102) *The Language of Instruction in Tanzania and South Africa (LOITASA).* Dar es Salaam: E & D Publishers.

Chick, K. (1996) Safe-talk. Collusion in apartheid education. In H. Coleman (ed.) *Society and the Language Classroom* (pp. 21–39). Cambridge: Cambridge University Press.

Ferguson, G. (2000) The medium of instruction in African education. The role of the applied linguist. In S. Makoni and N. Kamwangamalu (eds) *Language and Institutions in Africa.* (pp. 95–111). Casas Book Series No.5. Cape Town: The Centre for Advanced Studies of African Society (CASAS).

Grimes, B. (ed.) (1992) *Ethnologue: Languages of the World* (12th edn). Dallas: Summer Institute of Linguistics.

Heller, M. and Martin-Jones, M. (eds) (2001) *Voices of Authority: Education and Linguistic Difference.* Westport: Ablex Publishing.

Kaye, S. and Nystrom, B. (1971) Education and colonialism in Africa. *Comparative Education Review* 25 (2), 240–59.

Klaus, D. (2001) The use of indigenous languages in early basic education in Papua New Guinea: A model for elsewhere? Paper presented at the Annual Conference of the Comparative and International Education Society held in Washington DC. 17 March 2001.

Makoni, S.B. (2000) In the beginning was the missionary's word: The European invention of an African language. The case of Shona in Zimbabwe. In K.K. Prah (ed.) *Between Distinction and Extinction. The Harmonisation and Standardisation of African Languages* (pp.157–65). Casas Book Series No.1. Cape Town: The Centre for Advanced Studies of African Society (CASAS).

Mwinsheikhe, H.M. (2001) Science and the language barrier: Using Kiswahili as a medium of instruction in Tanzania secondary schools as a strategy of improving student participation and performance in science. Master of Philosophy thesis. University of Oslo: Institute for Educational Research. Spring Term 2001.

Mwinsheikhe, H.M. (2002) Science and the language barrier: Using Kiswahili as a medium of instruction in Tanzania secondary schools as a strategy of improving student participation and performance in science. Education in Africa. 10. Report No. 1. Oslo: Institute for Educational Research.

Mwinsheikhe, H.M. (2003) Science and the language barrier: Using Kiswahili as a medium of instruction in Tanzania secondary schools as a strategy of improving student participation and performance in science. In B. Brock-Utne, Z. Desai and M. Qorro (eds) (2003) *The Language of Instruction in Tanzania and South Africa (LOITASA)* (pp.129–49), Dar es Salaam: E & D Publishers.

Myers-Scotton, C. (1993) *Duelling Languages: Grammatical structure in code-switching.* Oxford. Clarendon Press.

Ndayipfukamiye, L. (1993) Code-switching in Burundi primary classrooms. *Working Paper Series.* Lancaster University, England.

Obanya, P. (1980) Research on Alternative Teaching in Africa. In E.A. Yoloye and K-H. Flechsig (eds) *Educational Research for Development.* (pp. 67–112). Bonn: Deutsche Stiftung für Internationale Entwicklung.

Osaki, K.M. (1991) Factors influencing the use of the environment in science teaching: A study of biology teaching in Tanzania. Doctor of Philosophy Thesis. Edmonton, Alberta.

Prah, K.K. (ed.) (2000) *Between Distinction and Extinction. The Harmonisation and Standardisation of African Languages.* Casas Book Series No.1. Cape Town: The Centre for Advanced Studies of African Society (CASAS).

Prah, K.K. (ed.) (2002) *Rehabilitating African Languages.* Casas Book Series No.18. Cape Town: The Centre for Advanced Studies of African Society (CASAS).

Prah, K.K. (2003) Going native: Language of instruction for education, development and African emancipation. In B. Brock-Utne, Z. Desai and M. Qorro (eds) (2003) *The Language of Instruction in Tanzania and South Africa (LOITASA)* (pp.14–35). Dar es Salaam: E & D Publishers.

Prophet, R. and Dow, J. (1994) Mother tongue language and concept development in science. A Botswana case study. *Language, Culture and Curriculum* 7 (3), 205–17.

Qorro, M. (2002) Language of instruction not determinant in quality education. *The Guardian.* Wednesday 29 May 2002. On www at http://www.ippmedia.com. Accessed 20.09.02.

Reh, M. and Heine, B. (1982) *Sprachpolitik und Sprachplanung in Afrika.* Hamburg: Buske.

Roy-Campbell, Z.M. (1998) Language as the repository of knowledge and culture: Deconstructing myths about African languages. Paper presented to the CIES annual conference in Buffalo, New York. 18–22 March.

Roy-Campbell, Z.M. (2000) The Language of schooling. Deconstructing myths about African languages. In S. Makoni and N. Kamwangamalu (eds) *Language and Institutions in Africa* (pp. 111–31). Casas Book Series No.5. Cape Town: The Centre for Advanced Studies of African Society (CASAS).

Rubagumya, C. (2003) English-medium primary schools in Tanzania: A new 'linguistic market' in education? In B. Brock-Utne, Z. Desai and M. Qorro (eds) (2003) *The Language of Instruction in Tanzania and South Africa (LOITASA)* (pp. 149–70). Dar es Salaam: E & D Publishers.

Rubagumya, C., Jones, K. and Mwansoko, H. (1999) Language for learning and teaching in Tanzania. Unpublished paper.

Serpell, R. (1980) Linguistic flexibility in urban Zambian schoolchildren. In V. Teller and S.J. White (eds) *Studies in Child Language and Multilingualism. Volume 345* (pp. 97–119). New York: Annals of the New York Academy of Sciences.

Tadadjeu, M. (1989) *Voie Africaine. Esquisse du Communautarisme Africain.* Cameroun: Club OUA.

Westley, D. (1992) Language and education in Africa: A select bibliography, 1980–1990. *Comparative Education Review* 36 (3), 355–68.

Chapter 11

Accommodating Tensions in Language-in-Education Policies: An Afterword

A. SURESH CANAGARAJAH

If there is one thematic strand running prominently through this collection of essays, it is the tensions in language policies and practices in postcolonial communities. We see tensions:

- within policy discourses: as in the conflicting priorities of pragmatism and multilingualism in Singapore [i.e. the pragmatic promotion of English as the language of economic capital and the validation of four official languages for national unity may reduce multilingualism as the other unacknowledged languages and dialects are defined unequal and dispensable (in Rubdy's chapter)];
- between policy-makers' intentions and the community's expectations: i.e. the Iranian political establishment's product-oriented promotion of English education, when the local people in fact value English for the communicative purposes demanded by globalisation (Riazi);
- between different orientations to the same policy: the ideological rationale of the state in promoting English as a force of modernisation and globalisation in the curriculum in Turkey and the technicist or product-oriented approach of teachers and students (Reagan and Schreffler);
- between *intended* policy effects and *realised* effects: as in the decline of various Chinese dialects in Singapore when the Speak Mandarin Campaign actually intends to empower local languages against the threat of English (Rubdy);
- between policy and practice: as in the deviations from the policy of using English only in classrooms in India (Annamalai), South Africa

(Probyn), Tanzania (Brock-Utne), Kenya (Bunyi), and Malaysia (Martin);
- between the policy effects on different social groups: rather than being a democratising force, English serves the vested interests of the elite in India, Singapore, and Hong Kong;
- and, at the most personal level, within identity: as in the conflicts we see within multilingual speakers (in almost all the communities presented in the book) who see themselves as native to English through their acts of localization and yet lack ownership over the language because of colonialist discourses.

Rather than perceiving these tensions as unusual, we have to see them as normal, as language planning involves a constant negotiation of the interests of different social groups and of the changing priorities of a community. Rather than treating them as a problem for policy formation, we should think of tensions as opening up more complex orientations to language in education (LIE). In fact, in some contexts, such inconsistencies enable minority communities to find space within institutions and discourses to achieve their interests even when policies are unjust (see Freeman, 1996). Before we proceed to explore more promising models of LIE policies that enable us to grapple with these tensions effectively, it is important to consider the shifts in our disciplinary discourse and social conditions that compel us to treat these tensions seriously.

Tensions are certainly an embarrassment for the dominant *rational or positivist tradition* in language planning and policy (LPP), which assumes that socially efficient policies can be formulated from objective assessments of the needs, processes, and outcomes of language relationships (see Ricento & Hornberger, 1996). The aim was to construct policies in a top-down fashion and to socially engineer desirable models of education and nation state. The project has miserably failed. Considerations of language allegiance, sociolinguistic identity, and linguistic attitudes are rarely rational, pragmatic, or objective. They are ideological. Since community needs and attitudes may be ambivalent, the processes of implementing policy can be multifarious and the outcomes of policy surprising. Therefore, the field of LPP is now moving towards a more localised orientation that takes these tensions, ambiguities, and paradoxes seriously to construct policies from the ground up, along micro social domains (see Cooper, 1989: 182). Hence the growing popularity of ethnographic approaches in LPP (as we see exemplified so well in many chapters in this volume).

In terms of social change, the tensions in the chapters are partly explained by the shifts indicated in the title of the book: decolonisation and globalisation. While non-Western communities were busy working on one project (decolonisation), the carpet has been pulled from under their feet by another project (globalisation). It is as if one historical process got subsumed by another before the first process was complete. There are significant differences in the project of both movements: decolonisation entails resisting English in favour of building an autonomous nation state; globalisation has made the borders of the nation state porous and reinserted the importance of the English language for all communities, through multinationals, market forces, pop culture, cyber space, and digital technology. Apart from the pressures the nation state is facing from outside (as mentioned above), it is also facing pressures from within (as the claims of diverse social groups and ethnic communities within the nation have become more assertive). Postmodern conditions have also created certain significant changes in discourse, calling for a different orientation to language planning. People are not prepared to think of their identities in essentialist term (as belonging exclusively to one language or culture), their cultures as monolithic (closed against contact with other communities), and their knowledge forms as pure (uniformly local or centralised).

All these changes call for a fundamental shift in LPP orientations. We realise now that the 'one nation-one language' model that has been with us for the greater part of modern history is outmoded. In the same breath with which the autonomy of the nation state has been questioned, the validity of prioritising a single language for national cohesion has also been debunked. Though we have advanced considerably from the narrowminded 'multilingualism as a problem' orientation to a 'multilingualism as right' perspective (and acknowledge the different languages in a polity), this is not enough. Contemporary social conditions demand that we move to treating 'multilingualism as resource' (see Ruiz, 1984). We have to recognise that being aware of as many languages as possible is an asset to postmodern citizens who are called upon to shuttle constantly between communities and contexts in contemporary communication. Even the practice of planning the place of languages as discrete and autonomous in education can be questioned. Multiple languages now jostle together in many domains of communication, functioning in a complementary, integrated, and fluid manner. The Internet is engendering hybrid texts where languages and symbol systems interact in dynamic new ways. Other forms of media in communication, created by new technology, have also contributed to creating a need for *multiliteracies* (Cope & Kalantzis, 2000). To be literate now requires competence not only in multiple modalities of communication (sound, speech, video, and photographs, in addition to writing) and multiple symbol systems (icons, images, color, and charts, in addition to words), but also in multiple registers, discourses, and languages. In such a context, we readily recognise that teaching literacy in a single language (English or vernacular) or a single dialect of that language ('Standard English' or nativised varieties of English) fails to equip our students for real-world needs.

In this context, how do we construct LIE policies? Like good ethnographers, we should first observe the practices that are developing in local situations to resolve the tensions in policy. We see *code-switching* in many communities (see Brock-Utne, Bunyi, Martin, Probyn), as teachers and students switch languages not only to facilitate communication but also to accomplish many other creative rhetorical and social functions. We see modes of *safe talk* in classrooms as teachers and students find convenient ways of accomplishing the lesson (i.e. through product-oriented and translation-type approaches) despite the linguistic challenges created by idealistic policies (see Martin; though Annamalai and Riazi don't use the term, their descriptions of existing teaching practices point to similar strategies). We even see new *hybrid codes* developing in certain communities – such as Singlish in Singapore, which serves as a nativised version of English and provides new forms of insider identity for disempowered speakers, despite the Speak Good English movement of the government (see Rubdy). These local strategies create a slight discomfort for the contributors to this collection as they cannot be accommodated in the traditional models of LPP. As Swigart (1992) has memorably observed, mixed codes are 'freak' forms of communication for traditional models in linguistics that favour discrete languages. It is understandable, therefore, that none of the contributors perceive these hybrid communicative practices as forming the basis of viable alternate LIE policies. While many contributors argue that code-switching may have certain positive functions in education (Martin), they think of this as a short-term or temporary solution at best to some of the conflicts in the classroom (see Brock-Utne). Some even point out the detrimental effects that such hybrid codes/practices may have for language acquisition (see Bunyi).

In general, the contributors hint at ways of putting together discrete languages to form a more effective multilingual policy for LIE. Though most authors are interested only in bringing out the problems descriptively without prescribing alternatives, those who do proffer alternatives are united in advocating a multilingualist policy which accommodates a combination of local languages and lingua francas, with different statuses and functions allocated to each of them. Brock-Utne considers this the direction in which the long-term policy alternative should proceed in South Africa. Her proposed 'three-language model' resembles the existing policy in India. Reagan and Schreffler show the merits of the policy in Turkey where English is phased into the curriculum at progressively more advanced levels of learning. Annamalai argues against the false dichotomy of indigenous versus global languages, and sees the need for providing an integrated and balanced place for diverse languages in the curriculum. The 'three-language policy' (which accommodates the vernacular, regional language, and Hindi or English as lingua franca at different points of the learning progression) is a step in the right direction – although it, like the policy in Turkey, faces problems of implementation.

However, to really rise to the challenges posed by globalisation we need a different way of orientating to LIE. A way to get a better handle on the pervasive tensions in postcolonial communities is offered by what is beginning to be called the *language ecology* model (see Hornberger, 2003; Mühlhäusler, 1996). Rather than constructing policies for discrete languages, treating homogeneous speech communities as the primary domain of policy formation, the language ecology model takes into consideration the geographical space as the locus for policies. From this perspective, we are ready to acknowledge that multiple languages live together in a specific locale, and that people have uses for all of them. An LIE policy with an ecological orientation will make policies for languages in their synergy–i.e. how languages interact and influence each other, and together affect a community's life. The ecological model would also be informed by the *history* of the languages in their environment, taking into consideration the fact that the languages contribute to their mutual life and death. Issues of language retention, shift, and decline need to be addressed in such a policy. The ecological perspective is thus concerned with possibilities of language endangerment even as it upholds multilingualism as a resource. Adopting this framework, Hornberger (2003) has recently developed a policy orientation to literacy. Her *continua of biliteracy* model features dichotomous communicative constructs like oral/literate, vernacular/literary, micro/macro, and contextualised/decontextualised as a continuum, with the latter representing the traditionally more powerful and the former the traditionally less powerful values. Hornberger demonstrates how this model can be used in research and policy-making as a heuristic to understand the ways these features are (or can be) negotiated by a community to define its needs and aspirations. It is important to note that the choice between vernacular or lingua franca, oral texts or written texts, and narrative or academic discourse is not mutually exclusive. Each community will have to develop the mix of languages, literacies, and discourses that best suits its interests. This will be based on the history of that community, and the relationship between the languages in its environment.

A distinctive feature of Hornberger's model is that policy is not made only for macro-social domains in education. Local life in the classrooms is also treated seriously. Recent LPP scholars acknowledge the place of the classroom as a powerful site that can creatively reconstruct language and educational policies in favour of minority groups (Freeman, 1996). In such micro contexts of teaching, Hornberger is prepared to accept code-switching. She shows how bilinguals textbooks, expressive writing from students in mixed codes, and oral code-switching between teachers and students in the classroom can develop important communicative and thinking skills. The artificial separation of languages is not sustained by practices of literacy, communication, or work in the contemporary world. If hybridity is a fact of life in postmodern society, we don't have to be squeamish about permitting code-switching in the classroom. Also, code-switching doesn't have to prevent students from developing fluency in both languages (as research from a variety of contexts has asserted, see Canagarajah, 1995). Till we have a formal pedagogy and curriculum in place for teaching these multilingual discourse strategies, we have to at least develop the everyday practices of code-switching and mixing for educational purposes [see suggestions for such activities in Lucas & Katz (1994) and Pease-Alvarez & Winsler (1994)]. A pedagogy for negotiating codes shouldn't sound fashionably postmodern. From precolonial times, certain local communities have practiced multiliteracies and hybrid codes quite effectively. Consider the examples of the *kene/dami* system of the Kashinawa (de Souza, 2002) and the *manipravalava* style in Tamil (Viswanathan, 1993). When such multilingual texts are engendered at the point of contact between different communities under unequal power relations, especially by minority communities to negotiate domination, Mary Louise Pratt (1991) calls them the *literate arts of the contact zone*.

Furthermore, LIE policies will have to be developed with considerable involvement from the local community. The place and mix of languages in education for its children needs to be negotiated by each community in relation to its history, needs, and aspirations. Finding that local communities have conflicting positions on the desire to retain their local languages and/or study dominant languages (from several ethnographic projects in literacy-for-development), Street (2001) concludes that the best that policy-makers can do is to start where the community is at. Though this doesn't mean giving in completely to the distorting influences from the dominant groups, it is still important to speak to the community's interests. Other LPP scholars, working in South American contexts, are also surprised to find well-intentioned policies for retaining indigenous languages not meeting the approval of local communities (Aikman, 1999; Hornberger, 1988; King, 2001). They too agree that it is important to work out the curricula, styles of learning, and materials that would implement a policy in consultation with the community. Freeman (1996) points out how even ill-devised policies can be modified to produce positive effects when parents and teachers collaborate on developing a suitable pedagogy for their children's learning.

It is important to note that dabbling in LIE policies without institutional changes in language status can be a recipe for failure (as Probyn is also wise to observe regarding South Africa in this volume). In her study in Peru, Hornberger (1988) finds that Quechua communities don't support the state's provisions for language maintenance even though the policy is pedagogically successful (in helping local students learn and value the indigenous language). She recommends providing more spaces for Quechua in institutional contexts to increase the community's valuation of their language and motivate them to use it more frequently. Such institutional promotion should lead to accessible and wide roles for indigenous languages, which would ensure social mobility without linguistic biases. Nations that are committed to giving all languages a place in their curriculum, and yet deny them a functional status in their social and economic life, should expect LIE policy failure.

All these conditions complicate the nature of LIE policy-making. We realise that a meaningful policy would be situated, collective, negotiated, and multipronged. While the actual policy proposals have to be constructed in each community from the ground up, with sensitivity to different interests and aspirations, the chapters in this volume help us to go beyond the traditional dichotomies that have stultified policy debates so far: English or mother tongue? Individual rights or group rights? Mobility or rootedness? Modernisation or preservation? Though these constructs are not mutually exclusive, they are not dispensable either (see Canagarajah, 2004). It is not impossible to imagine ways in which a student from a minority community can learn English and dominant discourses without neglecting proficiency in the indigenous languages. It is not impossible to imagine ways in which a state can provide educational facilities to democratise the acquisition of dominant codes, without neglecting protective group rights for disempowered communities and their languages.

References

Aikman, S. (1999) *Intercultural Education and Literacy: An Ethnographic Study of Indigenous Knowledge and Learning in the Peruvian Amazon*. Amsterdam / Philadelphia: John Benjamins.

Canagarajah, A.S. (1995) Functions of code switching in the ESL classroom: Socialising bilingualism in Jaffna. *Journal of Multilingual and Multicultural Development* 16 (3), 173–96.

Canagarajah, A.S. (2004) Language rights and postmodern conditions. *Journal of Language, Identity, and Education* 3 (2), 140–45.

Cooper, R.L. (1989) *Language Planning and Social Change*. Cambridge: Cambridge University Press.

Cope, B. and Kalantzis, M. (eds) (2000) *Multiliteracies: Literacy Learning and the Design of Social Futures*. London and New York: Routledge.

De Souza, L.M.T.M. (2002) A case among cases, a world among worlds: The ecology of writing among the Kashinawa in Brazil. *Journal of Language, Identity, and Education* 1 (4), 261–78.

Freeman, R.D. (1996) Dual-language planning at Oyster bilingual school: 'It's much more than language'. *TESOL Quarterly* 30 (3), 557–81.

Hornberger, N. (1988) *Bilingual Education and Language Maintenance: A Southern Peruvian Quechua Case*. Dordrecht: Foris.

Hornberger, N. (2003) Multilingual language policies and the continua of biliteracy: An ecological approach. In N.H. Hornberger (ed.) *Continua of Biliteracy: An Ecological Framework for Educational Policy, Research, and Practice* (pp. 315–39). Clevedon: Multilingual Matters.

King, K.A. (2001) *Language Revitalization Processes and Practices: Quichua in the Ecuadorian Andes*. Clevedon: Multilingual Matters.

Lucas, T. and Katz, A. (1994) Reframing the debate: The roles of native languages in English-only programs for language minority students. *TESOL Quarterly* 28 (4), 537–62.

Mühlhäusler, P. (1996) *Linguistic Ecology: Language Change and Linguistic Imperialism in the Pacific Region*. London: Routledge.

Pease-Alvarez, L. and Winsler, A. (1994) Cuando el maestro no habla Espanol: Children's bilingual language practices in the classroom. *TESOL Quarterly* 28 (4), 507–36.

Pratt, M.L. (1991) Arts of the contact zone. *Profession* 91: 33–40.

Ricento, T. and Hornberger, N. (1996) Unpeeling the onion: Language planning and policy and the ELT professional. *TESOL Quarterly* 30 (3), 401–628.

Ruiz, R. (1984). Orientations to language planning. *NABE Journal* 8 (2), 15–34.

Street, B. (ed.) (2001) *Literacy and Development: Ethnographic Perspectives*. London, New York: Routledge.

Swigart, L. (1992) Two codes or one? The insider's view and the description of code-switching in Dakar. In C. Eastman (ed.) *Code-switching* (pp. 83–102). Clevedon: Multilingual Matters.

Viswanathan, G. (1993) English in a literate society. In R.S. Rajan (ed.) *The Lie of the Land: English Literary Studies in India* (pp. 29–41). Oxford: Oxford University Press.

Index